A Language Teacher's Guide

A LANGUAGE TEACHER'S GUIDE

✱ ✱ ✱

Edmond A. Méras, Lic. ès L. Ph.D.
The Foxcroft School

Second Edition

HARPER & ROW, PUBLISHERS
NEW YORK, EVANSTON, AND LONDON

To Cecilia, Peter, and Christopher

CONTENTS

FOREWORD

This elementary book on language teaching is more a handbook for teachers or prospective teachers of modern languages than a methods book. It attempts to present in a simple, direct manner some of the principal ways that language teachers themselves have devised to solve their teaching problems. Most of the suggestions offered in these pages have been used successfully or observed by the author in a classroom. Some ideas will appear to be new, others quite old; for in spite of enthusiasts' repeated claims that they have found "the perfect new method," a long-range, impersonal, historical view will show only a steady improvement in techniques and an increased efficiency in presenting subject matter. This improvement in itself is worthy of great commendation. But greater emphasis on motivation is necessary, and greater social pressure and interest must be created to help combat the general public apathy, often open antagonism, to language learning. Only when such interest has been aroused will the many improved and progressive techniques of language teaching really become effective.

This book espouses no particular method. The principal

methods that have had or are now having some vogue are outlined in order to show prospective teachers the efforts that are always being made to vitalize language teaching. It is hoped that this rapid review will help them find in all these methods some common objectives that all language teachers will accept, thus ending the controversies that have raged so long over minor points of technique. These controversies have caused so much confusion about language teaching in the minds of educators, teachers, and the general public that language study has suffered greatly.

Another aim of this book is to point out to those who are willing to be convinced that not only has far greater efficiency than is generally supposed been attained in language techniques during the last fifty or seventy-five years, but that by the proper application of these techniques continued improvement can be made. It is more important now than at any moment in the history of the United States for languages to form a definite part of the educational program in our elementary schools, our junior and senior high schools, as well as in our colleges. Our prospective diplomats, engineers, scientists, business men, bankers, teachers, and military men will from now on travel and live abroad in ever increasing numbers. Their knowledge of foreign languages will enable them to be far more effective in their work and far happier as human beings. We cannot hope to maintain our prestige as a great nation, or to guide, as we seem destined to do, a great many other nations, if we have not mastered their languages and if we do not understand their peoples and customs. Whether we like it or not, we can no longer live in linguistic isolation; it is fruitless to expect to influence those who do not know our language if we do not know theirs.

All great and successful leaders must understand the people they guide; and as world leaders, everyone in the United States who comes into contact with other nations must understand not only their inhabitants but their languages. Otherwise efforts at cooperation and leadership can only meet with failure.

The State Department, recognizing this, has created the Foreign Service Institute. By using the linguistic-scientific approach, it offers practical, intensive language courses for all members of the Foreign Service, so that they will gain control of spoken and written languages in a minimum of time.

If in this book no single method is emphasized and as wide a range of techniques as possible is presented, it is because the author feels that techniques have to be changed depending upon social conditions, classroom conditions, community needs, national needs, and each teacher's particular abilities. Like a physician, the teacher must constantly keep in mind the many ways of obtaining the best possible results and, in accordance with the situation and his special talents, choose and apply them wisely. Many suggestions offered here are drawn from observations in secondary-school classrooms. With slight modification most of them can be applied to beginning college classes as well.

This book unfortunately contains a certain amount of unavoidable repetition because frequently similar techniques are used to obtain results in the language learning process. I hope these repetitions, as well as the unequal length of chapters, will be excused. The varying importance of the subject matter has made the latter necessary.

I am deeply grateful to my many friends and colleagues

for help and suggestions given me as they read the manuscript. Among them I should like particularly to express my thanks to Professors Stephen Freeman of Middlebury College, Henri Olinger, formerly of New York University, Mario A. Pei of Columbia University, Lois Gaudin of Brooklyn College, and Paul Langellier-Bellevue of Adelphi College; to Dr. James Grew of Phillips Andover, Miss Katherine O'Brien of Brookline High School, and Miss Maria Morales of Alexander Hamilton High School; to Professor Theodore Anderson of the University of Texas, Professors John D. Carroll and Edward Geary of Harvard, Professor Frederick Eddy of Georgetown, and Dr. Henry Lee Smith, Jr., of the United States State Department; and to my colleagues at Phillips Exeter Academy, Messrs. DeVaux DeLancey, William Jones, Harris Thomas, Zenas Neumeister, Percy Rogers, and Paul Gropp. I wish also to mention my particular indebtedness to the late Leslie Ross Méras for her patient reading and rereading of the original manuscript and for her kind and generous advice, criticism, and constant encouragement. Without her inspiration, this book would never have been completed.

EDMOND A. MÉRAS

January, 1962

A Language Teacher's Guide

* 1 *

A BRIEF HISTORY OF LANGUAGE TEACHING IN THE UNITED STATES

The teaching of languages in North America is nearly as old as the settling of the continent itself. As early as 1608 Catholic missionary priests were teaching in the part of the continent that is now Maine. Most French communities in the New World had their own church schools, and there the language and culture of Old France were taught to the children. The very wealthy colonists, on the other hand, brought with them their tutors and governesses and in that way maintained the traditional European educational methods of the seventeenth-century rich. By the early 1700s the Germans who settled in Pennsylvania after 1682 at the special request of William Penn were teaching German in their local parochial schools. But parallel with language instruction by religious groups, private tutoring in languages was always to be found. In what is now Florida, California, New Mexico, and other localities settled by the Spaniards, the Jesuits and other religious orders sought to maintain a knowledge of correct Spanish in the young as early as 1606. The University of Mexico, of course, must have had some instruction in language as early as 1552. These three languages—French, German, and Spanish—have played a fundamental role not only in the educational history but in the cultural development of our nation. Italian did not have the advantage of a transplanted native population until the nineteenth century, but it too has had an important part in our cultural growth.

The introduction and teaching of modern languages followed a different pattern in the secondary schools and colleges and must be treated separately. In the Latin grammar schools and the academies both French and German had their place among the studies from the beginning, although to a limited extent in comparison to the place occupied by the classics. As early as 1749, both French and German were taught in an academy in Philadelphia; Spanish was first taught there in 1766. In New England as well as in the southern colonies, French seemed to predominate, particularly in schools for girls. The cultural background of communities settled largely by persons of continental birth led them to maintain their native language in the schools they founded in the New World. This principle also influenced new settlers later in the West, although by that time French was quite generally included in most courses of studies.

Since colonial days, fluctuations in the fortunes of continental nations, as well as the state of our relations with various European countries, have been invariably reflected in the popularity of French, German, and Spanish in the secondary-school field. Thus French was popular during the War for Independence when the influence of the French philosophers Montesquieu, Rousseau, Condorcet, and others was at its height in America, and when both Frenchmen and France were aiding the colonies so substantially in their war against England; its popularity continued off and on for many years afterward, when our contacts with France were particularly friendly. Until Louis Napoleon's attempt to dominate Mexican politics, France also influenced our educational system directly as well as through the extensive adaptation and translation of French textbooks for use in our schools. Prussia's educational system attracted some attention as early as 1830, but it was not until the 1850s that German influence began to replace the French. The influence kept on growing, particularly in sections of the country settled by people of German origin, until the advent of World War I in 1914, when French educational ideas again began to gain ascendancy. In the period between 1918 and 1939 the United States experienced a sort of cultural and social renaissance, with French ideas and ideals predominating. In France likewise, the United States and its culture played a great role. American influence is still an important factor in the development of contemporary France. Between the two world wars the study of French in the secondary schools increased greatly (there were approximately 7 hundred thousand pupils in all the high schools) and the influence of France was also kept alive by the exchange of students and professors between the two countries. The French students and professors, distributed in schools and colleges throughout our country, interpreted as well as defended France's patterns of thought and action. American artists, actors, and literary men and women who lived in France helped to maintain our interest in French by their constant reference to French customs and manners in their writings and their frequent use of French words and phrases.

After 1924, during the Mussolini regime in Italy, the teaching of Italian in many large centers like New York grew phenomenally until about 1936. The rising importance of Germany as a European power under Hitler, however, did not seem to have a similar effect. It was not until after the return of our soldiers from the conquest of Germany in 1945 that teaching German began to regain a place in American schools.

Spanish at the secondary-school level was always prominent in the sections predominantly Spanish in origin. When, in 1914, Germany and England were forced to relinquish some of their commercial activity in South America, American business tried to fill the gap and Spanish became very popular, replacing German to a great extent, particularly in commercial schools. This gain was general throughout the country. Between 1918 and 1940 Spanish maintained the place it had gained, and after the defeat of France in June, 1940, it rose to first place among the modern foreign languages taught in secondary schools in most large centers.

Since 1942, some big high schools in large cities have introduced Slavic languages or languages that are popular with large portions of the city's population. Russian, in particular, is finding its way into more and more secondary schools. By the end of 1958 the number of enrollments on the college- and high-school level had greatly increased. Language institutes are now training specialists in Russian as well as in the Oriental languages so that teachers will be prepared on all levels.

In higher education, the story of language teaching is somewhat different. The teaching of modern foreign languages in institutions of higher learning began at Harvard in 1735 when

French was introduced. William and Mary was the first college to establish a professorship of modern languages in 1779; an Italian, Luigi Bellini, was appointed to the post. Little by little other well-established colleges and universities created chairs in modern languages. Columbia in 1784 appointed John D. Gros professor of German (although without salary); Williams in 1792 chose a professor of modern languages, as did North Carolina in 1795, Princeton in 1806, Yale and Virginia in 1825; Bowdoin in 1829 appointed Henry Wadsworth Longfellow professor of modern languages.

The first regular modern-language course of study was introduced at Amherst in 1824. After 1819, when Ticknor was appointed professor of modern languages at Harvard, Spanish and Spanish literature became very important studies. When Longfellow succeeded Ticknor, Italian took its place beside Spanish. In 1825 da Ponte was appointed professor of Italian at Columbia, and in 1832 at New York University, although Spanish had by this time become a fashionable language there. Scholars like Ticknor, Longfellow, Lowell, Norton, and others did much by their personal prestige to give to the study of modern languages a dignity that it might not otherwise have had. But young America's distrust of the Old World's political intrigues and antireligious philosophies lessened what might have been an uninterrupted enthusiasm for languages.

The study of languages in the United States has therefore had a fluctuating career, because education in this country is always responsive to public demand and public demand is not always based upon public need or collective wisdom. External influences, political expediency, and group pressure have in recent years dictated the inclusion or exclusion of languages in the school curriculum. Fortunately, a knowledge of languages is such a fundamental requirement for maintaining satisfactory commercial, diplomatic, and cultural relations with the rest of the world that, in spite of temporary reverses, the study of languages has always regained a prominent place in the school curriculum after each period of decline. Most attacks on language study have uncovered weaknesses in the methods used in teaching languages. Teachers of languages have, in general, accepted these criticisms as valid, and have made repeated and conscientious attempts to correct deficiencies that have been pointed out. As a result, there has been a steady increase in the efficiency of classroom techniques; and if a clear and permanent set of objectives can be maintained, the high degree of efficiency attained in more favored centers can be easily extended to the entire country.

Funds donated by the Ford Foundation and appropriations authorized by the National Defense Education Act to further research and experimentation with new techniques in modern-language teaching have made it possible for National Testing Services to standardize and raise language-achievement requirements throughout the country. It is very encouraging that loans and fellowships for studying here and abroad have been granted and that 35 special Language Institutes have been created. The Language Institutes are distributed in 30 states where they train teachers and supervisors to teach French, Spanish, German, Italian, and Russian for elementary as well as secondary schools. Their purpose is to improve the audio-lingual ability of foreign-language teachers by introducing new teaching methods and techniques, suggested to a large degree by the Linguistic Scientists, and by using new materials and new approaches to language learning.

Since 1942, first as a war emergency and now as part of an

expanded modern-language program in certain centers like Cornell, Colorado and Georgetown, and in government schools as well as in large universities, Russian and Oriental languages have been introduced, in addition to French, German, Spanish, and Italian which were already being taught. Practical instruction in all these languages is now offered.

Since 1883, when the Modern Language Association of America was founded, the teachers of modern languages have worked consistently toward making their subject useful to the community in which they live. This association has shared this task with the local language groups that in 1924 finally became the Federation of Associations of Modern Language Teachers, and with national single-language societies like the American Association of Teachers of French, Spanish, German, Italian, and Slavonic languages. They have been greatly aided by their publications—the *Modern Language Journal,* the *French Review, Hispania,* the *German Quarterly,* and *Italica.* Many of these language associations have worked with educational authorities, the public, students, parents, and teachers in adapting their subject to the changing needs of the community. They are well organized and are prepared to continue this work with enthusiasm. Their combined membership of more than 25 thousand teachers is carefully assessing these new experiments and adapting them to their local teaching conditions.

It has been largely through the influence of these associations that funds have been made available for scientific investigation of the methods in use, and for an evaluation of the results in relation to the demands of the community and the requirements of higher institutions of learning. These investigations and findings were embodied first in the *Report of the Committee of Twelve* (1901) and later in the long list of publications of the American and Canadian Committees on Modern Languages (1927–1932), as well as in the many contributions that have appeared monthly in modern-language periodicals. Extension of the work of the American and Canadian Committees continued as late as 1940. In 1952, the Ford Foundation gave the Modern Language Association a substantial grant for the restudy of modern-language teaching in the United States. The effect of the efforts of these professional groups and of these studies on teachers of languages has been manifested in their intellectual alertness and their willingness to accept changes in content and methodology. This progressive attitude toward their work is attested by the steady growth in membership of the various language associations, and by the increased attendance at special language summer schools like those at Middlebury, Mills College, Western Reserve, Colby-Swarthmore, and Fordham University—to name only a few. All these schools seek to maintain the closest possible contact with the intellectual life of the countries whose language they are teaching.

Some of them—Middlebury and Western Reserve in particular—train teachers in the field as well. Middlebury College has also organized courses for prospective language teachers, part of which are given at French and Spanish universities. Yale has set up an undergraduate summer course in Paris for students of French. The development of the Junior Year Abroad and the Fulbright Fellowships now gives the student of language the widest possible opportunities for complete advanced training in this field.

TEACHING OPPORTUNITIES ABROAD[1]

General requirements for teaching abroad are three years of teaching experience and a knowledge of the language of the country. Candidates with an M.A. degree for teaching or a Ph.D. degree for lecturing and research are given preference. Applications should be made from six months to one year in advance of the expected appointment date.

OPPORTUNITIES UNDER U.S. GOVERNMENT PROGRAMS

Fulbright and Smith-Mundt Educational Exchange (Department of State)

For university lecturing and advanced research for one year (occasionally one semester or a full summer session); Ph.D. degree and teaching experience required (Fulbright):

For specialists in fields of adult education, library service, museum and art gallery methods, nursing education and social work, to lecture or do research (for which doctoral degree is not necessarily a part of professional preparation) (Fulbright):

For lecturers under U.S. Information and Educational Exchange (Smith-Mundt Act) in non-Fulbright countries upon specific request of a foreign university:

For inclusion in register of scholars who expect within the next period of years to be available for lecturing abroad. Registration does not constitute application for particular countries at specified times:

Conference Board of Associated Research Councils
2101 Constitution Avenue, N.W
Washington 25, D.C.

For teaching in national and American-sponsored elementary and secondary schools abroad and in Canada (direct interchange of positions or one-way assignments) (Fulbright):

[1] Courtesy of the Institute of International Education.

For secondary-school teachers to attend summer seminars in France, Germany, and Italy:

> Division of International Education
> Office of Education
> Department of Health, Education and Welfare
> Washington 25, D.C.

BI-NATIONAL CENTERS (USIA)

For teachers of English, directors of courses, and administrators in centers in Latin America, Burma, Iran, Turkey, and Thailand:

> Chief, Recruitment Branch
> United States Information Agency
> Washington 25, D.C.

INTERNATIONAL COOPERATION ADMINISTRATION

For elementary-school, vocational-school, and teacher-training educators with at least five year's experience, to serve in under-developed countries:

> Division of International Education
> Office of Education
> Department of Health, Education, and Welfare
> Washington 25, D.C.

DEPARTMENT OF DEFENSE

For elementary- and secondary-school teachers qualified to teach two major fields; also for librarians, dormitory supervisors, and administrators to work in Army personnel dependents' schools in France, Germany, Italy, Japan, and Okinawa:

> Overseas Affairs Division
> Deputy Asst. Chief of Staff for Personnel
> Department of the Army
> Washington 25, D.C.

For elementary- and secondary-school teachers in Navy Personnel dependents' schools in Europe, North Africa, Newfoundland, the Caribbean, the Far East, and Pacific Trust Territories:

Chief of Naval Personnel
Department of the Navy
Washington 25, D.C.

For elementary- and secondary-school teachers and administrators in schools for dependents of Air Force personnel in Europe, Africa, Far East, Azores, and Newfoundland:

Overseas Employment Branch
Department of the Air Force
Washington 25, D.C.

OPPORTUNITIES IN U.S. TERRITORIES AND POSSESSIONS

ALASKA

Public Schools in Territory:
Territorial Commissioner of Education
Juneau, Alaska

Schools for Indians, Aleuts, and Eskimos:
General Superintendent
Alaska Native Service
Juneau, Alaska

City Schools:
Superintendent of Schools
Cities: Anchorage, Cordova, Craig, Douglas, Fairbanks, Haines, Juneau, Ketchikan, Kodiak, Nenana, Nome, Palmer, Petersburg, Port Alexander, Sitka, Seldovia, Seward, Skagway, Valdez, Wrangell.

CANAL ZONE

Chief of Office
Panama Canal Company
411 Tenth Street N.W.
Washington 25, D.C.

GUAM

Director of Personnel
Government of Guam
Agana, Guam, Mariana Islands

HAWAII

Superintendent of Public Instruction
Territory of Hawaii
Honolulu, T.H.

PUERTO RICO

Secretary of Education
Department of Education
Hato Rey, Puerto Rico

SAMOA

Director of Personnel
Government of American Samoa
Pago Pago, Tutuila, American Samoa

VIRGIN ISLANDS

Governor of the Virgin Islands
St. Thomas
Virgin Islands

Opportunities Under International Programs

UNITED NATIONS

For university teachers and secondary teachers in all fields interested in teaching abroad to be included in listing in *Teaching Abroad,* which is circulated to universities and other schools throughout the world:

Exchange of Persons Service
UNESCO
Place de Fontenoy
Paris, 7e, France

WORLD HEALTH ORGANIZATION

For teachers of nursing and public health, medical, and clinical sciences:

Personnel Office
World Health Organization
1501 New Hampshire Avenue, N.W.
Washington, D.C.

OPPORTUNITIES THROUGH PRIVATE ORGANIZATIONS

For appointments and occasional visiting professorships. Candidates must have Ph.D. degree and teaching experience at appropriate university level:
> President's Office
> American University at Cairo
> Cairo, Egypt

For teaching on junior-high-school to college level in Mission Schools in Asia, Africa, and Europe:
> American Board of Commissioners for Foreign Missions
> (Congregational Christian Churches)
> 14 Beacon Street
> Boston 8, Massachusetts

For short-term lecturing, and for specialists for observation and consultation, in Switzerland; fields of natural science and medicine:
> American-Swiss Foundation for Scientific Exchange
> 137 Summit Avenue
> Montclair, New Jersey

For two-year teaching assignments at colleges and universities in Cambodia, Japan, Korea, and Taiwan under the Asian English-Language Teaching Project. Only men candidates considered:
> Asia Foundation
> 105 Market Street
> San Francisco 5, California

For teaching and administrative work in American sponsored elementary and secondary schools in Latin America:
> Inter-American Schools Service
> American Council on Education
> 1785 Massachusetts Avenue N.W.
> Washington 6, D.C.

For teaching on various levels in Africa south of the Sahara:
African-American Institute
1234 Twentieth Street N.W.
Washington 6, D.C.

For university teaching in the British Commonwealth universities (The AUBC acts as the agency of its member institutions in inviting applications for advertised vacancies on their staffs, but does not operate as a general placement agency):
Association of the Universities of the British Commonwealth
36 Gordon Square
London W.C. 1, England

For university teaching in medicine in Nigeria and the British West Indies:
Secretary to the Senate Committee on Colleges Overseas in Special Relations
University of London
Senate House, W.C. 1, London, England

For teaching on secondary to university levels in seven colleges and universities in the Near and Middle East. Three-year appointments:
Near East College Association
40 Worth Street
New York 15, New York

For teaching in Swiss private schools, elementary and secondary level. Name is published in a list circulated among member schools:
Zentralverband der Schweizerischen Privatshulen
60 Hohenweg
St. Gall, Switzerland

Additional information concerning teaching opportunities abroad can be obtained from the following publications and offices:

Opportunities in all areas of the world
    Study Abroad, published by UNESCO
    UNESCO Publications Center
    801 3rd Avenue
    New York 22, New York

Opportunities in British Areas
    British Information Services
    45 Rockefeller Plaza
    New York 20, New York

Opportunities in Latin America
    Pan American Union
    Washington 6, D.C.

Annual listing of openings under mission boards of the National Council of Churches of Christ in the U.S.A.
    The Student Volunteer Movement for Christian Missions
    257 Fourth Avenue
    New York 10, New York

Awards for Study in Latin America (1956)
    Pan American Union
    Washington 6, D.C.

Fellowships in the Arts and Sciences (1959-1960)
    Association of American Colleges
    Edited by Virginia Bosch Potter of the University of Wisconsin

Fellowships and Scholarships (1957)
    National Foundation for Infantile Paralysis
    301 East 42nd Street
    New York 17, New York

Handbook on International Study (1961)
    Institute of International Education
    New York, New York

Scholarships, Fellowships, and Loans, vol. 1 (1949); vol. 2 (1951); vol. 3 (1955)
    S. Norman Feingold
    Bellman Publishing Company
    Cambridge 38, Massachusetts

Social Work Opportunities Abroad—Employment and Education (1958)
    National Association of Social Workers
    1 Park Avenue
    New York, New York

Teacher Exchange Opportunities (1959-1960)
    U.S. Department of Health, Education, and Welfare
    Office of Education, Division of International Education
    Educational Exchange and Training Branch, Teacher Ex-
        change Section
    Washington 25, D.C.

The *News Bulletin* of the Institute of International Education (subscription price $2.00) published monthly from September to May, occasionally prints descriptions of specific vacancies upon request of the foreign universities or organizations concerned.

1961-1962

FELLOWSHIPS OFFERED BY FOREIGN GOVERN-MENTS, UNIVERSITIES AND PRIVATE DONORS[2]

Three types of foreign study programs are administered by the Institute of International Education for U.S. students: U.S. government grants under the Fulbright Act; U.S. government grants under the Inter-American Cultural Convention and under the Smith-Mundt Act; and foreign government and university awards. The two former are described in detail in the booklet *U.S. Gov-*

[2] Courtesy of Institute of International Education.

ernment Grants. This booklet is primarily concerned with the fellowships offered to American students by foreign governments and universities. Students interested in applying for any of these awards are advised to read carefully this introduction to the listing of grants.

Primarily for graduate study, these awards are for one academic year, usually beginning in the fall. Since most of the awards offered by foreign governments and universities do not cover the entire expense of the period of foreign study, they are in the nature of grants-in-aid and candidates are expected to be able to pay their own travel expenses, incidental expenses and a part of maintenance costs, if these are not covered by the terms of the grant.

The grants are designed in the main to give U.S. students the opportunity to live and study in a foreign country and not to enable them to obtain foreign degrees. Two years of study are usually required to obtain a foreign degree and applicants for these grants who plan work toward a degree abroad should be prepared to finance their second year of study themselves.

At the time this summary goes to press, not all the awards offered by foreign donors or private foundations have been confirmed for the 1961-1962 academic year; they are listed as they were for the previous year, in the expectation that they will be renewed on the same terms.

General Eligibility Requirements

Although the qualifications for the awards vary, certain general requirements apply to the awards listed in this booklet. They are:

1. United States citizenship by date of application.
2. Unless otherwise specified, a bachelor's degree from a U.S. college or university, or equivalent training for candidates in the arts, by the time of departure to take up the foreign study grant.
3. A good academic record and demonstrated capacity for independent study.

4. The ability to read, write, and speak the language of the host country by date of application (unless the requirement is specifically waived).
5. Good character and adaptability.
6. Good health. All successful candidates are expected to have adequate insurance coverage.
7. Age limit is generally thirty-five years (for certain grants, a lower age limit is specified).
8. The marital status of a candidate has no bearing on his eligibility unless the terms of the grant specifically state otherwise. These grants are adequate to support only one person. Therefore, married candidates must be prepared to support their dependents during the study period. Under the terms of certain grants, dependents of grantees may not accompany them.
9. Candidates who have not previously had extensive experience abroad are, in general, given preference.

Application Procedures

SECURING APPLICATION FORMS AND DETAILED INFORMATION

(a) *Enrolled Applicants.* Anyone enrolled at an institution of higher learning should obtain information and application materials for the Fulbright Program Adviser at the institution of study.
(b) *At-large Applicants.* Prospective applicants not currently enrolled at an institution of higher learning may secure information and application materials by writing to:
 Information and Counseling Division
 Institute of International Education
 1 East 67th Street
 New York 21, New York
or by writing to the nearest regional office of the Institute.
 In writing to the Institute, applicants should be sure to specify the particular grant or grants in which they are inter-

ested. No application forms will be distributed by the Institute after October 15.

FILING APPLICATIONS

Enrolled applicants should submit completed applications to their local Fulbright Program Adviser by the deadline established at the particular campus.

At-large applicants are required to submit their completed applications to the Institute's New York office by November 1.

Since incomplete applications cannot be considered by the committees on selection, it is important that applicants make sure that all documents, including letters of recommendation, reach the Institute before the closing date. Candidates are urged to submit their applications as far in advance of the closing date as possible. No acknowledgment of receipt of applications is made.

Applicants are strongly urged to discuss their plans for foreign study with professors in their major fields as well as with other academic counselors. They should feel free to address inquiries pertaining to foreign study to the Information and Counseling Division of the Institute.

The statement of proposed study should be simply and precisely worded. The project should be one which can be completed in a year of study or research abroad.

Credit for study abroad should be discussed with applicant's own university. If the applicant plans to do research for a thesis, the approval of his university must be evidenced.

NUMBER OF APPLICATIONS PERMITTED

If a candidate is interested in a Fulbright award, he may apply for a grant to only one country. In the case of I.A.C.C. two countries may be applied for simultaneously. In the case of foreign government and university awards, application may be made for study in just one country, although a student may be considered for more than one award within that country. Another category of awards is the program sponsored jointly by the U.S. Government and the Irish Scholarship Exchange Board. Applications may be submitted in any or all of these categories simultaneously.

For information about U.S. Government programs, see the booklet "U.S. Government Grants."

Students applying for an award offered by a foreign government, university, or private donor *and* for a U.S. Government grant, providing the awards are tenable in the same country, need file only one application on the U.S. Government application form.

The one exception to this rule is that a separate application must be made for the assistantships offered by the French Government. The only form which can be used for this purpose is that entitled "Application for Study Abroad." This form includes a special sheet called the "Report on Spoken English." Students who apply for assistantships may also apply for U.S. Government grants but must file the U.S. Government application form as well as that required for the assistantship application.

Students applying *only* for an award offered by a foreign government, university, or private donor need file only the form entitled "Application for Study Abroad," which can be obtained on request from the Information and Counseling Division, Institute of International Education, 1 East 67th Street, New York 21, New York.

SOURCES OF FUNDS TO SUPPLEMENT PRIVATE AWARDS

VETERANS' BENEFITS

Candidates eligible for veterans' benefits, and wishing to use them to supplement awards listed here, should obtain information from the appropriate state branch of the Veterans Administration. They should verify that the educational institution abroad where they propose to study is approved by the Veterans Administration.

FULBRIGHT TRAVEL GRANTS

It is expected that the U.S. Government will offer travel grants, under the Fulbright program, to supplement the following awards:

Austrian Government Awards

Danish Government Awards
French Government Awards
German Awards (exception indicated)
Israel Government Awards
Italian Awards
Netherlands Government Awards

Students who wish to apply for a travel grant in conjunction with one of the awards listed above must do so by November 1. It should be noted that the receipt of a study grant carries no assurance of a travel grant. U.S. Government Travel Grants are not normally available to countries other than those listed above.

The application material for the Fulbright Travel Grant must be completed in full as well as the application material for the study grant.

NOTIFICATION OF NOMINATION

The Institute's committees on selection recommend candidates for the awards to the sponsoring governments, university, foundation or organization, with the final decision being made by the sponsor in each case. Candidates will be notified as soon as possible whether or not they have been recommended to the sponsor for final consideration; this notification is usually made by March 15 in the case of U.S. Government grants; in the case of foreign government and university awards, April 1.

Nominees for Fulbright Travel Grants will be notified direct of the final decision by the U.S. Department of State. Final decision on Fulbright Travel Grants cannot be made until after the confirmation of the awards which they are intended to supplement. Successful candidates must follow instructions for travel reservations which will be sent by the U.S. Educational Commission or Foundation abroad. Travel reservations will be arranged for them and must be accepted. No reimbursement is allowed for those who make their own reservations.

DEADLINE

Applications for the awards listed below must be received by November 1, unless otherwise specified.

AFRICA AND ASIA

Special Fellowships
Two awards for graduate study or research in the Far East, South
or Southeast Asia or Africa.
Amount of award to be determined by cost of living in country
of study. Maximum: $3,500.
Open only to candidates enrolled in an academic institution and
recommended by the chairman or director of his department.
Preference is given to candidates who hold a master's degree.

IRAN

University of Teheran Awards
Two awards.
Available at the University of Teheran.
Maintenance, tuition, and round-trip transportation from New
York. Men are given room and board at the University Club.
Open only to candidates with a working knowledge of Persian.

ISRAEL

Government of Israel Awards
One award to a graduate student engaged in a research project,
who does not seek a degree in Israel.
2,050 Israel pounds for the academic year, covering maintenance
and incidentals. Free tuition at the Hebrew University, Jerusa-
lem; the Technion, Haifa, and the Weizmann Institute of
Science, Rehovot.

EUROPE

AUSTRIA

Government of Austria Awards
Four awards.
Available at Austrian universities and other institutions of higher
learning.
2,600 Austrian schillings monthly for eight months beginning

October 15, and a travel allowance of 1,400 schillings.
Open only to unmarried candidates.

Salzburg Summer School Awards
Several full scholarships for a six-week session at Salzburg/Klessheim.
Open to candidates between the ages of 18 and 40 who have completed one year of college.

University of Vienna Summer School Awards
Several full and partial awards for a six-week session at the St. Wolfgang Campus in Strobl.
Open to candidates who have completed two years of college.

DENMARK

Danish Government Awards
Three awards.
Available at universities or institutions of higher learning in Denmark.
4,515 kroner for the academic year, including an orientation course starting August 1.
A knowledge of Danish is not a prerequisite.

FRANCE

French Government Awards

Fellowships

Approximately twenty awards.
Available at universities and other state institutions of higher learning, the majority of which are located in the provinces.
360 new francs monthly for eight months, and tuition.
Given through the Direction Générale des Affaires Culturelles (Ministry of Foreign Affairs).
Open to candidates preferably under thirty years of age, and preferably unmarried.
These awards must be considered partial awards that require a supplement from the grantee's own private funds.

Assistantships

Appointments in French secondary schools and teacher-training institutions.

350 to 380 new francs a month, depending on the location.

Given through the Office National des Universités et Ecoles Françaises of the Ministry of Education.

Open to unmarried candidates preferably under thirty years of age.

Positions are part-time and consist primarily of conducting classes in English conversation.

The stipend is sufficient for living expenses and minor incidentals. Board and lodging are provided at most schools except those in some university towns. Where assistants live in the schools, a charge of 55 to 93 new francs a month is made for maintenance.

Most assistants are assigned to schools in the provinces: assistants in or near university towns are entitled to enroll in the university, where tuition is waived except for minor fees. It should be stressed, however, that assistantships *are not primarily study awards.*

A recording of the candidate's spoken French and English must be submitted with the written application.

If a candidate's principal purpose is research he should apply for a *Fellowship*. If his principal aim is to teach, he should apply for an *Assistantship*.

GERMANY

Amerika-Kreis Muenster and University of Muenster Award
One award.

Tuition and DM 250 monthly for nine months beginning November 1 at the University of Muenster.

Bavarian State Scholarships
Five awards.

One each available at the Universities of Erlangen, Munich, Wurzburg, the technical institute in Munich, and at either the music academy in Munich or the art academy in Munich or Nuremberg.

Tuition and DM 250 monthly for twelve months beginning October 1, and round-trip transportation between German border and place of study in Germany.

Not open to candidates using veterans' benefits or with adequate private funds.

Deutscher Akademischer Austauschdienst Awards
Ten awards.

Available at universities and other institutions of higher learning in the Federal Republic of Germany.

Tuition and DM 350 monthly for twelve months beginning September 1, and an additional amount of DM 200 for transportation between the German border and the place of study in Germany.

Federal Republic of Germany Awards

(Dankstipendien)

Forty awards.

Available at universities and other institutions of higher learning in the Federal Republic of Germany.

Tuition and DM 350 monthly for twelve months beginning September 1, round-trip transportation between New York and Bremerhaven, and an additional amount of DM 200 for transportation in Germany between Bremerhaven and the place of study.

Free University of Berlin Awards
Two awards.

Tuition and DM 350 monthly for nine months beginning November 1, at the Free University of Berlin. Round-trip transportation between the German border and Berlin, or European harbor and Berlin.

Unmarried candidates preferred.

Germanistic Society of America Awards
Two awards.
$1,500 for the academic year in the field of German language
and literature at an institution of higher learning in the Federal
Republic of Germany.
For prospective teachers of German. Master's degree desirable.
Unmarried candidates preferred.

University of Cologne Award
One award.
Tuition and DM 300 monthly for ten months, beginning No-
vember 1 at the University of Cologne.
Not open to candidates in the field of theology.

ITALY

Italian Government Awards
At least 15 awards for advanced study or research.
720,000 lire and 50 per cent reduction on tuition for a period of
at least eight months. In some cases, 50,000 lire for tuition for
candidates in the field of music.
Open only to candidates with master's degrees or the equivalent
in advanced work. Applications will be accepted for study in
any field.

Collegio Borromeo and Collegio Ghislieri
One award each.
Tuition at the University of Pavia and maintenance at the college.
Open only to men under thirty years of age.

Scuola Normale Superiore, Pisa Award
One award.
Maintenance at the college and tuition at the University of Pisa.
Open only to men under thirty years of age, preferably those
planning to teach.

University of Padua Awards
Two awards.
Maintenance and tuition at the University of Padua.
Open to men and women, preferably under thirty years of age.

Fiat Award

Two awards for study at the Polytechnical School in Turin and the School of the Fiat Motor Company, Turin.

Maintenance, tuition, fees, textbooks and incidentals allowance provided by the Fiat Company for an eight-month period.

Open to candidates under thirty who have a Bachelor of Engineering degree.

Applicants must have some knowledge of Italian before taking up award.

THE NETHERLANDS

The Netherlands Government Awards

Three Awards.

Available at universities and institutions of higher learning in the Netherlands.

Tuition and 2,700 guilders for the academic year.

Preference is given to candidates under twenty-eight years of age.

Some knowledge of the Dutch language is desirable.

POLAND

Polish Government Awards

Approximately fifteen awards.

Available at universities and other institutions of higher learning.

2,400 zlotys monthly for ten months, tuition, living accommodations and medical care.

A working knowledge of Polish is required.

SWEDEN

Swedish Government Awards

Three Awards.

Available at universities and other approved institutions in Sweden.

4,500 Swedish kronor for the academic year, and tuition (except at the International Graduate School for English-Speaking Students, University of Stockholm, where tuition is approximately $60 for holders of these fellowships).

A knowledge of Swedish is desirable except for those wishing to study at the International Graduate School.

SWITZERLAND

American-Swiss Foundation for Scientific Exchange Awards
One or more awards.

Available for advanced study or research in the natural or medical sciences at Swiss universities.

Varying amounts, according to needs of applicants, maximum of $2,000.

Open only to applicants holding the Ph.D. or M.D. degree by the time of departure. Knowledge of French or German is required, depending on the language of instruction at the Swiss institution the student wishes to attend.

Swiss Universities and Organizations Awards
Tuition awards are available at the Universities of Basel, Bern, Fribourg, Geneva (including the Graduate Institute of International Studies), Lausanne, Neuchâtel, Zurich, the Federal Institute of Technology in Zurich and the School of Economics and Public Administration at St. Gallen.

Knowledge of French or German is required, depending on the language of instruction at the Swiss institution the student wishes to attend.

Partial maintenance awards ranging from 2,000 to 3,500 Swiss francs for the academic year are offered by Swiss educational institutions and bi-national organizations (Swiss-American Society for Cultural Relations and the Society of Swiss Friends of the U.S.A.).

UNITED KINGDOM

University Summer School Awards
Two or three full scholarships for graduate students, partial grants for undergraduates.

Available at Oxford, Edinburgh, London, Birmingham (at Stratford-upon-Avon).

Open only to applicants who would be unable to attend without aid.

Closing date: March 1. (Competition for admission of non-scholarship students closes March 31.)

NORTH AMERICA

CANADA

Canada Council Fellowships

Five awards for study in the arts, humanities and social sciences.

Available at universities and institutions of higher learning in Canada.

$2,000 (Canadian) and round-trip transportation between the student's home and the place of study.

MEXICO

Mexican Government Awards

Twelve awards for the academic year March 1 to December 15 offered through the Mexico-United States Cultural Commission to graduates, seniors and juniors. Graduate students will receive preference.

Only single students or married students who can prove their ability to support their dependents completely apart from the scholarship stipend are eligible.

Available for the National University of Mexico or other national institutions of higher learning in Mexico City.

Graduates will receive a stipend of 1,249 pesos monthly for maintenance and incidental expenses. Undergraduate stipends will be 1,185 pesos monthly. Both graduates and undergraduates will receive free tuition.

PRELIMINARY SCREENING AGENCIES

FOR GRADUATE STUDY ABROAD

Institute of International Education
1 East 67th Street
New York 21, New York

For Teaching in Elementary or Secondary Schools Abroad,
and for a Number of Summer Seminars for Teachers of
French, Italian, Spanish, and Classical Studies

U.S. Office of Education
Department of Health, Education, and Welfare
Washington 25, D.C.

For University Teaching, Lecturing or
Advanced Post-Doctoral Research

Conference Board of Associated Research Councils
2101 Constitution Avenue
Washington 25, D.C.

PARTICIPATING COUNTRIES

Fulbright Program

Australia	Iran
Austria	Italy
Belgium-Luxembourg	Japan
Brazil	Netherlands
Chile	New Zealand
China, Republic of	Norway
Columbia	Pakistan
Denmark	Peru
Ecuador	Philippines
Finland	Spain
France	Sweden
Germany, Federal	Thailand
Republic of	Turkey
Greece	United Arab Republic
Iceland	United Kingdom
India	(including colonial areas)

Awards also are available for study in IRELAND under a binational educational exchange program similar to the Fulbright program. U.S. Government application forms should be used.

INTER-AMERICAN CULTURAL CONVENTION

Bolivia	Dominican	Mexico
Brazil	Republic	Nicaragua
Chile	Ecuador	Panama
Colombia	Guatemala	Paraguay
Costa Rica	Haiti	Peru
Cuba	Honduras	Venezuela

FULBRIGHT TRAVEL GRANTS

Austria	France	Israel
Denmark	Germany	Italy
	Iceland	Netherlands

APPLICATIONS

Applications for grants may be obtained from the
Information and Counseling Division
Institute of International Education
1 East 67 Street
New York 21, New York

or from its Regional Offices:
116 South Michigan Avenue, Chicago 3, Illinois
1605 Pennsylvania Street, Denver 3, Colorado
731 Texas National Bank Bldg., 1300 Main St.
Houston 2, Texas
1530 P Street, N.W., Washington 5, D.C.
291 Geary Street, San Francisco 2, California

* 2 *

CHARACTERISTICS
OF LANGUAGE TEACHING
METHODS BEFORE 1939

There have always been several methods of teaching languages in the United States. Generally speaking, the more formal, academic, scholarly methods were used in the early days of language teaching in our academies, colleges, and universities. An exception was the method used by the very popular, nonacademic teacher Lorenzo da Ponte of New York, who, after being appointed to Columbia University in 1825, applied his personal method of teaching in the formal classroom.

About the middle of the nineteenth century, however, individuals experimenting with new and sometimes very original methods of teaching came to the United States from abroad and often established their own language schools. These private schools continued to thrive and to wield considerable influence on teachers in the public schools until about 1920. They kept the teaching of languages alive and maintained a popular interest in methodology until schools of pedagogy attached to the larger universities began experimenting with language teaching on a more scientific basis. These formal experiments in our colleges and universities, rare before 1900, became the vogue about 1910. Until the end of the nineteenth century our universities as a whole taught modern languages much as the classics were taught, emphasizing grammar and translation.

This *grammar method* attempted, by means of the study and even memorization of rules of grammar and exceptions to these rules, to give a firm basis upon which to build. As each rule was mastered, a vocabulary was learned, lesson by lesson. The vocabulary was then used to translate difficult sentences which tested complete knowledge of the rules that had been learned. Originally this system stressed neither accurate pronunciation of the foreign language nor ability to compose anything freely in it. The principal purpose of the study of both grammar and vocabulary was to enable the student to translate the foreign language into English, although exercises in translating English into the foreign tongue were almost always part of each lesson. The chief objective, however, remained learning the grammar rules. The application of a rule was often a secondary matter. Many of the sentences chosen to test knowledge of grammar were neither intelligent nor comprehensible, but they managed to include several almost insurmountable difficulties based upon exceptions to the rules or special interpretations. D'Arlon[1] quotes two that are typical: "The garden of my grandfather is larger than the pen knife of my uncle" and "The big dog wants but the little dog doesn't." Such sentences were more likely to confuse the student than test his knowledge. They were seldom designed

[1] H. Alpern and A. I. Katsh, *Audio-Visual Materials in Foreign Language Teaching*, New York University, 1950, p. 21.

to teach anything practical; rather, they served as obstacles
to be overcome. As soon as the grammar was mastered sufficiently, books containing excerpts from the classics, or the
classics themselves, were read for purposes of translation,
grammatical analysis, or even the parsing of the sentences in
the text. Here again the main objective was the study of
grammatical rules or of the verb forms. Living languages
were treated as dead languages—their purpose was to discipline the mind, develop the memory, and train the individual
in so-called logical thinking.

The grammar method never underwent any fundamental
changes. Its scope and objectives were well defined. It was
easy to use in a formal classroom; it appeared scholarly and
often was. It permitted the use of a simple, exact grading
system, fair to everyone alike and almost mathematical. It
could easily be defended as a "disciplinary subject" and hence
as of value to any student.

Akin to this method, but giving less emphasis to grammar,
was the *interlinear translation method* devised by an Englishman named James Hamilton, who taught in New York. He
was followed by T. Robertson, who in about 1852 prepared a
text containing a complete story divided into sections, each
with an interlinear and then idiomatic translation. Questions
and answers accompanied each lesson, and frequently there
were lists of cognates. The exercises consisted of translating
French to English and English to French. A short synopsis of
grammar appeared at the end of the book.

Disciples of these two teachers further developed this
method by attempting self-pronunciation exercises in the foreign language. Thomas Prendergast, another Englishman, emphasized the principle of a limited vocabulary of 200 to 300

words introduced in skillfully constructed sentences and repeated constantly to assure retention.

In about 1866 a rival method became popular, one which
discarded translation entirely in the teaching process. It was
generally known as the *natural method* and was used with
slight variations in private language schools rather than in
formal classes in academies and colleges. It stressed the spoken
language which the grammar-translation method had avoided;
it eliminated technical grammar at the beginning of the
course and used the foreign tongue to explain the meaning
of new vocabulary and even grammatical principles which
could not be taught in a functional way. No English was used
by the instructor and the student was discouraged from using
any himself. He was drilled in reading the foreign language
aloud and was taught the meaning of the text by inference
or by explanation, given in the language by the instructor.
Gottlieb Heness, a German who taught in the United States
from 1841 to 1885, experimented with this new method in
1866–1867 at New Haven, Connecticut. Heness' statement
of his principles of teaching in his book *Der Leitfaden* gives
a very clear picture of this new method.

This natural and familiar method . . . consists simply in questions spontaneously but naturally and logically connected and
built up one on the other, each suggesting the next, and their answers. . . . In the beginning, the teacher can point out the objects
he speaks about; after that he will have recourse to pictures; and
finally he should explain by questions and answers all new words
by means of the vocabulary already acquired. . . . One principle,
however, must guide him throughout the course—he must never
speak English. . . . He must withstand every temptation of exhibiting his erudition in grammar, philology, literature, etc., before
his pupils are prepared to understand what he says in German.

. . . My experience teaches me that by book we never can learn
to speak. Speech, like music, is acquired by ear. . . . Therefore
let us put aside the book, and use it only to read. In the natural
order, reading and writing come after speaking, grammar and
dictionary after reading and writing. . . . Grammar serves to correct
mistakes, and the dictionary only assists in the recovery of words
which cannot be recalled without it.

In 1868 Dr. Lambert Sauveur joined Professor Heness at
New Haven. Dr. Sauveur was the first popularizer of the
natural method in this country. His *Causeries avec mes Elèves*
(1874) became the model for future textbook writers interested in following his principles. Like Heness, he used an
inductive and conversational method. To familiarize his pupils
with the sound of French, he asked questions about the *hand*
and the *fingers* of the *hand,* which he himself answered first
as a model, and then led his pupils to answer, supplying them
with the necessary vocabulary which they repeated after him.
No English was used. Comprehension came only through the
foreign language and gestures. From the *hands* and the *fingers,*
Sauveur went on to the *arm,* the *shoulder,* etc. By the sixth
chapter he had begun to discuss *objects in the classroom,* then
meals; later he introduced the principal tenses by asking questions beginning with the words *today, tomorrow,* and *yesterday.* The grammatical explanations that were given were
presented by questions or remarks by the instructor. When the
pupils had acquired sufficient vocabulary to understand simple
stories, Sauveur introduced them to Grimm's and Perrault's
fairy tales and La Fontaine's fables; from there he went on to
"literature and philosophy." The real study of grammar, he
tells us, "must be deep, very serious, and cannot be begun

before the moment that the pupils understand the language." Sauveur also believed in translation, but only when the pupils "were ready for it. . . . When the pupils understand and speak the language, when they read a French book with ease, when they have acquired the spirit of the language, the time for translation has come."

Dr. Sauveur also initiated the idea of the language summer school. The first such school was founded at Plymouth, New Hampshire, in 1876, but his greatest achievement was the language summer school established in 1877 at Amherst College; sessions were held until 1883. His energy brought him many disciples who, by founding similar schools for the winter as well as the summer, spread his method or sister methods all through the East and as far west as Chicago. Among these disciples were Paul Bercy, C. Fontaine, W. Montague, Sigmon Stern, and B. Méras.

When Professors Stern and Méras presented their *Etude Progressive de la Langue Française* (1882) to the public, they expressed their objective in specific terms:

It being the aim of a teacher of languages to enable his pupils: (1) To receive the thoughts of others: (a) Thoughts which are communicated to us in writing, in the literature of the languages (also the letters), (b) Thoughts which are communicated to us by the spoken word; (2) To communicate his thoughts correctly to others in spoken or written words; (he has to seek and to prepare for the pupil the most direct and the most pleasant way to reach this result). . . . Every lesson ought, as a rule, to contain Conversation, Reading, Writing, Grammar, and Questioning by the teacher and by the pupils. . . . In teaching grammar, the instructor should be guided by the following principle: "The formation of the language must not be given in advance, but should be developed from the living organisms of the language."

Like Sauveur's book, the book was divided into chapters, each chapter being made up of basic information or material and questions and answers. A great deal of material was crowded into one lesson, but it was not supposed to be mastered at once and was frequently repeated in succeeding lessons. New vocabulary was introduced in each lesson and the themes chosen contained easily comprehended words such as the names of animals, cities, rivers, streets, and as many words as possible that were alike in both French and English and which would help convey the meaning of the paragraph. This method was superficial; however, it was intended for students who were satisfied with approximate comprehension and were willing to continue their study for many years; they spoke with many errors but used the language fluently and enjoyed themselves the while. They had a sense of accomplishment and confidence in their ability to understand and make themselves fairly well understood. Since many of them traveled abroad, they had an opportunity to test themselves and to practice what they had learned.

Paul Bercy's *La Langue Française* (1886) applied the same conversational method but began with a discussion of fruit and fruit trees and progressed to the study of the names of flowers, the use of numerals, and material based on geographical names. An outline of the grammatical points introduced in each lesson appeared in small print at the foot of each page.

These two methods, the grammar and the natural method, remained in vogue for many years, but neither was completely satisfactory. Modern languages were becoming increasingly important as a part of the secondary-school and college curriculum. In 1892 a committee of ten prominent teachers of language, under the chairmanship of Professor C. H. Grandgent, met in Washington and drew up a report outlining a method which might be called the *translation method* and which stressed the following points:

1. Children should, if possible, begin their study of German or French by the time they are 10 years old.
2. French or German should from the very first be part of the high-school course.
3. During the first year there should be five recitations per week, during the second at least four, and during each of the other two at least three.

The objectives of elementary high-school language courses were (1) familiarity with the rudiments of grammar and the conjugation of regular and the more usual irregular verbs, (2) ability to translate simple prose at sight by reading not less than 400 pages from three dissimilar works, (3) ability to pronounce and to recognize foreign words and easy sentences when spoken.

The objectives of advanced language courses were (1) proficiency in more advanced grammer and idiomatic phrases, (2) ability to translate by reading not less than a thousand pages, (3) ability to write a paragraph in the language on a subject chosen from the works studied in class, (4) ability to follow a recitation conducted in the language and to answer questions asked by the instructor.

The teacher's efforts were to be directed toward preparing students to translate at sight and ultimately to read foreign languages directly. To acquire the necessary vocabulary the need for a great deal of reading and for rapidity in reading was stressed. Sight translation was undertaken at the outset in the first year and was supposed to proceed as briskly as possible, with the teacher helping the students with the hard passages. Abstruse or technical passages were to be either skipped or translated by the instructor. There was to be some practice in pronunciation, conversation, and composition. From the beginning, carefully graded, isolated sentences based upon the texts used were to be translated into the foreign tongue and converted into connected passages. The language was to be used as much as possible in the classroom, and in the lower classes reading was to follow translation. Grammar rules were not to be studied until the pupil had had 3 months' reading and thus become familiar with the language.

The recommendations of the Committee of Twelve in 1898, a committee composed largely of the same men who drew up the report just summarized, presented a method with a four-fold aim—speaking, writing, understanding, and reading a language—but stressed the importance of reading and abundant practice in sight translation. Great importance was attached to the use of good English in translating.

From 1890 to 1914 textbooks were also greatly improved. In the field of French were published Chardenal's *Complete French Course* (1892) and Fraser and Squair's *French Grammar* (1901), both of which aimed at a more thorough mastery of grammar for purposes of translation. Downer's *First Book in French* presented grammar by the inductive method, and Aldrich and Foster's *French Grammar* offered the idea of frequent review lessons to clinch points of grammar studied in a given series of lessons. In Spanish, Ramsey's *Text Book of Modern Spanish* (1894) and *Spanish Grammar* (1902) and also Hills and Ford's *Spanish Grammar* (1904) all followed the grammar-translation method. In German the most popular grammars used in colleges were E. S. Joynes' *German Gram-*

mar and Calvin Thomas' *German Grammar,* the latter a very comprehensive book corresponding to the Fraser and Squair in French and the Ramsey in Spanish. Grandgent published an Italian grammar, the object of which was to prepare students to read Dante. In fact, wherever the reading objective was stressed these grammars were quite generally used until after World War I.

There were also many books devised for study with or without an instructor, such as the Otto grammars and the Ollendorff grammars, which were translations or adaptations of popular European texts. Such books appeared in several languages and promised extraordinary results. Some popular language schools like the Berlitz and Cortina Schools published their own books which were used by their teachers and were also sold to the general public for study at home.

The followers of the natural method, not being fortunate enough to have a fixed clientele like college and university instructors, were usually more receptive to new ideas and sought to improve their methods of instruction in every possible way. When François Gouin published his *L'Art d'Enseigner et d'Etudier les Langues* in 1880, the new ideas embodied therein were soon adopted in this country by supporters of the conversational method. Its influence was exerted principally by a translation by Swan and Bétis, and it came to be known as the *psychological method.* This method was truly revolutionary. It consisted of a *series* of statements dealing with one subject but developing the action by the use of a different verb in each statement. The subjects were also novel. They dealt, for the most part, with commonplace daily *actions* such as "going to the pump for water" and contained all the vocabulary related to that activity. A *series* on that topic followed this general pattern: The woman *takes* the pail by the handle; the woman *lifts* the pail; the woman *crosses* the kitchen; the woman *opens* the door; the woman *crosses* the threshold; the woman *leaves* the kitchen; the woman *turns around;* the woman *closes* the door, etc. Gouin and his disciples believed that by association students would easily recall more of this useful vocabulary and that by acting out, repeating, and telling in the foreign tongue what they were doing, they would retain the verb because they had heard it, repeated it, and acted out its meaning. The other vocabulary they would retain because of the sequence. "Do not attempt to obtain a perfect pronunciation at the first lesson," said Gouin. "Talk yourself. Talk constantly. . . . Address the ear then, first of all, and principally. Afterwards, take as auxiliaries the eye and the hand in writing and reading. The ear is the prime minister of the intelligence." Mercier, Mankiewitz, Chankin, and many others adapted these ideas for the classroom, either as part of a basic method or as a teaching device. O'Brien and LaFrance in their *First Year French* have revived and modernized the whole idea; they use it in the first ten lessons.

This vigorous emphasis on training the ear led naturally to an attempt to standardize the teaching of pronunciation so that it also might become an integral part of the language lesson. Dr. Wilhelm Viëtor, professor of philology at the University of Marburg, was the first champion of the scientific use of phonetics as an aid in teaching the pronunciation of a foreign tongue. His vigorous denunciation of methods of foreign–language teaching, published anonymously in 1882, not only gave courage to others but helped create a school of disciples. Among them was Dr. Max Walter, who came to America in 1911 as a visiting professor and greatly influenced the teaching of languages in this country. The principles of the Viëtor phonetic method has been incorporated in the *méthode directe* as described in the official circular of the French Minister of Public Instruction in 1901, and used in France. In Germany, what was essentially the same method had been officially used since 1902. It was the Viëtor principles that Dr. Walter brought to the United States; Dr. Herman Rapper of the University of Halle summarized them as follows:

1. Language consists not of letters but of sounds, therefore phonetics belongs in the school.

    Through the sounds of the foreign language the road must lead to the speaking of that foreign language. Not through the eye but through the ear the foreign language must come.
2. The living language consists not of isolated words, but of sentences full of meaning. As material for instruction, connected discourses and not incoherent sentences should be used.
3. One can never learn a living language through grammar and translation. It should be learned as a child learns its mother tongue. Translation is an art that does not concern the school.
4. Grammar should be taught inductively—in fact, the pupils should make their own grammar and must be made to think in the language they are studying.[2]

In practice this method usually began with a thorough drill in the pronunciation of the vowel and consonant sounds of the language being studied. These sounds were studied by means of phonetic symbols used as isolated signs or grouped into words and sentences. These phrases, once learned correctly as to both sound and sense, were combined into stories or dialogues. In the early stages, texts printed in the phonetic

[2] Herman Rapper, *Psychologische Grundlagen des Neusprachlichen Untesrichts*, Leipzig, 1914.

symbols were preferred. Visual aids in the form of familiar objects—pictures of interiors, railroad stations, shops, etc.— were displayed and used in class as a basis for conversation and vocabulary building. Phrases and sentences which had been learned orally were then written down in composition form; this was the first step toward free composition in the foreign tongue. The formal study of grammar came last and only as a corrective process. Translation was also used to correct inaccuracies.

As the number of students in secondary schools and colleges increased with the war prosperity of 1915, outstanding teachers of language, given the opportunity to experiment with larger numbers of students, sought to apply some of these new techniques and to perfect their methods of teaching. The popular appeal of the natural method for adults, the prestige of the direct method in French and German schools, and the impatient criticism of college graduates who after 4 years' study with the grammar method found themselves unable to use the language orally or even to correspond in it with foreigners began to swing most foreign-language teachers, especially in the secondary schools, toward any method that emphasized the oral and aural objectives first. There were, of course, marked differences in the methods proposed by such teachers as A. G. Bovée, E. B. de Sauzé, Charles A. Downer, A. A. Méras, Louis Mercier, W. R. Price, and Jacob Greenberg, but for the most part they followed the same general pattern.

1. Pronunciation was stressed, either by means of phonetics or merely through imitation during the first weeks of the first term. It was never abandoned as an objective, and perfect

pronunciation was believed possible.

2. Initial instruction was always given through the ear rather than through the eye. All reading matter was presented orally before being shown to the pupils.

3. Grammar was still taught, but by the inductive method, and the functional approach was favored even in the study of verb forms.

4. As soon as a sufficient amount of vocabulary and phraseology had been assimilated, composition exercises which would put these phrases to practical use were assigned as written lessons.

5. Initial study of vocabulary was presented directly through objects displayed to the class rather than through the medium of translation. Translation was avoided as far as possible, even in more advanced classes. Discussion of the text, summarizing of the lesson, and explanation of the vocabulary, all in the foreign tongue, were used to test comprehension.

6. In addition to the objects used for teaching vocabulary, picture charts reproducing scenes from life in the foreign country, typical material gathered there, and other audiovisual materials were used to bring local color into the classroom.

The conclusion of World War I, the opening of foreign universities to American students, and the great European travel boom seemed to give purpose to the direct method, and teachers and pupils raised their objectives higher as their proficiency in foreign languages increased. Teachers in secondary schools sought to improve their methods, increase their efficiency, and build still greater enthusiasm for the foreign language being taught, its country and people.

Partly as a compromise to satisfy the more conservative teachers who clung to the grammar and translation methods, and partly to eliminate wasteful practices in their own teaching, many instructors and textbook authors sought to create a new method which they called the *eclectic* or *complete method*. This was supposed to include the best and most successful characteristics of all the other methods. Maintaining the fourfold aim—speaking, writing, understanding, and reading—the eclectic method called for oral practice, reading aloud, questions and answers, and the use of audio-visual materials, but it did not insist upon the elimination of translation; it even encouraged it as a purposeful exercise. Nor did it frown too determinedly on the use of the deductive method of explaining grammar when economy of time was essential. In a sense, the teacher's intelligence and experience were to be his guide. Although not published until 1935, *Language Learning* by Peter Hagboldt gives in substance the principles and practices of the eclectic method at its best.

On the secondary-school level, Phillips Exeter Academy has modernized the eclectic method with an aural-oral approach, which is followed by a presentation of grammar, mostly through the foreign tongue. This is supplemented by extensive reading (nine or ten complete texts in 3 years) that is treated in the main with an *explication de texte* technique. The reading is used to increase passive and active vocabulary and develop oral facility in the foreign language. Gifted students are advanced rapidly according to their ability. Thus many of the upper classes cover material usually taught at the college level.

In 1924 the Modern Foreign Language Study began an

investigation of the whole field of modern language study in the United States, and in 1929 Professor Algernon Coleman published *The Teaching of Modern Foreign Languages in the United States*. The conclusions reached in this volume affected the teaching of modern languages most fundamentally until the outbreak of World War II.

Experience and statistical evidence on teaching the vernacular indicated that the amount of reading that pupils did was directly related to achievement, both in rate of silent reading and in comprehension. Furthermore, experiments showed conclusively that by increasing the amount of required reading, rapid progress resulted in both reading rate and comprehension. Experimental data in the modern-language field seemed to warrant the hypothesis that there was close correspondence between limited reading experience and poor attainment in reading among large numbers of second- and third-year students. This was substantiated by the American Council Reading Tests and by teacher opinion. It seemed fair to assume that if, as a result of a shift in emphasis, the amount of reading were considerably increased in modern-language classes, a more rapid increase in rate and comprehension would result, as had been clearly demonstrated in the case of classes in the vernacular.

Statistics apparently indicated that 2 years of language was the maximum taken by 87 percent of the secondary-school students; and many educators felt that by limiting the objective to reading, more would be accomplished.

Since reading ability appeared to be the principal objective of most of the methods then in use, classroom efforts during the first 2 years were henceforth to be centered primarily on developing ability to read. Coleman outlined this objective for practical application in the classroom and summarized it in his report as follows:

OBJECTIVES OF THE FIRST TWO YEARS (SECONDARY SCHOOL)

IMMEDIATE OBJECTIVES

Progressive development:
1. Of the ability to read books, newspapers, and magazines in the modern language within the scope of the student's interests and intellectual powers.
2. Of such knowledge of the grammar of the language as is demonstrated to be necessary for reading with comprehension.
3. Of the ability to pronounce correctly, to understand, and to use the language orally within the limits of class materials.
4. Of a knowledge of the foreign country, past and present, and of a special interest in the life and characteristics of its people.
5. Of increased knowledge of the derivations and meanings of English words, of the principles and leading facts of English grammar, and of the relationships between the foreign language and English.

ULTIMATE OBJECTIVES

1. Ability to read the foreign language with moderate ease and with enjoyment for recreative and for vocational purposes.
2. Ability to use orally in an intelligible fashion a small stock of foreign words, phrases, and sentences.
3. A special interest in the history, the institutions, and the ideals of the foreign country; a better understanding of its contributions to civilization, and a less provincial attitude toward the merits and achievements of other peoples.
4. Increased curiosity about the literature and the art of other nations, and greater ability to understand and enjoy them.

5. Greater interest in the accurate use of English.
6. Increased understanding of the development and the structure of the mother tongue and of other languages.

OBJECTIVES OF THE THIRD AND FOURTH YEARS

IMMEDIATE OBJECTIVES

1. Further development of speed and of range of silent reading ability, to a point more closely approximating attainment in the vernacular.
2. Development of an increased functional knowledge of the forms and of the syntax of the foreign language, with speaking and writing more definitely in mind as ends in themselves.
3. Increased development of the ability to pronounce, to understand, and to use the language orally.
4. Development of a larger active stock of vocabulary and idioms for use in writing and speaking.
5. An increased knowledge of the foreign country, its people, and their achievements in various fields of activity.
6. A more mature knowledge of the history of the foreign language and of its various relationships with English in word meanings, in derivations, and in grammar.

ULTIMATE OBJECTIVES

1. Ability to read the foreign language with considerable ease and enjoyment, both for recreative and for vocational purposes.
2. Especial interest in the foreign country and its people, considerable knowledge of its past and present, and a broadened attitude toward civilizations other than our own.
3. Ability to use orally and in an intelligent fashion a larger stock of foreign words, phrases, and sentences.
4. Increased ability to understand and enjoy the literature (in the original or in translation) and art of other nations, and greater curiosity about such matters.

5. Greater interest in the accurate use of English.
6. Increased knowledge of the development and structure of English and other languages.
7. Ability to write the language with the aid of a dictionary and other helps.[3]

To the layman this program and its objectives did not appear to vary much from the program of teachers who advocated the modified direct method or the eclectic method. The stress was very defintely on more training in reading, however, and there was an understatement of the maximum possible attainment of the average student; but all the old objectives were included in the program, most of them more clearly defined than at any previous time, and there were a few new ones, like those pertaining to the fuller understanding of foreign people and their civilization.

These objectives when interpreted in the average classroom produced very unexpected results. The introduction of the idea of reading for comprehension and approximate understanding soon set up a goal of quantity rather than quality. In many texts ten simple questions in English were the only test of comprehension for a 50- or 60-page book. Students were limited in their acquisition of an active vocabulary; they learned most vocabulary passively and much of it only approximately. The stress given to speed and quantity of reading naturally resulted in less emphasis on oral and aural language.

As time went on, many teachers began to devote more time to teaching *about* language, but gave increasingly less time to the language itself, although this was not part of the Coleman method. More and more time was devoted to studying the

[3] Algernon Coleman, *The Teaching of Modern Foreign Languages in the United States*, Macmillan, 1929.

structure and nature of language in general, especially in the beginning classes, and there was an increasing tendency to discuss the peculiarities of foreign people in an effort to make students tolerant of other nations. In some courses an attempt was made to incorporate language study into the social arts, primary emphasis being given to the history of the country's civilization and to popular phrases in its language that had found their way into English, and only enough information about the language itself was provided to enable the student to recognize it and its linguistic characteristics. This drifting away from learning a language itself to learning about it led to the introduction of general language courses in junior high schools and in elementary classes of secondary schools. After presenting some elementary facts about the language in general, especially in relation to the study and understanding of English, some of the textbooks in this field offered a series of ten short trial lessons in several of the languages most usually taught in secondary schools, such as Latin, French, German, Spanish, and Italian. The purpose of these lessons was to inform the students about the nature of the various languages so that they might choose the one they considered most attractive or most useful to them.

Other methods proposed in the late 1930s were Tharp's direct reading method and Hendrix' cognate approach. Tharp sought to develop ability to read from the beginning, bringing in pronunciation incidentally and teaching essential grammar inductively as it appeared in the reading text. By means of a basic French vocabulary of cognates which was used by the student in writing free compositions and in oral drill from the very first, Hendrix gave his students a sense of power and led them into reading rapidly and easily.

By the beginning of World War II a great number of methods of teaching language had been discovered, experimented with, tested, and found wanting in some particular. Each method contributed something to increased efficiency in presentation, usually because it stressed a particular phase of language teaching and perfected methodology in that respect. The teacher who knew these many methods found them invaluable if he could adapt them to special problems that arose in his class or school. But some young teachers and educators not very familiar with language teaching saw only confusion and controversy in the variety of methods in this field. As a result a great deal of criticism was leveled against language teaching and the importance it was given in the curriculum. However, during World War II a new impetus was given to language study because of the sudden pressing need for linguists.

* 3 *

LANGUAGE TEACHING METHODS
SINCE 1939

As early as 1925, members of the Linguistics Society of America, in their research on the languages of the American Indians, devised learning techniques which were to play a leading part in revitalizing language teaching after 1939. These new techniques were based on the belief, originating with Professor Franz Boas and supported by Professors Edward Sapir and Leonard Bloomfield, that written language is seldom a reproduction of actual speech and that the only way to learn a language as it is spoken is to imitate as accurately as possible the conversation or speech of natives talking naturally and freely. While the controversy was raging about the relative merits of the reading versus the direct method, little attention was paid to these new ideas; but the American Council of Learned Societies realized their value. Some of their members developed some interesting innovations in teaching which were applied to language learning by the Army and Navy.

In brief, the innovations stressed in their Intensive Language Program were: (1) insistence that students spend most of their time in small drill sessions, imitating a native speaker or informant; (2) extension of the language course to 15 or 20 hours per week; (3) reduction of the study of grammar to what is essential for the intelligent imitation of a native speaker; and (4) less emphasis on the study of reading or writing, which might interfere with learning the *spoken* language. When there was great similarity between sound and spelling, reading and writing might be taught from the beginning. When there was great difference in sound and spelling, a temporary, "stop-gap," purely phonemic spelling was sometimes devised and used until the spoken language had been largely mastered. This new approach[1] also broadened the field of language study to include the Slavic and Oriental languages which, because of orthographic difficulties and great variations from the spoken language, had been generally neglected.

In an effort to awaken popular interest in language study, two linguists, Professor Mario A. Pei of Columbia University and Professor Frederick Bodmer of the University of Cape Town, made use of similar approaches. Their books made these theories plausible and comprehensible not only to the layman but to many teachers who were wearied by the long wrangle over methodology. Pei's *Languages for War and Peace*[2] (1943) and Bodmer's *The Loom of Language* (1944) were intended for the layman who found himself in need of a second language and desired to learn enough of it quickly to understand it and make himself understood. The basic principle underlying both books was that several languages

[1] Cf. Bloch and Trager, *Outline of Linguistic Analysis*, and R. Hall, *Descriptive French Grammar*.

[2] A new edition of this book was brought out in 1948 under the title, *The World's Chief Languages*.

should be taught at once; the books brought out the similarities and stressed the ease with which languages can be learned.

Pei's book was wider in scope that Bodmer's; it dealt with languages in the Germanic group, the Romance group, the Slavic group, and with those of the Middle and Far East. Pei stressed the practical value of his book, for it presented "the world's main languages and their geographical distribution, the linguistic families and the elementary relationships among their members, the identification of the written and possibly the spoken form of several important tongues, and lastly the description of the sounds and grammatical structure, together with a limited vocabulary, of seven of the world's most widely-spoken languages." In presenting these languages to a class, Professor Pei used a native informant who pronounced all the vocabulary and expressions for the students. Pei made no attempt to give a full grammatical outline of the language; instead, he gave only the grammar that he deemed essential in using the vocabulary of about 800 high frequency words and expressions which was included. These words were not chosen by a frequency count in reading, as were those of the Modern Foreign Language Study. Rather, they were popular words used daily by the average person seeking to make himself understood by his fellows.

Bodmer's book contained much more pedagogical theory. He limited the languages studied to the Teutonic (Swedish, Danish, Dutch, and German) and the Romance (French, Spanish, Portuguese, and Italian), and compared them with English. Stressing the fact that learning a language is not a difficult task for the ordinary man, Bodmer tried to break down the fear of it that most people have. He emphasized the principle of association and advocated the study of several languages in the same family at once. He urged the student to approach language study as a new adventure. The fault of academic teaching, he said, was that it had adopted a perfectionist attitude and set its goal too high. The usual language instruction, he said, failed to realize that language study requires three kinds of skills: (1) "learning to read easily," (2) "learning to express oneself in speech or in writing," and (3) "being able to follow the course of ordinary conversation among people who use a language habitually." Bodmer accepted the principle that a basic vocabulary of 850 words, similar to C. K. Ogden's list for English, should be taught first, for it would "suffice to convey the meaning of any plain statement"; but his own basic vocabulary of close to 3 thousand words is three and one-half times as large as Ogden's and considerably larger than Professor Pei's. Bodmer was willing to reduce grammar for practical purposes to only such essentials as were necessary to make oneself understood. Fundamental among these are the rules governing word order, because it is desirable that from the first the student learn the natural word pattern of the foreign language. Although much of what Bodmer advocated might result in dangerous inaccuracies if followed blindly in the classroom, he tried to instill new enthusiasm in language study and to give it a leading place among normal human accomplishments. He tried to strip it of all that is unessential and pedantic, select fundamentals, and explain them in the simplest and most comprehensive terms, hoping that the student would drill, study, and learn with the confidence and assurance that he could attain the goal set.

When general mobilization was ordered shortly before our entry into World War II, the Army faced the problem of giving our soldiers a practical working knowledge of foreign languages in the shortest possible time, and it believed that the techniques advocated by the American Council might be the answer. Dr. J. Milton Cowan, then of the American Council of Learned Societies and now of Cornell University, prepared and directed much of the initial work. By having our soldiers memorize an essential working vocabulary, certain expressions (there were explanations in English on the side), and an apprixomate pronunciation of the language, the Army expected to teach the average soldier enough so he could make himself understood. This method contained many of the principles in both the Pei and the Bodmer books; in fact, many of Pei's chapters on single languages were reprinted as pamphlets for use by the Army.

Some of the ideas introduced in the Army Specialized Training Program (A.S.T.P.) were similar to the Navy's earlier experiments in language teaching. The Navy had introduced at two universities—Harvard and California—its own curriculum which was designed to train translators and interpreters of Japanese and Chinese. The course was intensive and lasted for 12 months; it was designed to teach students to read a Japanese newspaper easily, to converse fluently, and to write and understand the language readily. It therefore had a fourfold objective: speaking, understanding, reading, and writing. Eighteen hours were spent in the classroom each week. Reading was the basis of the work. Each sentence was read and translated and the grammar was explained by the instructor, the students imitating and repeating what he said. This procedure was continued until the end of the hour. Sentences were memorized by the students and hence were understood through memorization rather than through analysis. Questions and answers in Japanese, or translation exercises based upon the reading lesson tested mastery of the reading. Japanese was also used for commands. Five hours a week were spent on dictation, writing being taught from the first day. Japanese was used exclusively after 3 weeks. The reading lesson of the preceding day was the basis of conversation. This was only one form of the constant repetition used to insure mastery of vocabulary and sentence structure. Pronunciation was taught by imitation. The teachers were regular instructors, not informants as in the A.S.T.P. Students who did not meet the requirements were dropped; one out of every eight failed to graduate. The classes were small. There were four or five students in each Japanese class and three in each Russian class; for Chinese, one student had two teachers. In 1946 the Japanese course took 14 months, the Chinese 18 months, the Russian and German 6, the Italian and Portuguese 4, and the French and Spanish 3.

The A.S.T.P. differed from the Navy's program mainly in its stress on the contemporary history, institutions, and geography of the area in which the language was spoken. The general objectives of the Foreign Area and Language Program of the Provost Marshal General were briefly as follows:

1. Special knowledge of characteristics and conditions in areas of occupation.
    a. *Place*—transportation facilities, climate, soil, minerals, etc.
    b. *People*—race, birth and death rates, religion, politics, international relations, etc.
    c. *Means of making a living*—industries, labor supply,

effect of government on daily life, financial control, etc.

d. *Government*—degree of local self-government, position and authority of local officials, role of elections, political parties and party programs, civil service, legal system, government finance, forms of taxation, etc.

e. *Manner of living*—family life, religious influences, schools, degree of literacy, reading habits, architecture, arts, music, dress, sports, literature science etc.; sanitation, use of money.

f. *Historical background and contemporary world affairs* —historical relations to adjacent areas and to the U.S.; most important current theories and ideologies.

2. Language training.

Officers with speaking or reading ability in the language were to be given further instruction so far as required. All other officers were to be given instruction in the language of major importance in the area—German, Italian, French, Japanese, Malay, or Melanesian Pidgin. All instruction was to be in accordance with modern methods of intensive language teaching, native speakers being used unless not available.

3. Special application of previous civilian training to military government situations.

The specific objective of language instruction was to impart command of the spoken form of the language so that officers would have the ability to speak it fluently, accurately, and colloquially, with an acceptable approximation to the native pronunciation, and so that they would also have almost perfect auditory comprehension of the language as spoken by natives. This was to be achieved in 6 to 9 months. Study of the orthography of the language was not an objective in itself.

Any method which could achieve the objective was acceptable. The 17 hours of instruction per week were divided as follows: (1) 1-hour demonstrations 5 days a week by the senior instructor in pronunciation, grammar, syntax, word formation, etc.; (2) 2-hour drill sessions 6 days a week with a drillmaster, preferably native-born.

In the demonstrations, the essential structural characteristics of the language were to be presented in order of difficulty for the American learner. In drill sessions the principles discussed in the demonstrations were to be practiced in conversation, with constant review of material previously studied. No drill sessions were to have more than ten students. Drillmasters were to be natives, but not necessarily trained teachers. Whenever possible, students of the same language were to live together and to be encouraged to use the language at all times. Reading and writing, except in the form of dictation, played a minimum role. In the drill sessions the drillmaster read a few new questions and answers at normal conversational speed. After two or three such readings aided by gestures, intonation, and facial expression, the class repeated each sentence in chorus. Then the printed copy was passed out and the class read the text aloud in unison for 10 minutes. The class was then divided into two groups of five, and these groups repeated the questions and answers. Mistakes and mispronunciations were corrected by members of the group. After 10 minutes of this drill, the printed copies were put away, key words were placed on the blackboard, the class was divided into five groups of two, and five separate dialogues were carried on, the instructor passing from group to group, listening and correcting. Mimicry and memorization were a vital part of the drill. Impromptu dramatics, skits, lectures on politics or economics, discussion of current or controversial topics were used to stress the practical application of the language. Reading without translation was emphasized except in Oriental and eastern European languages where translation was used to clarify the meaning.

Grammar was taught as early as possible by the inductive method and the analysis of drill sentences or dictation. It was also taught functionally by means of a model sentence stating the grammatical rule in its simplest form; this was added to or varied to develop the idea. Vocabulary lists based upon everyday needs took the place of word frequency lists; words were learned in short phrases rather than separately. This vocabulary seldom exceeded 1500 words. Phonograph records, shortwave broadcasts, March of Time recordings, and records to accompany the language courses with pauses during which the student could repeat the phrases were all used. Drillmasters often made their own records to help students in review and self-instruction. Lectures by foreign visitors, soirées, club meetings, meals, church services, meals in foreign-language restaurants, singing groups, and the editing of foreign-language newspapers also stimulated extracurricular learning.

After the war, the Naval Intelligence School in Washington devised a still more concentrated method for training language specialists. Captain A. E. Hindmarsh, the late Professor Jean Pulver, and others have revised the original Navy program; it now offers many features that may be useful to language teachers in general.

Since all the students in this school are acquiring a tool that is absolutely necessary for them and are preparing themselves to establish and maintain direct and intimate contact with the people they will have to observe and with whom they will have to work, they must therefore be able to read and write the language without any effort. They must be able to use and understand the spoken word exactly and automatically. They must never be forced to depend on a translator or interpreter. This is a new and important step in naval language training.

The aim is to teach a great deal to a very few students, all of whom are capable of absorbing a maximum with the minimum effort in the shortest possible time. Hence, candidates are carefully screened before they are allowed to register for this course. Such a procedure is seldom possible in the average secondary school or college, although some large cities are taking steps in this direction. Thus Hunter College in New York has selected its language specialists very carefully for many years, and it has been suggested that a language high school be built for boys and girls who have special language aptitude.

While learning a language in the Naval Intelligence School the students have no time to do anything else. Conferences with their instructors and the preparation of the daily assignments consume the entire day and demand all their effort and attention. As soon as the first difficulties are overcome, results begin to appear and the students learn to distribute their effort. Although the assignments are long and difficult, they are all in the same subject and there is more concentration, less confusion, and less tendency to forget what has been studied and hence less waste of time in reacquiring lost material.

To acquire complete knowledge of a given word or phrase,

all the forms of memory are used so that the visual, the auditive, the graphic, and the spoken images of the word will coincide to give a total and automatic impression. Particular emphasis is placed on oral work because a student who pronounces correctly has, as a rule, greater facility in spelling correctly and in lining up words in the right order. The Naval Intelligence School does not use both an instructor and an informant. All the instructors are teaching their native tongue but are fully aware of the differences between it and English.

The method is based upon the principle that a language is made up not of detached words but of phrases, or groups of words. The emphasis therefore is not on the memorization of separate words but on the retention of *expressions*. The result is that after only a few weeks the student usually ceases to "string words one after another," with a pause between each word, in order to express an idea. He has learned to express that idea as a whole, as a single concept. He does not analyze the thought and go through the process of building up a sentence by translating the various elements in it and, in a second operation, slowly put them in their proper place. He says the phrase directly, exactly as a child would say it, without giving any thought to syntax or idiomatic usage.

Correct usage, the Naval Intelligence School believes, does not depend on the application of fixed grammatical rules. On the contrary, grammar summarizes correct usage and is derived from it. That is why a minimum of grammar is taught, but *only* after correct usage has been established by means of countless examples. Moreover, the few essential rules that are included are not explained, but are given to the students as facts peculiar to the language they are learning. This eliminates all the exceptions over which pupils generally stumble.

So far as possible, no student effort is wasted. In a period varying from 3 months to a year for European languages, depending upon his natural aptitudes and the difficulty of the language, a student succeeds in establishing himself thoroughly in the language and in feeling at home in it.

When his basic language course is over, the naval officer is given a course on the country in which he will live. This complementary course, known as "Area Study," is given entirely in the foreign language, no effort being made to simplify either the vocabulary or the syntax. The course consists of a series of lectures followed by question periods. By this time the student finds no difficulty in expressing his thoughts fully when he asks and answers questions concerning the subject at hand.

The Army Language School at Monterey, in California, accomplishes similar results. The school teaches twenty-four languages divided into four departments: (1) Russian; (2) Romanic-Germanic—that is, the five Romanic languages and Norwegian and Swedish; (3) Middle Eastern and Slavic languages—Albanian, Arabic, Bulgarian, Czech, Greek, Hungarian, Persian, Polish, Serbo-Croatian, and Turkish; and (4) Far Eastern languages—Cantonese, Mandarin, Japanese, and Korean.

The longest course calls for 46 weeks, with 6 hours a day in the classroom and 20 hours of homework a week. An examination is given every 2 weeks. The Romanic-Germanic languages are learned in 23 weeks. These courses are the equivalent of 4 to 8 years of study in the ordinary college course. Emphasis is on the spoken language, but neither translation nor writing is neglected. The textbook, which is mimeographed, was prepared by the staff especially for the school's needs; it is reproduced on records by natives. The classroom work is similar to that in other Army and Navy language schools, but in preparing their work the students listen to records of each lesson during the evening, in order to master it. One classroom innovation to test proficiency involves the use of comic strips. A comic strip is shown the students and they are then required to act it out, supplying their own dialogue based on the vocabulary they have learned. This comic strip technique could be profitably used in any conversation class, as well as in tests of oral proficiency.

Many of the techniques adopted by the Army and Navy were introduced in various forms in American colleges after World War II. The difficulty always lay in fitting a concentrated program which demanded a minimum of 10 hours of classroom work into a curriculum built on a series of basic 3-hour courses.

One college solved the problem by maintaining the traditional 3-hour course for beginners—there were 50 to 70 in one class—and replacing the usual homework with four drill sessions in groups of ten. Selected intermediate students were permitted to take double courses of 10 to 12 hours. The drill sessions, which were conducted entirely in the foreign language, were informal and produced great enthusiasm for the language. The drill instructors were changed frequently to give the students the advantages of different techniques and different pronunciations.

Another college offered a double course of intensive study for 10 hours a week. The number of students was limited and they were carefully selected. In French there were four recitations and six drill periods; in German and Russian there were two recitations and eight drill periods. The drill classes had eight students apiece and were conducted entirely in the foreign language; they consisted of discussion and conversation between students and teacher on practical topics such as the purchase of an article of clothing or a trip by rail, boat, or automobile. The necessary vocabulary was supplied by the teacher. Unison reading, repetition of questions and answers without books or mimeograph sheets, and ordinary questions and answers on old or new material were also used.

The French section of the Yale plan, directed by Professor Jean Boorsch, was also a 10-hour unit, but it was divided into 7 hours of practice and 3 hours of explanation. In general, this new plan, as adopted by the colleges, changed from the old theory-practice method to a practice-theory method. At Yale the drill classes were directed by informants or native teachers. The course was based on the memorization of model sentences and the creation of new sentences growing out of these basic sentences; the elimination of seldom-used vocabulary and expressions; the use of a phonetic system in which symbols were replaced by the letters of the alphabet of the language being studied; structural analysis of sentences and explanation of essential grammatical rules; and constant repetition, by teacher and pupil, of the application of the rule in a model or in original sentences until complete familiarity was achieved. Disks, recording machines, and other aural aids were used to supplement the work of the informants. A similar plan was introduced for the study of German, Spanish, Italian, and Russian. Professor Paul Langellier-Bellevue of Adelphi College further adapted this method, making it fit even more easily into the regular college curriculum while retaining most of the new features.

Another college gave a course calling for 9 hours a week—

3 hours of explanation and 6 hours of drill. Six credits were given for the course. Reading, writing, and oral work were begun as soon as possible, the material being made up and mimeographed by the teacher and distributed each day. Sometimes the material was suggested by the students themselves. After a basic vocabulary had been mastered, the students were questioned about what they did when they went home —how they got home, whom they saw, how they spent their time—and from their answers a mimeographed story was prepared which taught new vocabulary and gave practice in the various tenses. Whenever possible the class work was supplemented by language houses and clubs, the Junior Year Abroad, and the use of the language by attending foreign-language theaters and moving-picture houses. The important change then for the college was the addition of these contact hours for language study which corresponded to the laboratory work required of science students.

A new scientific approach to language teaching, developed through the research of such scholars as Bloch, Hall, Trager, Jakobson, Smith, Walker, Twadell and Cowan, has been put into practice in the comprehensive civilian language programs of the School of Foreign Service of Georgetown University. Language instruction is under the direction of descriptive linguists and native speakers. The introductory intensive courses require 15 clock hours of class per week supplemented by at least an equal number of hours of laboratory drills, using language recordings on tapes. Other courses require 8 hours of class and 12 of laboratory. Cognate languages like German require 6 hours of class and 9 of laboratory. At the intermediate level class hours are reduced to 5, laboratory to 7; at the advanced level, 3 and 3.

Introductory courses under the special intensive schedule

provide 1200 to 1500 hours of instruction and drill during the 12-month period; regular program courses in Arabic, Chinese, and the Slavic group, 600 hours; Germanic and Romance languages, 450; all of these as against 80 hours of class instruction in most institutions at the elementary level. In many cases the written language is not introduced for several weeks; when script is unusually difficult, oral instruction extends over several months and phonemic transcription is often used to aid in retaining the spoken language. The language laboratory tape recordings are used for audition, imitation drills, and more recently for analytic work. The descriptive recordings are prepared by the linguists and native speakers and contain a summary of analytical material presented during class. Individual laboratory drills relieve the class of much of the monotony of repetitive drills. Recordings by students are "spoken themes" and are reviewed and commented upon by instructors. At the Institute of Languages and Linguistics recording on tapes correspond in the teaching of the spoken language to the printed page in the teaching of written language.

Frequent dictation exercises given by tape recordings and taken by individual students leave the class free for other work. The papers are brought to class for correction. Literary selections heard over tape enable the student to better appreciate their meaning and value. Ability in translating, interpreting, and digest writing is developed. Reading is taught by the use of recordings on tapes of the English version of foreign language texts. The student reads the foreign language version while he listens to the English translation. This is repeated often, and recordings are progressively faster until comprehension is complete without use of the English version.

The widespread introduction of language laboratories is stimulating further experimentation and a perfection of these techniques. The establishment of the many Foreign Language Institutes under the Defense Education Act will undoubtedly bring more innovations in what is now being recognized as a new method of teaching languages. The tape recorder is accepted as a study aid, and in many cases as a new form of textbook. It has become an effective method for drilling students in pronunciation and aural comprehension, for perfecting patterns of speech drill, and for presenting new testing techniques.[3]

On the secondary-school level, the difficulties of increasing the class hours enough to make the intensive course effective detracted from the advantages of the new method. At first only 5 hours per week could be devoted to language study in the public schools, and the number of pupils in each class ranged from 36 to 41. Nothing very unusual could be accomplished. The oral method was used, and memorization, dramatized dialogues, paraphrases, the Gouin series, and functional grammar were stressed. The active vocabulary required was limited to 300 words and 30 idioms; this was very small. There were no written exercises and all the tests were oral. Some private schools increased the number of hours for language study, and others adopted a full-year intensive program in which the students devoted all their time to language study; this was followed the next year by intensive work in

[3] Marjorie C. Johnston, *Foreign Language Laboratories in Schools and Colleges,* U.S. Department of Health, Education, and Welfare, 1958.

history or mathematics. This approach is still in an experimental stage, although the initial results were very good for language.

Phillips Academy (Andover) has recently experimented with an aural-oral approach to language teaching. No textbook is used, but the material studied at Andover during the first year of French, is completely covered. Two instructors are employed. One presents the vocabulary and grammar through pictures, action, and conversation and initiates the necessary drill for retention; the other reviews each day's material at a later hour usually devoted to study. Reading material is presented aurally; no laboratory is used. The total course requires 9 hours, but no home study is assigned. At the end of the first year of the experiment, it was found that the students were able to carry on unrehearsed conversation with a group of French exchange students who were visiting the United States.

As a result of the great emphasis on the practical phases of language study, particularly on the importance of the spoken language, many secondary-school teachers have adopted a new method—the unit approach to the teaching of modern languages. Here the subject matter of each lesson is organized so that it centers about a unit of interest that is essentially practical. By either the decision of an elected committee or class vote the unit of study is chosen for the following day; it may involve such topics as a visit to the grocery store, an evening at a dance, buying a ticket or reserving a seat on a train or plane, riding in a taxi, etc. A committee of students then prepares a dialogue in English containing 20 to 40 lines of text. The teacher translates this dialogue into the foreign language, trying to include in the sentences the practical vocabulary, idioms, and whatever grammatical points seem to fit the subject matter best. If, for example, a grocery store unit is being taught in French, the partitive will naturally form part of it:

—Avez-vous *de la* farine?
—Non, monsieur, nous n'avons pas *de* farine, aujourd'hui.
—Eh bien, avez-vous *du* sucre et *du* lait?
—Non, monsieur, je peux vous vendre *du* sucre, mais nous n'avons pas *de* lait.
—Avez-vous *de l'*eau en bouteille?
—Non, monsieur, nous n'avons *plus d'*eau.
—Alors, avez-vous *des* olives et *des* sardines, au moins?
—Oui, nous avons *des bouteilles d'*olives et *des boîtes de* sardines en conserve.
—Avez-vous *des* pommes de terre en conserve?
—Non, monsieur, nous n'avons pas beaucoup de demandes pour cette sorte de marchandise.

From this the pupils first list the grocery store vocabulary, and then a supplementary vocabulary for a series lesson. They next list all the new grammatical constructions and all the idioms in the text. This preparatory work is often done during study period or consultation hours and then organized for presentation to the class in mimeographed form. In class, the vocabulary is learned first, by a direct method if possible, with concrete objects to help make it real. Then the phrases with the partitive are repeated until most of the class knows them by heart. These phrases are then studied inductively to see whether any students have discovered the grammatical peculiarities of the partitive; if not, they are explained by the teacher. Next the whole scene is acted out and the second vocabulary list is put on the board or read from the mimeographed sheet for use in free composition, translation of sentences containing the vocabulary and grammatical points, fill-in exercises, or collateral reading that contains this vocabulary and grammatical material. In language teaching the unit method of presentation lies wide open for experimentation and may offer an excellent way of revitalizing language study. This approach demands from the teacher not only complete mastery of his subject but great technical skill in presenting it. Hence it should not be undertaken by the inexperienced teacher.

The unit approach often requires the reorganization not only of several weeks' work in the textbook but of the whole term's assignments in grammar. In his *Planning the Modern Language Lesson,* W. H. Rice[4] presents another treatment of the unit approach.

If the unit chosen is the position of the direct object pronoun in French, the teacher may bring to class books and apples representing objects of masculine and feminine gender. The lesson presupposes knowledge of the present tense of *avoir, donner,* and *prendre.* Picking up a book, the instructor says, *"Je prends le livre."* He then asks, *"Qui prend le livre?"* The students answer, *"Vous prenez le livre."* Then, asking one or two students to join him, he covers the first person plural and the third person singular and plural. He follows the same procedure with the apple. Then he replaces the name of the object by the pronoun—*le* for the masculine, *la* for the feminine—in his statements and questions; the class in answering makes the same substitution of pronoun for noun. When the form and position of the pronouns are mastered orally by the class, a student or the teacher writes on the board

[4] W. H. Rice, *Planning the Modern Language Lesson,* Syracuse, Syracuse University Press, 1947.

dictated sentences containing the pronouns. The class is questioned concerning the position of the pronoun in relation to the verb. The instructor follows the same procedure with the plural forms. When they have been mastered and written on the board, he proceeds with the object pronouns used with *avoir*. He asks questions that bring out the elision before a vowel, and this form is written on the board. After the questions and answers have been repeated until the new grammatical fact seems clear, the class is divided into two groups for a period of questions and answers supervised by the instructor. Finally the class is broken down into pairs; these pairs, under the supervision of the instructor who goes around the class room, have a conversational drill on pronoun objects. When this phase of the work is completed, several students are sent to the blackboard in the rear of the room to write similar dialogues covering all phases of the lesson—the three verbs, the masculine and feminine forms, singular and plural, with and without elision. At the same time, the students who are seated also write dialogues. When they have finished, the dialogues on the blackboard are corrected. The seated students are permitted to correct their own sentences if they discover errors similar to those made on the blackboard. All papers are then corrected. If the grammar has fill-in questions and if time allows, these are used, or they may be assigned to the students as preparation for the next day, together with any other exercises that may fit, including the translation of sentences. If the reading material used by the class gives examples of the use of the pronoun object, the class may be asked questions on these passages, which require the use of object pronouns in the answers. Thus, study of the object pronouns may cover several periods and at the same time bring in verbs and vocabulary review in a practical form as dialogue or conversation.

One of the great advantages of the unit method is the fact that it requires integration to really succeed and that it stresses activity and the practical quality of language study. It makes language functional and eliminates much of the artificiality that so often deadens the language classroom.

Both the intensive and extensive reading lesson can be treated similarly, provided they contain a unit of thought or action that can be stressed. For example, depending on its difficulty, a short story unit from one and one-half to two or three pages can be developed in an elementary class in many ways under this plan. When the lesson is assigned, the instructor can discuss the new vocabulary by questions and answers in the language, either by asking for meanings or giving the explanations outright. Probable difficulties in pronunciation can be explained or drilled on through the use of questions and answers in the language.

The lesson itself, which may cover several class hours, can be taught for content and vocabulary (1) by preparing a long list of detailed questions, as many as 50 in number; (2) by asking the class to rewrite the story unit in dramatic form, or by choosing a small group to prepare a dramatization and then act it out in class; (3) by isolating idiomatic expressions, using several of them in sentences, then asking the students to use them; (4) by preparing English sentences containing the idioms and having them translated by the students; (5) by picking out salient grammatical points in the lesson and questioning the class about them in order to assure practical understanding and ability to use them correctly; (6) by isolating spelling difficulties and stressing them in exercises; (7) by translating a summary of the story in English; (8) by stressing the vocabulary through study of synonyms and antonyms; and (9) by asking for a resumé of the whole story in the foreign language.

The Linguistic Scientists have continued their research since their contributions to language study during World War II and have offered their findings to language teachers for adaptation to the classroom. Because of this an increasing number of language teachers have become aware of certain previously overlooked facts concerning language. Contemporary linguists have presented language as a living, vital, everchanging force that is intimately involved with human beings and their civilizations. The static concept of language, made up of isolated sounds, words, and grammatical rules and out of which the classroom students slowly created an instrument of human communication in a foreign tongue, has, they contend, failed to teach the foreign language as it really is. To attain their goals they insist first upon an aural-oral approach—that is to say, a phonemic analysis of characteristic foreign sounds as pronounced by a native—followed by phonetic variations of sounds which are caused by their position in a word or sentence when influenced by stress and pitch. This, the Linguistic Scientists claim, is necessary in order to reproduce the meaningful harmony of the complete foreign phrase. They insist further that individual words be incorporated in and taught as part of a thought sequence, that grammar be mastered through cultural patterns of speech, and that, before these words are analyzed, the student be thoroughly familiar with them as a particular form of human communication. Transferring them to a written form or understanding them through the printed page, linguists consider to be of secondary importance; for they believe that reading and writing should be attempted only after a sufficient number of structural patterns have been memorized to permit easy comprehension of the printed page.

Edwin T. Cornelius presents an excellent statement of the principal objectives and general techniques of the new school. They are, with some curtailments, substantially the following:

1. The objective of the teacher of a foreign language is to expose students to the language as it is spoken.
2. The ability to read and write a language may come as a by-product of the process of learning the spoken language.
3. The terms "correct" and "incorrect" are not helpful in language learning and teaching. It is important to know whether a given form or construction is a part of the particular language system or not.
4. The model to be used in teaching a language is always the speech of a native speaker of that language.
5. A knowledge of grammar rules and terminology is independent of the ability to speak and understand the language. . . . Children learn to master the spoken language of their country before they learn to tell the difference between reflexive pronouns and subjunctive clauses.
6. No one language is more difficult to learn than any other. Some languages have a more difficult and more complicated writing system than other languages, but the process of acquiring the spoken language is essentially the same.
7. The process of learning a language is chiefly the process of learning by heart innumerable forms from the language. In this sense, learning a new language is essentially memorizing the language in the same way the native tongue is memorized.
8. The study of Latin will be helpful in understanding the terminology of . . . certain foreign language textbooks. . . .
9. The most important activities of classroom study are continuous imitation and repetition of the model of the spoken-

language provided by the teacher.

10. The teacher of the foreign language must make a conscious distinction in class between techniques of teaching and testing.[5]

Nelson Brooks[6] has suggested ways in which these objectives can be applied to the classroom. He recommends a modeling first of all of new material by the teacher in the foreign language, and demands that the mother tongue be subordinated to the second language. He also believes that language training should be begun early, for this will train the students ear and tongue before he is too old to be receptive to an unfamiliar language. This aural-oral training should be continued indefinitely so that students can learn the structure of the language by practicing patterns of sound and speech; not through explanation. Once the sounds have been mastered, graphic symbols may gradually be substituted for the sounds. The main principles of structure can be summarized for the student when he is thoroughly familiar with the language; as mastery increases, the time span between performance and correction can be shortened. Emphasis on vocabulary should be minimized until the student has learned all the important structure; and even then vocabulary should be taught and studied only in context.

Professor Brooks feels that all practice in using the language should remain aural-oral, since translation should be practiced only as a literary exercise, and then only at an advanced level. He also points to the importance of a supervised language laboratory that is integrated with the classroom work in such

[5] Edwin T. Cornelius, *Language Teaching*, Thomas Y. Crowell Company, 1953.

[6] Nelson Brooks, *Language and Language Learning*, Harcourt, Brace & Co., 1960.

a way that the student not only hears the materials—dialogue, pattern practice, or reading matter—that have been covered in class, but is prepared by the tape for greater proficiency in his next class period. Well-defined and effective testing is also stressed as an essential part of this new approach. Tests, Professor Brooks points out, should measure proficiency in special as well as general skills, irrespective of training. In addition to our present achievement tests in written and aural comprehension, he urges setting up those that will record the student's ability to repeat what he has heard, to make statements and answer questions according to a suggested pattern, to read the foreign language, and to answer general questions about himself.

Most of these suggestions are being adapted to classroom use and experimented with in the Federal Defense Education Act Language Institutes in Teachers' Colleges, and in Language Methods Courses. Special committees are preparing new procedures and techniques for testing, and other committees are constructing textbooks based upon this new interpretation of the aural-oral approach and its reorganized objectives.

There are other methods and approaches that have had their vogue over the years, but only those which seem distinctive and have gained prominence have been discussed. All these methods have performed, and to some degree are still performing, a service in the teaching of languages, either directly or by their incorporation into some other techniques. The importance of reviewing those with distinctive principles lies in the fact that from them it may be possible to evolve a permanent set of objectives and techniques that will have enough flexibility to make them adaptable to changing conditions and emergency needs.

* 4 *

PERMANENT BASES AND
OBJECTIVES IN LANGUAGE
TEACHING

The principal objectives of all these methods seem to be to give the student the ability to _understand_ a foreign language, both spoken and written; to give him the ability to _communicate_ his thoughts in oral or written form; _and_ to give him enough information about the people, geography, and culture of the nation whose language he is studying to inspire in him an understanding of the people and an appreciation of their civilization and accomplishments.

Because the United States has been placed in a position of world leadership and because the present and coming generations must accept this position, their interest in language stems from their desire to know more about the various nations —their people, economy, politics, geography, distinguishing psychology, customs and manners, and culture. Since more than ever before in business, diplomacy, engineering, medicine, administration, education, and human relations, they are finding themselves in more intimate contact with other nations, our people seek a means—any means—to hasten the development of their powers of communication with other nations, aural and oral as well as written. The emphasis must now be placed on complete knowledge and understanding of a people as well as their language.

A basic error of all our language teaching has for a long time been the almost continuous quarrel between language teachers concerning what the *primary* objective should be, and the attempt to rally all the teachers around that objective— reading, speaking, or grammar—often to the exclusion of the others. Most language teachers seem to have forgotten, except for very brief periods, that to teach a language in all its phases is really not too great a task. They have failed to consider the cooperation they can expect from the student if the subject is presented with multiple appeal. As soon as the student realizes that he is really gaining knowledge which can be used in a practical way, he has an incentive to learn, and as a result he absorbs much of the language unconsciously. The student who feels that he is being driven learns with difficulty. In order to obtain the best possible results in teaching modern languages, we must abandon the idea that any *one* method with a limited objective can be the open sesame to all language learning. Every classroom has its share of students whose previous training has been essentially visual, as well as those whose training has been oral or aural. Language study, as a vital part of general education and culture, should train all the faculties, and, whenever possible, develop any faculty that may have been neglected in earlier training. There is no sound educational or psychological principle which insists that, because some students or teachers have logical minds that tend to learn language primarily through the study of grammar, all the pupils should be forced to learn by this method. The fact that one student or teacher has great facility in acquiring vocabulary is no reason for concentrating on the study of vocabulary in every course. Nor should we, because one teacher or pupil finds imitation of sound more fascinating than comprehension of the printed page, build our foreign-language courses entirely on the principles of phonetics.

We should seek to teach a foreign language as we wish every foreigner to know our own language. This cannot be done by trying to force all the students to follow one pattern of study, no matter how successful this pattern may be in special cases. We must cease imposing a unique approach on all the students, because those who cannot follow are left to limp along after the more adaptable students; hence they learn to dislike the subject. Language learning is as natural and necessary a process as eating, walking, or sleeping, and should be presented as naturally as these other human needs. Learning a language should follow the same pattern, whether the student is amplifying knowledge of his own language or learning a new one. To attain the necessary mastery, our slogan should be: "Any method is valid that brings the maximum results."

The now vastly extended FLES program also demands that we consider the integration of FLES pupils into the secondary-school program. Since there is very little uniformity in the curriculum content of language instruction in the elementary school, and even the junior high school, the only way to transfer students from one level of achievement to another is through the national adoption of the MLA Educational Testing Service Examinations. These tests of the various language skills should accurately measure the pupils' achievement as they advance from level to level. Tests covering the four language skills should be prepared at least for pupils in the seventh, ninth, and twelfth grades. Since achievement in each of the skills can now be measured, students can be transferred into more advanced classes on the basis of their tested achievement in each of the language skills. If schools are able to vary the contents of classes—within each level, and if they can distribute students according to the findings in these tests, weaknesses in any of the skills may be overcome without neglecting the other skills in which students are proficient. This process of equalization may be continued until a national standard of college entrance or its equivalent is attained.

In other words, pupils who, on the elementary level, have achieved high proficiency in aural-oral language but who, as they have passed from level to level, have achieved little in the graphic skills, might be placed in compensating classes; students whose training in the graphic skills has been very good might be assigned to classes which, while maintaining the high level of these acquired skills, will stress the unlearned aural-oral skills. However, scheduling these special classes within the framework of the high-school curriculum, as has already been done for gifted students, becomes an administrative problem. If it were possible to test language skills at levels still lower than the seventh grade, the transition to higher levels would certainly be more efficient. Also, a far greater degree of uniformity in teaching and accomplishment could be achieved nationally than is at present. Such a program would gradually train language students of real ability on a scale large enough to enable them to compete with students in other countries. It would prepare the way for introducing in the United States a general 6-year language program based upon achievement in all skills. This program would contrast with the haphazard and unequal certification that is unfortunately so typical today. As instruction on the elementary-school level becomes more effective and more uniform, standards of achievement can be raised uniformly and progressively throughout the United States, continuing to the end of the secondary school.

Although the following report of the New Jersey Modern Language Teachers Association does not, in outlining its objectives, include the achievement that is possible in the elementary school, its requirements are such that, pending the standardization of courses and aims on that pre-high-school level and the introduction of a 6-year course or its equivalent, it can very well serve as a model.

OBJECTIVES: LOWER LEVEL[1]

SECOND YEAR OF HIGH SCHOOL AND FIRST YEAR OF COLLEGE

1. Conversation: Ability to converse with confidence in the foreign language in simple idiomatic sentences about subjects of everyday interest or matters already thoroughly assimilated in classroom discussions.
2. Reading: Ability to read and comprehend, without translation into English, a variety of moderately difficult passages in the foreign language.
3. Composition: Sufficient skill in written composition to demonstrate capacity for well-organized thinking in the foreign language, and ability to use less familiar words in correct relationships and with correct connotations.
4. Usage: Knowledge of basic structural grammar adequate to

[1] The following is adapted from a mimeographed report presented by the Committee of the New Jersey Modern Language Teachers Association at the Princeton Language Conference on April 5, 1952.

insure on standard tests a score higher than the nationally required norms.

5. Culture and civilization: Some knowledge of the outstanding personalities, events, and contributions of the people whose language is being studied.

OBJECTIVES: UPPER LEVEL

THIRD AND FOURTH YEAR OF HIGH SCHOOL AND SECOND YEAR OF COLLEGE

1. Conversation: Progressive fluency and confidence in speaking the foreign language.
2. Reading: Facility in reading, without translation into English, the more appealing classics which have been carefully selected to approximate the intellectual and emotional level of the students.
3. Composition: Ability to demonstrate, in writing, the effective application of all the elementary goals on the more advanced level.
4. Usage: Proficiency in the use of basic structural grammar patterns and familiarity with advanced syntactical combinations met within material read but not specifically drilled as grammar.
5. Culture and civilization: Definite understanding and appreciation of the outstanding personalities, events, and contributions of the people whose language is being studied.

Language learning must be made adaptable to all students and it must reach, by using a multiple approach, every student in any given class, whatever his individual aptitudes may be. The task may seem difficult to many, but in reality it is not. It merely means a little less formalism and artificiality in teaching and a little more thought applied to the needs of the class, which is considered as a group of individuals rather than an impersonal unit. Personalized teaching is easier in small classes, but even in large classes the increased amount of time and energy required at first will be compensated for by the greater enthusiasm of the students and their greater eventual achievement. Although the teacher may be led to use many different approaches in order to reach every student effectively, no single essential phase of the language need be neglected. The only element of language study that is flexible from the point of view of time of presentation is the cultural. Although culture is probably best taught as an introduction to language in order to stimulate and motivate interest in the linguistic subject matter, it may in some cases be used at the conclusion of the course to emphasize the importance and implications of the completed work. The cultural element may also be presented simultaneously as a feature of the language learning process itself.

Every language lesson can be conducted so as to bring in repeated references to the customs, manners, and psychological characteristics of the people. Everything read can be made the basis for a commentary on the life and culture of the country and its people.

The multiple-objective approach leaves room for stressing particular phases of language study which may require more emphasis than others. It permits flexibility of emphasis in accordance with the nature of the community and the intelligence and age level of the students. It even permits consideration of the students' previous general training which may have developed one ability more than another. If all the teachers of language would accept the fact that the primary purpose of language study is to facilitate communication between people and that this communication must be oral as

well as written, much of the artificiality and apparent pur-
poselessness of our teaching would disappear.

It is gratifying to find in Marjorie C. Johnston's article on
promoting international understanding through the study of
modern languages the following summary of the aims of the
Modern Language Association's Steering Committee (1953).

The study of a foreign language, skillfully taught under the
proper conditions, provides a new experience, progressively en-
larging the pupil's horizon through the introduction of a new
medium of communication and a new culture pattern, and progressively adding to his sense of pleasurable achievement. This
experience involves:

1. The acquisition of a set of skills, which can become real
   mastery for professional use when practiced long enough. The
   international contacts and responsibilities of the U.S. make
   the possession of these skills by more and more Americans a
   matter of national urgency. These skills include:
   a. The increasing ability to understand a foreign language
      when spoken, making possible greater profit and enjoyment
      in such steadily expanding activities as foreign travel,
      business abroad, foreign language movies, and broadcasts at
      home and abroad.
   b. The increasing ability to speak the foreign language in
      direct communication with people of another culture, either
      for business or for pleasure.
   c. The ability to read the foreign language with progressively
      greater ease and enjoyment, making possible the broadening
      effects of direct acquaintance with the recorded thoughts of
      another people, or making possible study for vocational or
      professional, e.g., scientific or journalistic purposes.
2. A new understanding of language, progressively revealing to
   the pupil the structure of language and giving him a new
   perspective on English.
3. A gradually expanding and deepening knowledge of a foreign

country—its geography, history, social organization, literature, and culture—and as a consequence, a better perspective on American culture and a more enlightened Americanism through adjustment to the concept of differences between cultures.[2]

To attain the goal set by this objective we must abandon both the 1- or 2-year limit imposed on language study in some secondary-school systems and any other short-sighted compromises which force teachers to accept unintelligent objectives. It is true that such limits on language study in the secondary-school curriculum often make it fit into the total program better; but if sufficient time is not allowed for proper assimilation and understanding, any time spent on it is wasted. In a 2-year course the student is given no opportunity to learn anything of the psychology, thought processes, and civilization of the nation whose language he is studying —knowledge that is essential for successful cultural, diplomatic, and business relations.

Both the 1960 report of the National Education Association and the Modern Language Association recognize this, and they recommend that gifted pupils begin studying foreign languages in the third grade and continue studying them for 10 years, or until the last year of high school. They also suggest that the common practice of studying a foreign language for 2 years only be discontinued, and that at least 4 years of language study be required. It is fortunate for language teachers that these suggestions have been made, because for some years these teachers have been handicapped by the defensive attitude they have been forced to take toward their subject.

[2] Marjorie C. Johnston, *Bulletin of the National Association of Secondary School Principals*, December, 1956.

As a result of isolationism, many people have accepted the unrealistic belief that we could remain independent of the rest of the world, and that if we were forced into communication with other nations we could impose our language upon them. This cannot be done if we wish to maintain other nations' good will. When we have needed the friendly cooperation of other countries in an emergency, we have suddenly become language-conscious and have tried to master their language in record time. But this has been done only by spurts, when the situation demanded it. Now that we have accepted world leadership to some degree and have become a dominant figure in world affairs, it is essential not only to raise the standard of linguistic accomplishment in our classrooms but also to broaden the study of languages in our elementary and secondary schools.

Henceforth our elementary- and secondary-school program should cover a sequence of at least 6 years, carefully integrated so that there will be no loss of time or skill in transferring from one level to another. Even at the earlier levels, our program should include not only important European languages but Slavic and Oriental languages as well. Language must no longer be considered a luxury in the elementary- or secondary-school curriculum. It has now become a necessity.

With our changed position in the world, giving students a knowledge of foreign languages has now become a vital part in educating our citizenry. Without more and better linguists in this country our leadership in world affairs cannot be truly effective. Every educated American should be master of at least one modern language besides his own. To attain this goal we must maintain a permanent set of practical objectives—objectives which will seem practical and worthwhile to everyone, not merely to a selected or provincial group, and ones which will lead to true mastery of the language in all its phases, to ability to *comprehend* it in both spoken and written form, to *communicate* thought both orally and in writing, and to understand sympathetically the psychology, customs, and manners of the people who speak the language.

Studying a modern foreign language with the opportunity it offers to learn about a nation's economic, political, and social problems; its scientific, commercial, artistic, and diplomatic successes and failures; the psychology of its people, its customs, and manners; and the medium by which we can communicate effectively with its people is daily becoming a more important part of our educational pattern. What excellent lessons in tolerance and international understanding can be learned from such a study—lessons that are so essential in our rapidly shrinking modern world!

* 5 *

PRESENTATION AND METHOD IN RELATION TO SCHOLASTIC AND INTELLECTUAL LEVEL

From a practical point of view, another basic error in teaching foreign languages has been the failure to develop specific methods or approaches to meet the needs of various intellectual levels. Teaching languages in the elementary grades and in junior high schools offers problems which are quite different from those encountered in either senior high schools or colleges. These differences should be dealt with from the point of view of psychology, method of presentation, and method of procedure, as well as from the point of view of the content of the curriculum. This applies not only to teaching grammar but to the choice of textbook and of reading material and the manner of presenting cultural material.

Some of the statements that follow may not seem to agree with the opinions drawn from scientific psychological experiments, but like all the classroom procedure described in this book, what is said grows out of personal classroom experience and the actual observation and interpretation of what other teachers have done. There may, of course, be some variations from what appears to be a norm, but there should not be many.

In dealing with the junior-high-school student—that is, students of the seventh, eighth, and ninth grades—we must keep in mind that their intellectual experiences have been limited but that they have great curiosity of mind and tremendous energy. Most of them have few inhibitions and hence are free to show their dramatic talent if they have any. They are very lively and react favorably to any program that gives them an opportunity for physical activity. They are eager to please and to help their teachers. For the most part, they want to talk a great deal.

All these characteristics can, of course, be used to advantage in presenting the subject. Pupils of that age like to play and to feel that they are having a good time; this permits the use of songs and games with considerable success. The junior-high-school boy or girl arrives at a conclusion quickly, but his comprehension of a subject, even though it has been explained, is usually incomplete. This leads to confusion in ideas and to failure really to understand things already explained until they have been repeatedly explained and frequently tested.

The young student needs to form habits; and although there is a natural aversion to doing so, this tendency is more easily overcome at this stage than later. These boys and girls become tired very easily. Because their powers of concentration are limited, great variety in method of presentation is necessary. They have good memories; hence impressions made upon them should be lasting. Their sense of logic is elementary and not very sure. At times they surprise us by the conclusions they reach, but often these conclusions are not sound and are based, generally speaking, on rather limited experience. They have great imagination and this often creates for them a world that is more real than the world in which they actually live. As a result, they frequently confuse the two. There are, of course, exceptions to this description of the psychology of these young people, but they are relatively few. This age group also has great ability to imitate, a fact that enables them to pronounce a new language easily and well. For a group of students with these characteristics, what method of language teaching is most effective?

The grammar that is required should be presented as clearly and as simply as possible. Only one idea should be introduced at a time and it should be repeated often and as dramatically as possible, by means of drawings, pantomime, colored chalk, and any other devices which appeal primarily to the senses. This must be followed almost immediately by drill on the new idea—drill in as many different forms and with as much physical activity as possible.

For teaching verbs or the days of the week, a method like the Gouin method is very effective. A little improvised dramatic scene will help to teach vocabulary such as that used at a meal, in a grocery store, at home, or in the classroom. Popular games like bingo, in which the whole class participates, can be used to test vocabulary and grammatical points. Flash cards should be used frequently. Pupils should be encouraged to make drawings of a house, boat, store, animal, parts of the body, or articles of clothing, and to label the various objects in them. Questions and answers amuse and stimulate the pupils. The rapidity of drill excites them; they enjoy vocabulary, verb, and grammar matches similar to spelling contests, and programs that resemble our popular "Information Please" and "Double or Nothing." They have few inhibitions about giving oral compositions within the limits of their vocabulary, and they enjoy writing free compositions either on the board or at their desks or at home. They are willing to do translation, but they do not particularly enjoy it. They learn songs, short poems, and proverbs very easily. They learn and are willing to act out short practical conversations and short plays that are not too artificial.

A simple form of the unit approach is very effective with these pupils. They enjoy working out projects together, cooperating in writing a class notebook or in making a large map of the country whose language they are studying, including on it all the products and the characteristic features of each province. They have more facility for accurate pronunciation than older children. They should be taught sentences or groups of words rather than single words, in order to acquire the proper intonation. They are at an age when they can imitate so easily that they should be encouraged to mimic in order to approximate correct pronunciation. Picture cards can be used like flash cards to correct sounds which the pupils do not pronounce well. Songs remedy many errors in pronunciation, and chorus reading—particularly choral recitations—is helpful in improving it. Grammatical functions can sometimes be made clearer by being correlated with similarities in English grammar. But terminology must often be taught first. Classrooms for these grades should have many pictures; foreign proverbs, maps, drawings, and photographs pertaining to the country should be put on the walls. These should be changed at least once a week and questions should be asked on the material to see whether the students have examined it.

There should be plenty of conversation based on the sentences learned, and these sentences should be constantly repeated so that they may be retained and used for oral or written composition. It is difficult for children of this age to construct sentences except by imitation, and it is unwise to ask most of them to apply a rule; it is easier for them to learn a model or pattern sentence and imitate it. Frequent dictations, short and simple, based on either the grammar lesson or the reading lesson, help to fix correct spelling forms and certain grammatical points in their minds. Very frequently, if a student who has remedial reading difficulties in his own language really applies himself and becomes interested in mastering a foreign language, he will have no unusual difficulty in learning it. Many students, properly motivated, become accurate spellers in the new language and hence realize that their poor spelling in English can be remedied if they are willing to make the effort.

Civilization when taught at this level should, for the most part, deal with personal anecdotes or stories told by someone who has recently returned from the foreign country. The life of children who are approximately their own age interests these pupils. They find pleasure in examining the stamps of the country, its money, dolls, ships, and airplanes in the form of models, drawings, or photographs. Pupils of this age enjoy giving short reports on assigned topics which they can look up in an encyclopedia. They like to listen to short, simple stories, particularly funny stories and anecdotes, and they have far less difficulty in understanding them than might be supposed. These stories should of course be told in the foreign language.

Although they are not able to handle purely cooperative activities, these children enjoy conducting the class by means of committees or in the form of a club or a socialized recitation in which they can feel that they are directing the affairs of the classroom and taking responsibility.

The textbooks for these classes must be simple and very repetitious; they should cover nothing but the main elements of grammar, and, if possible, they should contain an element of fun. There should be great variety in the exercises, and as many illustrations as possible. The same features hold true in the choice of reading material; it should not be childish but full of life, activity, adventure, mystery, and keyed to the children's natural reading interests.

Only recently have efforts been made to prepare foreign-language textbooks for the different levels of learning. There is still, however, much confusion in the textbooks themselves and in the way they are used. Thus many of them still attempt to serve the junior high school, the senior high school, and the first year of college. Textbooks are much more successful when they are written specifically for the age and intellectual capacity of the students who will use them.

Reading material for the junior high school should not be limited, as has too often been the case, to stories told in words of one syllable or to subject matter based on fairy tales. Junior-high-school students should be treated like adolescents, for they read and comment on much of what appears in the daily papers, and their attendance at movies has given them a content interest which is fairly mature; consequently, although their vocabulary is limited and the style with which they can be reached in a foreign language must be simple, neither the subject matter nor the style of writing should be childish. Although, as has been said, children of this age particularly enjoy adventure, mystery, animal, and humorous stories, they are critical of the construction and the conclusions reached in these stories. In elementary work comic book material may be used profitably. Most historical novels of the nineteenth century—those by Dumas, Hugo, and Erckmann-Chatrian in French, and South American novels and stories in Spanish —when properly simplified, hold the attention of the pupils. If the longer descriptive passages can be eliminated, any short stories with a good plot are likewise popular with these youngsters. Interesting biographies of great men and the stories of national heroes that emphasize the dramatic, heroic, or adventurous aspects of their lives, and their human qualities, can also be used to advantage, especially when the incidents can be given an element of suspense.

high school

In dealing with students on the high-school level—that is, the second, third, and fourth year of high school—we must bear in mind that to some degree they are at a different psychological stage, generally called adolescence. Students at this level are likely to be confused mentally, to be subject to involuntary distractions and romantic dreaminess. They are basically timid or self-conscious; they lack frankness and are usually very sensitive but hate to admit it. They are motivated either by great ambition, probably out of all proportion to their capabilities, or by extreme laziness caused by the fear of not succeeding or attaining their objectives. Fundamentally they want to be kept busy but they refuse to admit it. They are frequently the victims of poor earlier training, and this makes every effort doubly hard. They are usually willing to work, but they hate to work without obtaining the results they think they should obtain. Their critical faculties are beginning to develop and they are critical of their instructors and of the materials they are given to learn. They are beginning to feel the pressure of time; and although they seldom say so, they really want to be consulted and given an opportunity to direct their own affairs, but they need considerable guidance. They seldom admit that they need this guidance and they frequently rebel against it, but if it is intelligently offered they accept it with enthusiasm. If they are healthy, they are capable of long periods of concentration and an extraordinary amount of work. They are trying, most of them, to form political ideas and they have a tendency to be either extremely idealistic (which is usually another term for radical) or conservative, blindly accepting what their fathers and grandfathers believed in. It is in this period that students can be most easily and permanently influenced. It is the period in which they form strong attachments for their teachers. Their outlook on life is usually extremely exaggerated. They are either far too modest and retiring, or extravagantly boastful. They are much more susceptible to the influence of a strong personality than to that of a great intelligence. Of all periods of life, this is what may best be called the "plastic age."

To teach on this level it is essential that every detail of the work be carefully prepared, and that the presentation of each lesson be clear and simple but appeal to the intelligence of the pupil. Explanations should awaken a form of adult curiosity, for pupils of this age are very willing to make personal efforts in research.

To succeed in teaching at this level, one must be a fine teacher. A mediocre teacher will generally be tolerated, but to have any real influence and to be completely successful, a teacher must be very deeply admired. In teaching routine material, drill must be given, but without monotony. Teachers can obtain excellent results by showing personal interest in their students, by being sincere and honest in their relationships with them. Students appreciate a teacher's efforts in organizing student clubs, in working with them outside of class hours, in showing genuine interest in helping them. The teacher at this level should be very conscientious. He must be friendly and informal, but he must always be dignified. It is always helpful for him to make an effort to know and understand his students and to know their families. It is wise for him to work with them on big school projects such as dances, bazaars, and shows of any sort for which his aid and effort are solicited. Students of this age appreciate invitations to the teacher's home or to dinner somewhere. This is an opportunity for a language teacher to introduce his pupils to a phase of the foreign culture by inviting them to a meal that is characteristic of the country whose language is being taught. He can also take them to museums where its art is being exhibited, or to the theater where foreign plays are being given. Many students are very appreciative of the opportunity to see a teacher's library of foreign books. They react to his enthusiasm for his subject as well as to his enthusiastic interest in them. They are grateful for prizes that are given for good work, prizes that are personal and seem to be a gift for them alone. Again, the language teacher has an opportunity to put his students to work on language newspapers, to have them read in class the articles that other students have written for these papers, and to display any special talents they may have. High-school students can master grammar, but the exercises that illustrate the rules should be practical. The teacher should express confidence in his pupils and should make them feel that they have great possibilities. He should never consciously discourage them. He may accuse them of laziness, but if he insists that they can be sure of ultimate success if they work, they will usually work.

As a general rule, students, at this age at least, tend to make an instructor believe that they are less capable than they really are, that the tasks he assigns are too hard. He should not fall into this trap, for students usually admire an instructor more if he does not give in to their demands. In spite of their protests, they enjoy taking tests, particularly those that put them on their mettle and make them solve problems.

In choosing reading material for the secondary school, select subject matter that is interesting and, whenever possible, informative with regard to the country and the life of the people. If exciting stories with good plots can be found, contemporary material may make up the bulk of the reading matter. Many contemporary plays present problems that high-school students understand and enjoy discussing. This is seldom true of even the best plays of the middle nineteenth century, for their problems hold no interest for youth today, and their vocabulary, manner of speech, and interpretation of life seem outmoded. Many textbook writers and teachers fail to realize that more than 50 years of the twentieth century have now passed and that what still seems modern to them is very old-fashioned to the teen-ager. Generally speaking, boys do not like love stories, but girls do. Books that have a purely artistic, poetic, psychological, or ideological basis should be avoided for the most part. The majority of boys and girls at the high-school level are incapable of understanding the philosophical problems that some authors like to discuss, unless they are presented in very simple terms. Students at this level like adventure, history, realism. They enjoy learning about the history, geography, and politics of foreign countries. In French,

Dumas, Hugo, Rostand, Daudet, Loti, Mérimée, Sartre, Gide, Camus, Romains, Anouihl, Pagnol, or Saint-Exupéry interest these students, even though some of these authors wrote during the nineteenth century. In Spanish, short stories by almost any South American provide good material. In German, contemporary literature or that of the earlier part of this century is most successful. In all three languages, however, it is often necessary to simplify the vocabulary for classroom use.

Students at this level like to write compositions, but they want to write on subjects that they think are intelligent. They may be asked to choose their own subjects, which are then assigned to the entire class. At this age, students are capable of undertaking projects of their own, and they like to—not class projects, but individual projects. Most of them like to design things, to create things.

It is unwise to progress too quickly in teaching any important detail. There should be a great deal of repetition and much reviewing. Students at this age level forget easily and hence need to repeat the same material from several different angles. They tend to be self-conscious; but if they are taught early enough to express themselves, they enjoy working out conversations. They can still learn by heart, but they should be encouraged to learn with the idea of a perfect reproduction of the text, as well as with accurate pronunciation. They are interested in understanding things; they want to know the causes of things. But in whatever they are taught, they should be guided toward absolute accuracy. The desire to know things thoroughly should be instilled in them so that they will never be satisfied with anything superficial. They are likely to ask many questions. These questions should be encouraged and answered, provided that they are not introduced merely to waste time. The students may be encouraged and even forced to do written work, for fundamentally they like to work. They will tend to do nothing unless they are pushed into action. Since most of them are very interested in dramatics, lessons can be dramatized in class. The class can begin to improvise; the students enjoy making personal reports which they have prepared at home. Frequent dictations and exercises in oral comprehension may be given to them. The teacher should speak to them in the language as much as possible, for that is a phase of language which seems practical to them. Every effort must be made to be just to all the students and to avoid having any prejudices. In spite of their apparent sophistication and disillusionment, they believe strongly in justice, and if they lose confidence in their instructor he will fail in his relations with them. As far as possible, the teacher should try to discourage them from working merely for better marks. They should realize the need for knowledge itself and be shown that by seeking greater knowledge they automatically attain their goal of high grades, which is their measure of knowledge.

The senior-high-school student needs grammar with a minimum of rules and much stress on drill exercises and practical vocabulary—vocabulary which he can use in making up sentences, carrying on a real or imaginary conversation in the language, or reading a book or magazine in it. The essential verbs should be taught, as should pronunciation. Memorized songs and poems may also be used in teaching pronunciation. The senior high school today prefers a functional grammar in which the rules and exercises are not confusing to the student but complement each other. Pains should be taken to avoid statements and exercises which lead the student into error or give information that can be interpreted in several ways. Too many grammars, by over- or under-emphasis of certain points, lead students into error or mis-interpretation that is hard to correct.

College

In dealing with students of college age the attitude of the teacher must be quite different. These young men and women are adults, or believe themselves to be so. Their minds are quite well formed. Either they have good memories or else they have very little ability to retain facts. They either comprehend very easily or have great difficulty in understanding quickly and accurately what is told to them. Those who have the ability and will power can do whatever they set out to accomplish. The instructor has much less influence on the characters of these students than he has on their minds. They tend to admire his intelligence and his ability as a teacher. They think themselves more or less his comrades, his equals; they enjoy his witticisms and understand irony. They are, for the most part, grown men and women, and they make use of all the talents and abilities that men and women use in making their way in the world. Men students frequently flatter their instructors or ignore them completely; girls will flirt with male instructors, hoping to win favor and special consideration. A woman instructor often finds that her influence is greater among her men students. There are no subjects on which one cannot speak to these students; they understand all aspects of discussion. In general, they tend to believe that the instructor is old-fashioned, not very experienced, and has far less knowledge of what really goes on in the world than they have. It is always helpful for him to disillusion them early and have them understand that he has had experience and that life is no novelty to him. They react easily to his enthusiasm about his subject and to his superior knowledge. At this level a good instructor can change the whole career of his students. They seek to be inspired and, once inspired, are capable of tremendous work; in their enthusiasm they will even come and suggest work that they may do. They, too, need to be guided, but they must be guided without their realizing it, because many of them are convinced that they need no guidance. In dealing with them, an instructor must avoid forcing himself upon them. They seek independence and, for the most part, wish to go their own way. They, too, prefer honesty and justice. They understand the existence of falsehood and injustice; some of them have already abandoned all idealism, but most of them are still willing to return to it. They are far less sophisticated than they appear to be. They are very difficult to know and particularly difficult to convince, unless the teacher's personality is such that he can inspire them very deeply. They should be made to realize the importance of the work that is assigned to them and the possible value of that work to them. They accept discipline, but in much the same manner that an adult accepts the social restrictions of life. They protest—at times vigorously, at times lightly. In general they are always willing to submit. They are reasonable and serious, and more grateful for what is done for them than students at either of the earlier levels. They understand the importance of whatever sacrifices of time are made for them.

In teaching these men and women of college age, any child-ishness, any games, should be avoided. The exercises that are used must be adult in nature. For the most part, these students do not enjoy lessons based on activity programs or dramatics. They seek clear, complete, adult explanations, lots of written work, lots of correction, and, in particular, conferences and explanations of work based on their own difficulties. Most students feel that it is an honor to be asked to work with the instructor on his own research projects. (Incidentally, none of this research should be published without giving credit to these students.) They take great glory in anything that they themselves accomplish and are easily encouraged to go on beyond this point. If they feel that they have been deceived or tricked they may never continue in the field of research. They enjoy working on individual projects which they believe will lead somewhere, but they want to receive full recognition for their work.

At this level, conversation in a foreign language can be a corrective exercise based upon their own preferences. Written compositions can be imitations of the work or style of authors whom they have studied and analyzed. College students enjoy translating difficult passages, passages that test previous as well as current knowledge.

At this level students can be encouraged to do not as well as the instructor, but better. They are perfectly capable of being taught to appreciate literature and to develop a fine critical sense, but this cannot be done quickly. The development of a critical sense that is based upon knowledge as well as personal taste requires several years, in some cases the full 4 years of college. Courses on civilization may also be given at this level. In discussions of literary and philosophical material, the instructor should not hesitate to admit a student's point of view, even though it may be contrary to his own, provided that the student can defend it. The instructor should stimulate discussion but never dominate it.

There is no limit to the amount of knowledge and inspiration that a teacher can offer a student in college. Since the student is preparing for life and a career, this is the instructor's last opportunity to emphasize the importance of perfection and high ideals of accomplishment.

Any class can progress as rapidly as the intelligence of its members allows. Most college students prefer to feel that they are covering ground rather than being held back by constant repetition which seems unnecessary to them. They want to be doing something serious, to be doing adult things in an adult manner. They are willing to take the consequences of the responsibility that is placed entirely upon them.

A teacher's realization of what may seem to be unimportant psychological differences in these three age groups may determine his success or failure as a teacher. A careful analysis of his own ability to deal with these groups, of the effectiveness of his teaching at the different levels, and of his personal happiness in his social and intellectual relations with one or another group may determine the success of his entire teaching career. Proper choice of the teaching level is of paramount importance to the ultimate efficiency of our educational system.

On the college level, appeal can be made more directly to the intelligence. More grammar can be explained, although today a minimum of rules—the minimum including only the essential—is more popular. Here, as in the secondary school, every effort should be made to avoid creating confusion by discussing too many exceptions, and the learning process should be made effective through drill. The amount of vocabulary in each lesson may be increased, as may the grammatical material, so that the textbook selected will lead the students as quickly as possible into substantial reading matter which will enable them to take more advanced courses in literature. Reading material may have a broader appeal, be chosen with an eye to scholarship, and follow a thread of literary history or the evolution of a literary genre in order to provide a basis for studying literature as well as understanding the culture of the people. In order to better prepare students for reading contemporary literature it is helpful to introduce them to small units like the short story, where variations in style and construction can be studied more profitably.

If great care is not taken in the choice of textbooks, the teaching will be much less effective, and students of average intelligence will for the most part lack the enthusiasm that encourages them to read the material they are taught and to read and study beyond what is assigned in the classroom. This care in selecting texts should apply to classes made up of students of superior intelligence and especially students whose interests are very special. Every care must be taken to choose texts that will fit the particular interests of these students, if such textbooks are available. The difficulty in choosing textbooks has been one of the most serious handicaps to effective modern-language teaching in the United States.

* 6 *

LANGUAGE TEACHING
IN THE ELEMENTARY SCHOOL

Foreign languages have been taught to a limited degree in the public and private elementary schools of the United States for many years, but new impetus has been given to this phase of language teaching by Dr. Earl J. McGrath, formerly U.S. Commissioner of Education. As a result of his encouragement, volunteers as well as veteran teachers in the field have introduced courses in foreign languages from the kindergarten up to the seventh and eighth grades. According to a bulletin published by the Modern Language Association of America in May, 1953, 28 states and 99 cities and towns have introduced language study in the elementary schools.

Since then language study has been extended at the elementary-school level to several hundred communities, and more than half a million boys and girls at that level are now learning foreign languages, including Russian.

In most communities these experiments in language teaching on the elementary-school level have caught the imagination of the public and through them have been brought to the attention of educational administrators who are examining the need for curriculum adjustment which the general introduction of language study in the pre-school and elementary school might involve.

The widespread and serious nature of these experiments has brought a number of questions to the attention of educators which should be kept in mind by those interested in this phase of language teaching. According to reports from the two school systems that have had the longest and widest experience with languages in the elementary school, the best results are obtained when language study is started in the pre-school years or in the first grade. If classes are limited to daily 15-minute periods, the children's progress is regular and their enthusiasm is maintained beyond the classroom so that by the time they enter junior high school they seem quite generally to elect the foreign language they studied previously. Very few fail to continue language study if a foreign language is offered.

It would seem, then, that if the main objective of modern language teaching is to give American boys and girls real mastery of a foreign language, one of the most effective means in our power is to introduce them to languages at a very early age and encourage them to continue their study through high school and college. This is no new discovery, for from time immemorial the children of royal families the world over have been taught languages painlessly by preceptors and governesses. Ability to converse in several tongues was essential diplomatically to the ruling families of Europe and they met this need simply and directly. In view of our national position in the world today the average citizen finds himself in a similar situation, and command of a second and even a third language has become a commercial, economic, military, and diplomatic necessity for the younger generation. Royalty learned what has been proved psychologically today, that a high degree of intelligence is not necessary for the mastery of a foreign tongue at an early age and that the essentials of language can be acquired in early life with a minimum of that obstruction caused by self-consciousness.

Present-day experiments in elementary-school language teaching are proving that teachers in this field must be well prepared not only in their subject matter but in their ability to handle children. Professor Theodore Andersson in his book on the *Teaching of Languages in the Elementary School* sets a high goal for teachers in this field if they are to succeed. In addition to knowing the language and pronouncing it well, being well acquainted with the history, civilization, and culture of the foreign country, and being fond of children, he feels that they must understand the philosophy of the elementary school, be creative, enthusiastic, and broadly educated.

The most serious problem that has confronted administrators seeking to introduce language instruction in elementary schools has been finding well-prepared teachers. The demand far exceeds the supply.

Professor Andersson has also outlined what he believes to be the best general approach in each of the elementary-school years. The first 2 years should be used to train the ear and vocal organs; in the second and third years the aural-oral method is most successful and can be supplemented by notebooks in which cut-outs may be pasted or objects drawn. In the fourth, fifth, and sixth years the emphasis should remain on aural-oral instruction, but since children are eager to read and write, blackboards, notebooks, filmstrips, and simple texts may be used effectively. The main points of grammar are best learned through practice. In the <u>seventh grade</u> the 12-year-old shows great curiosity and begins to analyze what he reads and hears. He can read more interesting material and do more writing; he should hear and speak the language constantly. By the <u>ninth grade</u> the pupil should understand easily and be able to speak fluently, as well as write easily, on general subjects. His skill in reading and writing should equal that of a good 2-year high school student whose mastery of the oral and aural phases of language study have been stressed. In the <u>tenth grade</u> the geography, history, economics, politics, science, art, literature, and philosophy of the country whose language has been studied can be discussed. As far as possible the personal interests of the student should be kept in mind and points of comparison between Americans and foreigners dwelt upon.

The Modern Language Association of America has made, in conjunction with specialists in the field, individual schools, and some municipal school systems, a thorough study of the approach and methods best adapted to successful language teaching at the pre-school and elementary-school level.

Experimentation in this field has also brought the realization that foreign-language instruction in a daily period of 15 to 20 minutes tends to strengthen and stimulate interest in other elementary-school subjects when integrated with them, an easy and natural task in the early years. It has further been shown that bilingualism in the primary grades causes no difficulties. This belief, which most linguists and teachers of language have held for centuries, was shattered for the average man by the publication in the 1940s of many popular articles on the evil effects of bilingualism. Out of the experience of hundreds of elementary-school experiments has also come the assurance that the study of a second language at that level seems to improve the pupil's comprehension of his own language and its grammar, rather than otherwise. And finally, it has been found that the languages introduced in elementary schools are more popular in the school and community when they correspond to the interests of the parents as well as of the pupils.

Much of this research has been concentrated on the third grade since so many schools have found that level a convenient place to introduce a foreign language. One of the most carefully prepared of these programs, and one which has been tested and revised, comes from Glastonbury, Connecticut. It was developed under the chairmanship of Mary P. Thompson. Although the program has been designed for several languages and covers all grades from the third grade up, most of the principles governing the teaching are the same. The foreign language used is authentically foreign and taught in real situations. The language is spoken at normal speed. The audio-lingual approach is emphasized, and reading and writing is postponed, at least in the third grade. Every unit is designed to revolve around a living situation which the child can understand and in which he can take part. The vocabulary is limited and contains a great deal of repetition of the same basic words. The utterances are short so that the language can be learned by speech patterns rather than by words. Progress is made slowly, but every utterance must be mastered completely, that is, until it becomes automatic.

Each of the ten units, which consist of only 16 or 17 utterances apiece including repetitions, spread over 2 or 3 weeks at the third-grade level. The ear is trained first, so that, through the senses, associations can be made directly between objects or activities and the new language. Each pupil in turn is encouraged to play the part of the teacher or take part in a chain in which the first pupil repeats the teacher's question to a second pupil who then asks the same question of the first and third pupils; the third pupil then follows the same procedure. Choral practice is stressed to reduce individual embarrassment.

One of the first dialogues might center about a key utterance such as: *Bonjour, Comment t'appelles-tu?* and its answer, and end with *Au revoir.* However, variations of these utterances will develop into a conversation. At this level, several weeks of 15-minute daily sessions will be required to master the patterns, stress, intonation, and pronunciation.

Following is a conversation between teacher and class that might result if such a method is used.

MME. X.:	(1) Bonjour, mes enfants.
TOUTE LA CLASSE:	(2) Bonjour, madame (monsieur, mademoiselle).
MME. X. (*à Jacques*):	(3) Comment t'appelles-tu?
JACQUES:	(4) Je m'appelle Jacques.
MME. X. (*à Suzanne*):	(5) Comment t'appelles-tu?
SUZANNE:	(6) Je m'appelle Suzanne.
MME. X.:	(7) Ah, bon! Au revoir, mes enfants.
MME. X.:	(1) Bonjour, Jacques.
JACQUES:	(2) Bonjour, madame.
MME. X. (*à la classe*):	(3) Comment s'appelle-t-il?
TOUTE LA CLASSE:	(4) Il s'appelle Jacques.
MME. X:	(5) Comment s'appelle-t-elle?
TOUTE LA CLASSE:	(6) Elle s'appelle Suzanne.
MME. X.:	(7) Au revoir, mes enfants. A bientot.

Un, deux, trois, quatre, cinq.
Comptez de un a cinq.
Quel est ce numero?

To conduct this lesson the teacher must not only use gestures to obtain the answer desired, but must often give the answer, and ask a pupil or the class to repeat it, until the teacher is sure that each child in the class can understand, repeat, and answer every utterance perfectly.

The ten units, dealing with such subjects as "Classroom Objects," "Colors," "Classroom Activities," "A Visit," "A New Friend," "A Telephone Call," "An Invitation," or "A Picnic" are developed in much the same manner. The Glastonbury units seems to be the shortest and simplest yet devised.

"Living French," a record album prepared by Crown Publishers (1960) under the direction of Mary Finocchiaro and Suzanne Jacob, and designed for pre-school and elementary-school children, contains longer units, longer utterances, and simple children's stories for comprehension. A picture vocabulary and printed booklet of lessons, with an English translation on the reverse page for consultation, accompany the records and are an aid for home study. "French for Children," prepared by Ottenheimer Publishers (1957) under the editorial direction of Professor Frederick D. Eddy and tested experimentally in some of Maryland's elementary schools, contains 12 short units of 7 to 17 utterances each, and covers such topics as "Pets," "The Family," "Counting," "A Birthday Party," "Breakfast," "Dinner," "The Doctor's Visit," and "A Movie Date." The beginning utterances are as short as those of the Glastonbury program. They are also idiomatic and colloquial, and very authentic since they make use of children's voices and phraseology. Since the set is intended primarily for home use, English precedes each utterance. Directions are first given in English. Each unit allows time for repetition in French, and before proceeding to the next unit a comprehension test is offered. If the test is not understood, it is suggested that the unit be repeated until it has been mastered.

Professor Andersson's sample lessons move even more slowly than the Glastonbury program, since they spread the normal first unit vocabulary over three lessons. Helen Kelso Carney's experiments in Tulsa, Oklahoma, have produced a seventh-term French text with tapes, which uses each unit as a basis for drill. The vocabulary is limited, and although the situations in the 23 units vary considerably, the short utterances of "Pour Parler aux Français" keep repeating in successive units the key words and phrases previously introduced. Each unit contains some grammar, fill-in exercises, pattern-of-speech drills, and completion and oral comprehension exercises. The vocabulary is practical, the situations French, and the conversation animated.

The diversity of approach exhibited by these several programs of study for the elementary school proves how uncertain we still are about what we should try to accomplish at that level.

With every additional day of experience and conscientious effort towards concrete achievement, language teachers in the elementary schools are moving nearer to uniformity. The most difficult problem ahead is to build up carefully-planned sequences leading to and fitting in with the secondary-school language curriculum. With some pupils now beginning foreign languages in the pre-school grades, others in the first grade, and still others in the third, sixth, and seventh grades, the difficulty of evaluating the achievements of each of these different series of sequences, so that every pupil can profitably continue his language study in high school without being penalized for proficiency in one skill rather than another, is very great. If all language teachers constantly keep their ultimate objectives in mind—to teach pupil's to comprehend, speak, read, and write the spoken language as much like a native as is humanly possible, and finally to understand and appreciate the people whose culture and intellectual accomplishments they are studying—even this difficult integration will be achieved, although less effectively than if progress is measured regularly by four skill tests.

As an aid to the young teacher struggling with his first elementary-school classes in language, the following diary of a very successful and experienced teacher, Dr. James Grew of Phillips Academy, should serve as an inspiration. From a careful study of pupil reactions, many valuable techniques and procedures can be obtained.

The record of progress, which has only been slightly edited, shows graphically what can be taught, how the boys and girls react, and what was finally accomplished. This Andover experiment awakened such enthusiasm in the community that language teaching was introduced in the public elementary-school system the following year.

AN EXPERIMENT WITH TEACHING ORAL FRENCH IN GRADE III[1]

Monday, October 6:

Class of 28 were well prepared psychologically as their room teacher had imbued them with the idea that they were a privileged group to be having French and had an advantage over the other grades. This spirit was typical of the entire set-up on the

[1] Class in the Andover Central Elementary School. The class met four times a week, the class period ranging from 15 to 20 minutes a day. The report begins with the fall term, 1952.

part of all concerned—principal, room teachers, parents, and pupils.

Began by giving them their French names; not too successful as too many of them did not lend themselves to Gallicization (Karen, Beverly, Marshall, *et al.*). Then taught numbers, o to 6. Much interest; caught on quickly; attention excellent; no silliness or recourse to English.

Tuesday, October 7:

Great enthusiasm, numbers well retained. New words: 7 to 10, le crayon, le livre, bonjour, au revoir. Followed such instructions as: levez-vous, comptez, asseyez-vous, allez au tableau, écrivez.

Thursday, October 9:

Past words well retained. New words: la craie, la gomme, le tableau noir (latter difficult). Very good following of directions. Only a few caught on to the idea of replying by a *oui* or a *non* to "Etes-vous un garçon, êtes-vous une fille?" Most repeated question.

Friday, October 10:

Good retention; more inclined to answer a question than to repeat it. Good on doing things. New words: le professeur, le pupitre, la chaise, la pendule, 11, 12, merci. Trouble between *un* and *une*. Asked to learn how to tell time.

Tuesday, October 14:

All words well retained; great enthusiasm; still having trouble answering *oui* or *non* to a direct question. Learned to count up to 30 as a prelude to telling time.

Thursday, October 16:

Past words well retained. Learned hours from *une heure* to *midi*. Very few said "douze heures." *Montrez-moi* led to their repeating the question rather than using *voilà*. Less trouble, however, getting a *oui* or a *non* from a direct question. Good at following commands.

Friday, October 17:

Restless and inattentive except for six or seven. Because it is Friday? All past words retained except difference between *un* and *une.* Did time up to 29 minutes past, except for the quarter. New word: la pendule.

Monday, October 20:

Good on old words but least pep and greatest restlessness to date. Learned *le quart* and *demie* easily. Drilled on questions: *Qui êtes-vous? Etes-vous un garçon ou une fille?* Slow at first (question repeated or simply *oui* or *non* given), but eventually caught on.

Tuesday, October 21:

Best class to date. All old words retained except *demie.* Animals at class' request: le chat, le chien, l'âne, la vache.

Thursday, October 23:

All past words well retained except *âne* and *vache.* Counted up *to* 50; not much bothered by the *et* in 41, no *et* in 42, etc. Good on answering "êtes-vous?" questions, but tendency to omit the *je suis* in the replies.

Friday, October 24:

First weekly quiz à la spelling bee. Won by Thomas Doucette. (Despite name, he had never spoken French but had heard it spoken by his Canadian grandparents.) Trouble with *garçon, âne,* difference between *chat* and *chien,* time. Rest well retained. Continued with counting up *to* 60. Request for alphabet next time.

Monday, October 27:

Much enthusiasm, very alert. Pleased to have another vocabulary game; decided it would become a regular Friday feature. Learned alphabet easily and with zeal. Spelled their first names in French. All old words retained except 50; still confuse *chat* and *chien.*

Tuesday, October 28:

Again most enthusiastic and alert. Hard letters (G and J) well retained; some pronunciation trouble with easier ones (A and T). New words: la lampe, la fenêtre, la porte, la table. Counted up *to* 60. *Chien* and *chat* now assimilated; not 50. Four boys poor in answering "Etes-vous un garçon ou une . . . ?"; rest have it right.

Thursday, October 30:
New words: le drapeau français, le drapeau américain, rouge, blanc, bleu. Good unison response to all past words. Individual errors with letters, never G or J. Much keenness for tomorrow's test.

Friday, October 31:
Test won by Dorothy Easton. More "finalists" (i.e., to qualify for same each pupil had to spell given name correctly in French and finalists stayed in longer). Runner-up said *onze* after *neuf*. Started *je ne suis pas*. Slow going. Restless (Hallowe'en), children talking together, scribbling, etc.

Monday, November 3:
Good class. All keen to be this week's winner. New words: jaune, vert, numbers through 79. Got *soixante-dix* idea easily. Caught on pretty well to *je ne suis pas*.

Tuesday, November 4:
Excellent class. Negatives better. New words: le stylo, noir, numbers through 100. Want days of the week next.

Thursday, November 6:
Again good, except for *le stylo*, 80, 90. Much better with negative. New bad habit: putting *un* before numbers and colors. Slow but enthusiastic in learning days of week.

Friday, November 7:
Dorothy Easton again the winner. Other two finalists: Paul Daugherty and James Doyle (the boy who put his head down during the first two weeks and refused to participate). Problem words: A, 80, 90. Most qualified for finals by *je ne suis pas*. . . . Much interest in but difficulty with days of week.

Monday, November 10:
Restless (rain and no recess). Very keen and all eager to dethrone the champion. All past words letter-perfect. Much drill on days of the week; starting to get them, but it comes slowly.

Thursday, November 13:

One half knew days. Voted 5 to 1 to do months next. Started "de quelle couleur est . . . ?" for *il est* or *elle est* answer. Much interest in counting by fives. New words: le chapeau, le sac. (Equipment in room for Thanksgiving play.)

Friday, November 14:

About ⅘ of class qualified for test. Tie between Dorothy Easton and Barbara Auchincloss. Great interest. Started months; much enthusiasm.

Monday, November 17:

Restless (rain). New student from Methuen who had had no French. Slight silliness for first time (screaming answers). Very slow on months; only 5 or 6 really interested, despite lip service to the contrary. Perfect on all past words. New expression: je me lève.

Tuesday, November 18:

Great enthusiasm. Three (Dorothy, Paul, Thomas) qualified for Friday's test by reciting the 12 months. *Je me lève* well retained; trouble mouthing *je m'assieds*. New words: l'arbre, le bateau, le cheval (from a Thanksgiving drawing on the wall). Words quickly learned and well retained; phrases go much more slowly. Are they too young for the latter? They could easily take two 20-minute periods a day.

Thursday, November 20:

Seven more (all girls) qualified. New words: le plancher, le plafond. Great enthusiasm. Almost all knew *je m'assieds*. Tuesday's new words retained; months still giving trouble.

Friday, November 21:

Thirteen (3 boys) in finals; Dorothy again the winner. Greatest stumbling block to qualification; last four months. Contestants fell more rapidly and on easy words; runner-up on 71. Request for next week: *Alouette*.

Monday, November 24:

All old words retained except *la montre*. New words: la boîte, le papier. *Alouette,* a great success; much keenness. Used five parts of the body: la tête, le nez, le bras, le dos, le bec. Also, l'oiseau. Easily learned after singing song.

Tuesday, November 25:

All old words retained except for a few *Alouette* terms. New words: la bouche, la dent, la langue, le cou. Great enthusiasm for song.

Monday, December 1:

Messrs. Teakle and Caron from Canada visited and each took over class which lasted 30 minutes with great enthusiasm. Pupils had requested test but were consoled by having real Canadian visitors! They explained "boy words" and "girl words," and stressed verbs to suit actions, je vais, je prends, etc. Their verdict: our pupils have a larger vocabulary than theirs, but know less "grammar," i.e., verbs.

Tuesday, December 2:

Another keen class. New *Alouette* words: la patte, la jambe. Drilled on allez, je vais, touchez, je touche; former came easier than latter.

Thursday, December 4:

Drilled on aller and toucher. Most reply "je vais," but very few "je touche," majority repeating "touchez." This the requirement for tomorrow's test.

Friday, December 5:

Fewer qualified than usual; many went out on *jambe* and *patte*. Dorothy again champion. Drilled *montrez-moi* for *voici* or *voilà*.

Monday, December 8:

Drilled *voici* and *voilà*. Considerable progress. Still shaky on latest *Alouette* words, jambe, doigt, main. Few words: le front, le menton. Some have difficulty with recognition (montrez-moi votre ncz, et al.); some excellent with new cognates (le miroir la canne le téléphone, etc.).

Tuesday, December 9:

More voici-voilà drill. New words: Noël, le Père Noël, le ski, la canne, le téléphone, le miroir. Students took over class to everyone's delight; some very good.

Thursday, December 11:

Class at its best to date, *all* participating. 12 qualified for test (replying by voici or voilà, changing votre to mon). Good retention.

Friday, December 12:

Twin champions: Dorothy and Barbara. More qualified and stayed in longer than heretofore. Requests: (1) for another song, (2) more objects, (3) more sentences. Gave them *Frère Jacques* (many already knew it), je prends, j'écris. Champions led singing of *Alouette*. A simple poem to memorize was suggested.

Monday, December 15:

Very good class. New words: gris, brun, Joyeux Noël, le bonhomme de neige (requests), la pipe, le renne. Enthusiastic singing of both songs, student led.

Tuesday, December 16:

New word: le phonographe. Excellent class. Much drill on *qu'est-ce que je fais? Vous vous asseyez, levez, écrivez, touchez,* etc. Also drilled *levez-vous,* etc., for answers. *Asseyez-vous sur le pupitre de* . . . met tremendous laughter and interest. Drilled use of complete sentences.

Thursday, December 18:

Last class and great excitement because of school Xmas party in afternoon. Presentation of French card signed by all 29 pupils and PTA gift wallet by Dorothy. Enthusiastic singing of *Alouette* and *Frère Jacques*. Explanation, in English, of French Xmas customs. Much disappointment there could be no test. Great enthusiasm and zest.

Monday, January 5:

New girl, Maureen, from Shawsheen; she had had no French but her mother used to teach it.

Reviewed fall-term words, surprisingly well retained, very few errors except for the letters G and K. Class voted about 2 to 1 for learning songs rather than sentences. Drilled use of *il* or *elle* with se lever, s'asseoir, aller, écrire, etc. Attention better than I had anticipated for first post-vacation class.

Tuesday, January 6:

Whitney came to teach class "Savez-vous planter les choux?" Great success. New words: le pied, les cheveux, la joue. More drill on *il* and *elle*.

Thursday, January 8:

Tune of "Savez-vous planter les choux?" forgotten. New words: le coude, le genou, l'étoile (request); new phrase: *je* (il, elle) *retourne à ma* (sa) *place*. Tuesday's words well retained; *il* and *elle* fairly well.

Friday, January 9: no school because of blizzard.

Monday, January 12:

Great desire for a test as both champions were absent. Winner: Tom Doucette; runner-up: Paul Daugherty. Most went out on numbers and letters; days of week and months well retained. Drilled parts of body, il, elle, verbs.

Tuesday, January 13:

Cheers when I opened the door, putting an end to their recess play; groans and lamentations when I announced there would be no class Thursday or Friday. Beverly brought farm picture. New words: le coq, la poule, le poussin, le lapin. Sang both songs, but a few are losing interest in *Frère Jacques*. Much drill on parts of the body; less confusion between *cou* and *coude*; better on verbs and pronouns. Restlessness, however, due to no outdoor recess.

Monday, January 19:

Test by popular demand. Triple winners: Barbara, Beverly, and Dorothy. Most went out on *patte, joue,* numbers. Words well retained considering hiatus, except *poussin* and *lapin*. *Alouette* again requested. New words: oreille, droite, gauche. Former difficult to pronounce; most very confused by left and right; probably not too sure of it in English.

Tuesday, January 20:

New words: le disque, le mouton, la chèvre, la ferme, le dindon. Request to count up to 200 so we went all the way to *1000* and did *1492* and *1953* with *mil.* Played Paul's Christmas record (*Alouette*) and my record of *Savez-vous planter les choux?* Acted out latter and also sang *Frère Jacques* by request. Good enthusiasm, most old words remembered. Confusion between *mouton* and *menton.* Classes now lasting 25 minutes without any decrease of interest.

Thursday, January 22:

New words: les yeux, le cochon, la fleur, l'écureuil, but last very difficult. Good retention of all past words. Triple digits too much for them, i.e., 285. Sang all three songs by request. Great enthusiasm for "parlez comme un âne, etc.," with chorus response.

Friday, January 23:

Dorothy again champion. Beverly and Paul, the runners-up, went out on *quatorze.* New words: le veau, le nid, l'œuf. Most past words remembered, but *yeux* and *écureuil* give trouble. Much better on actions, difference between *il* and *elle.* Children played teacher, great success.

Monday, January 26:

Most of them listless (no recess?); words well retained except *écureuil.* Added: *la rivière.* Drilled numbers as too many had gone rusty. Then drilled *se lever, aller, toucher, retourner à sa place, s'asseoir,* the requirements for this week's quiz.

Tuesday, January 27:
   More alert and keener. New words: la branche, l'aile. Drilled verb actions.

Thursday, January 29:
   Very good class. 16 qualified for test by doing and saying: je me lève, je vais au tableau, je touche (some object in farm picture), je retourne à ma place, je m'assieds. 2 or 3 didn't try and 2 or 3 missed. Almost letter-perfect on past words.

Friday, January 30:
   Shortened test. Four winners: Dorothy, Barbara, Beverly, and Tom. We then sang our three songs and reviewed all we have learned. Visitors impressed by large vocabulary and ability to follow instructions. Amazed so much had been learned since "September." (We started October 6.)

Monday, February 2:
   New words: le cœur (seasonal!), le commutateur (hard to pronounce), allumer and éteindre, last three this week's test requirement. Great joy in acting it out. New direction: allumez ou éteignez *toutes* les lumières. New bad habit: allez *au* Carol, *au* Tom, etc.

Tuesday, February 3:
   Light words not well retained. Much drill on them. Other past words near perfect. Added "je" and "vous" forms of *prendre, écrire, mettre*. Restless today in contrast to yesterday; no recess either day.

Thursday, February 5:
   To qualify for test the proper action had to accompany je me lève, je vais au commutateur, j'éteins, j'allume, je retourne à ma place, je m'assieds. 15 qualified, two trying twice. Only one other volunteered. New words: la lèvre, l'épaule, la flèche (seasonal). Good class except for continuing to put article before proper nouns.

Friday, February 6:

Test won by Dorothy. Others went out mostly on yesterday's new words. Began: *ouvrez, fermez, tournez la page, sortez de et entrez dans* la salle de classe. The last two a great success especially when couples did it hand in hand.

Monday, February 9:

Drilled *entrer, sortir,* etc. Last week's words well retained. Also drilled *merci* and *il n'y a pas de quoi,* latter very difficult.

Tuesday, February 10:

Drilled with doors, good progress, new verb: *frapper.* Also taught *grand* and *petit.* Great amusement drawing a "grand" or a "petit" number or letter on the board. Still having great trouble with *il n'y a pas de quoi.*

Thursday, February 12:

Least rewarding class this winter: Lincoln's birthday and Valentine party tomorrow, snow and no recess, announcement through loud speaker that afternoon school would be called off. Only 7 qualified for test. Recent words well remembered, however, except *il n'y a pas de quoi* and *frapper.* New game: donnez la craie à une fille (ou à un garçon) qui est beau (stupide, intelligent, etc.). Not too successful as child hesitated too long to decide, although it did amuse them.

Friday, February 13:

Still listless. Only two more qualified for test. Four-way tie: Dorothy, Beverly, Tom, and—for the first time—Carol Cheever, Started washing: *le lavabo, le morceau de savon, le robinet, la serviette* (paper), *le panier.* Loved doing things like "mettez le panier sur la tête de . . ." and "prenez la serviette dans la bouche et mettez-la dans le panier." This seemed to restore usual pep and made them forget afternoon party. *Il n'y a pas de quoi* now pretty well absorbed.

Monday, February 16:

Excellent class. Much following of directions: allez au lavabo, tournez le robinet, prenez un morceau de savon, lavez les mains, rincez les mains, prenez une serviette, séchez les mains, mettez la serviette dans le panier. Also: allez au tableau et dessinez une tête, etc. Every command repeated with "je." Great enthusiasm.

Tuesday, February 17:
  On stage for rehearsal of program our room is to put on for the PTA March 11.

Thursday, February 19:
  Stage in use, but worked on PTA program in the room. Class wanted a test, but room teacher insisted we try to perfect program before going on stage again tomorrow.

Friday, February 18:
  On stage. Went very well. Piano teacher to accompany *Alouette*. Children seemed to enjoy it.

Monday, March 2:
  Terrific ovation upon my entrance! Strong desire for both a test and a rehearsal. To qualify for former, children had to count from 1 to 20. Those who failed went too fast and skipped; only 2 really flubbed it. Tie between Dorothy and—for the first time—Karen Franz. Equal enthusiasm for the rehearsal. Most remembered their lines. Good retention also of last term's words.

Tuesday, March 3:
  Another ovation! Went over playlet. Drilled "de quelle couleur est . . . ?" and other sentences. Most retained, but they did better on harder than on easier directions. New words: le ciel, la feuille (from bird pictures on wall). Very good class.

Thursday, March 5:
  Rehearsal on stage. Went very well. Children enthusiastic and cooperative.

Friday, March 6:
  No class.

Monday, March 9:
  Rehearsal on stage before an audience. Went very well.

Tuesday, March 10:

"Dress rehearsal" before grades 4, 5, and 6. Went very well. Audience attentive (although knowing no French) and enthusiastic. Very few mistakes.

Playlet given at 8:30 P.M., Wednesday, March 11, before parents and teachers. It went very well, only one error and much applause; the children seemed to be enjoying themselves hugely.

Thursday, March 12:

Class not as tired as I would have expected. All keen for a test and more French. Several who had not been so enthusiastic now among the most. Test consisted of counting, going around the class. Five winners: Dorothy, Beverly, Tom, and—for the first time—Marshall Darling and Gloria Hasleton. Started: *la maison, le toit, la cheminée, la fumée*. Amused by saying (their idea), "C'est la fumée de la cheminée du toit de la maison de M. Grew." Much demand for sentences.

Friday, March 13:

Another enthusiastic class. New words: le volet, le jardin, le mur, la sonnette, sonner. Great disappointment at not having another test.

Monday, March 16:

Class voted 4–1 for test, but felt they didn't know latest words well enough to have them count. Parts of body first which only eliminated 2 or 3. Numbers next. Most went out on careless errors, such as giving 45 after 43, or misusing the *et*. Triple winners: Dorothy, Beverly, Carol. News that the playlet was to be recorded on tape gleefully received: girls wanted to know what to wear, boys regretted they couldn't go on TV! Went over playlet, well remembered

Tuesday, March 17:

Playlet recorded. They did well considering it was "warmed over" and there was no audience.

Thursday, March 19:

Spent period "showing off" what the class can do. Very keen and enthusiastic. Remembered "Savez-vous planter les choux?" which we had not sung for nearly two months!

Friday, March 20:

Test by overwhelming demand. Parts of body to qualify; about ⅓ failed, all on *genou*. Then numbers again; those who failed did so through carelessness. Five winners: Dorothy, Tom, Beverly, Carol, Gloria. Two of the heretofore "slow" came close to winning test.

Monday, March 23:

Introduced no new words, but asked them innumerable questions, particularly about staff artist's drawing of a house. Their response and attention were excellent.

Tuesday, March 24:

Added *l'auto* and *le garage* to the scene. Also, "Je lève la main droite; je baisse la main gauche; je touche l'oreille droite, gauche; etc." They caught it very quickly.

Thursday, March 26:

Did not meet the class.

Friday, March 27:

They clamored for a test, but were disappointed. We reviewed the house and its appurtenances, also the business of *droit(e)* and *gauche*. Introduced *l'avion* and *le hibou* as part of the scene on the board. Then, "l'avion vole; l'oiseau vole; le hibou vole." Had the class rise, wave arms in the manner of flight—and hence: "Je vole!" As usual, the class was most alert and orderly. They are a marvelous group.

Monday, March 30:

No class.

Tuesday, March 31:

Class very sluggish, although apparently avid for a test. No recess; salle surchauffée. Very few qualified for test on words taught the past week. Four winners: Dorothy, Beverly, Barbara, Gloria. New words: la cravate, le soulier, le mouchoir, la robe. All found them difficult.

Thursday, April 2:
Best class to date, all participating, all keen and alert. Past words well retained, except *soulier*.

Friday, April 3:
School closed.

Monday, April 6:
Restless despite first outdoor recess in weeks. Room far too hot. Triple tie in test: Dorothy, Barbara, Beverly. Most went out on recent words. Added *le journal, les lunettes*. Much acting, always popular.

Tuesday, April 7:
Better class despite rain. New words: le pont, la poche. Old words retained except *les lunettes*. Sang "Sur le pont d'Avignon."

Thursday, April 9:
Excellent class. No new words, but more complicated directions. Past words retained, but more trouble with gender than usual.

Friday: April 10:
Taught "Sur le pont." Great success. "Mettez un trois, etc., sur le toit au tableau" easily and pleasantly done. New words: le rideau, le col, la chemise. Started *aimer* and *embrasser*. Slow going as no one seemed to like anyone in the class except himself, but enjoyed, as a result, going to mirror and kissing reflection.

Monday, April 13:
New boy, Peter, just back from the Argentine; knows no French but says he does know Spanish. Dorothy to go to Grade IV after vacation, but will be allowed to return to Grade III for the French. Test, very quick, as we used farm words and they were rusty. Tie between Dorothy and Carol. Acted out dialogue of meeting in the street: *Bonjour, je vous serre la main, comment allez-vous? Je*

vais très bien, merci, et vous? *Aimer* and *embrasser* now mastered. Great enthusiasm.

Tuesday, April 14:
  No school because of snow.

Thursday, April 16:
  New word: *la pluie*. New direction: requesting one child "Dites à X de se lever." Two or three got the idea of "X, levez-vous," right away, but the majority had trouble. Very good on all past words and commands.

Friday, April 17:
  Class at its very best.

SCRIPT OF PLAYLET
(Given before the Central School PTA, Wednesday
Evening, March 11, 1953)

To the accompaniment of the *Marseillaise*, class filed in and stood in two groups on either side of the steps leading up to the stage, Dorothy and Barbara (most frequent "champions") in the center. Only prop a blackboard. As each instruction was given, the individual would rise and act out what he was told to do, stating in the first person what his action was.

Bonjour, classe.
Asseyez-vous.
Carol, levez-vous, allez au drapeau américain, saluez le drapeau.
Beverly, levez-vous allez à la porte, sortez, maintenant rentrez, retournez à votre place, asseyez-vous.
Paul, donnez le crayon à Gloria. (Merci, Paul. Il n'y a pas de quoi, Gloria.)
Tom, parlez au téléphone. (Allô, allô.)
Joyce, parlez comme une vache; Mary-Bob, parlez comme un chien; Marie-Louise, parlez comme un âne.
Karen, qu'est-ce que c'est? (*Indicating the clock.*) Quelle heure est-il à la pendule?

Louise, qu'est-ce que je fais? (Vous vous asseyez, vous vous levez.)

Ronnie, allez au tableau, dessinez une tête.

Maureen, les cheveux; Howard, les oreilles; Mary K., les yeux; Barrie, le nez; Douglas, la bouche; Marshall, le cou.

Pat, de qui est-ce le portrait? (De M. Grew.) Alors, effacez-le.

Dorothy, faites le professeur. (*Dorothy gets her group to stand up and repeat les jours de la semaine. Barbara has hers repeat les mois de l'année.*)

Dorothy then asks the pianist: "Jouez *Alouette* s'il vous plaît" and the entire group sings four verses, la tête, le cou, le coude, le pied. Class then says "au revoir" and exits in single file, again to the accompaniment of the *Marseillaise*.

Monday, April 27:
Not too bad a class considering that it was the first day after vacation, and raining. New word: la poupée. New actions: jeter, attrapper, asseyez-vous, à cheval.

Tuesday, April 28:
Test on all old vocabulary. Five winners: Dorothy, Beverly, Pat, Carol, and Tom. Yesterday's verbs retained. New actions: *monter sur* and *descendre de* la chaise.

Thursday, April 30:
Excellent class. New words: le soleil, l'arc-en-ciel, tirer, les mains *propres* et les mains *sales*. Chose two pupils, one with clean hands and one with dirty, and then sent the latter to the "lavabo" to wash them. New game: one child sits with his back to the room and his eyes closed; another is chosen to "tirez les cheveux" or "touchez l'épaule gauche," etc., of the first who tries to guess who it is by the voice. Great success.

Friday, May 1:
Another excellent class. New game: one child leaves the room, others pick an object, first returns and goes around the class asking "est-ce la . . . ?" Great success, and directions quickly understood. New action: "mettez deux chaises dos à dos." New

verb: gifler. Past words well retained, although only a few remembered "arc-en-ciel."

Monday, May 4:
 Test won by Dorothy, Karen, Barbara, and Tom. Most went out on recent words. New words: le parapluie (from drawing on wall), la pierre (used as paperweight), le rideau, ramasser. Keen class, interested in following directions.

Tuesday, May 5:
 Good class. Showed off mostly. Past words well retained except "parapluie" and "attraper."

Thursday, May 7:
 Class very keen and on its toes. Again showed off. Argentine boy participated for the first time.

Friday, May 8:
 New words: le pot, le vase (both on table), laisser, tomber. Many directions, lots with new words mostly cognates. All participated and all very keen.

Monday, May 11:
 Good class. Tie between Dorothy and Marie-Louise Currier. More finalists and new runners-up. New words: les ciseaux, couper. Most recent words retained except "le lait" which even Dorothy had forgotten! Her first error, I think, since the first month.

Tuesday, May 12:
 All past words retained, but class sillier than usual, others answering than those called upon, poor on new words: le poisson (room décor), nager, la roue (boy's toy auto). After being shown that an auto has four wheels, they couldn't or wouldn't answer such question as "combien de roues a une bicyclette?" Spring fever? The word "lait" now retained.

Thursday, May 14:
 New words: le manteau (one on table), rire, sourire, pleurer. Much "faites danser, voler, etc., la poupée." All recent words retained. Excellent following of directions both new and old.

Friday, May 15:
Went through our "for visitors" paces, a sample of all we have done during the year. Excellent response. Few words forgotten.

Monday, May 18:
Tests won by Dorothy alone; most went out by mixing "je" and "vous" in questions and answers. Otherwise it was a spirited, eager class.

Tuesday, May 19:
Drilled on difference between "je" and "vous." Not so troublesome as previous day. New words: la ville, le village. Complicated directions well followed.

Thursday, May 21:
To qualify for final test (May 26) child must know: l'assiette, le verre, le couteau, la fourchette, la cuiller. Drilled on them. About half got them very quickly.

Friday, May 22:
Six knew the salle à manger words. Spent most of class drawing on board. Remembered "ville" from Tuesday.

Monday, May 25:
Six more qualifiers. About eight showed no interest in trying, something new. Used "flèche" and "coeur" for first time since circa February 14. Most remembered them. Rest of period spent on actions.

Tuesday, May 26:
Decided to postpone test sine die because of important visitors and because class had to be limited in time for practice alert. Thus I avoided any tearful farewells. Followed the usual "for visitors" routine, and the results were the best to date, a perfect swan song.

On Thursday, May 28, the three groups who have been having the French attended a special showing of the film strip used in the Protestant Schools of Quebec, "Boucles d'Or et les trois Ours."

* 7 *

METHODOLOGY AND PRESENTATION IN RELATION TO PUPIL INTEREST

In schools that train pupils in the vocations and in special techniques, in those devoted entirely to the arts or sciences, and in those offering specialized courses and training for other than an academic degree, great care must be exercised not only in selecting textbooks but in drawing up a course of study which will be in harmony with the particular interests of the students. Unfortunately very few specialized language textbooks are available for such schools, but material can be mimeographed and distributed to the students.

In some large centers variety in the course of study has already been achieved. Nevertheless, every teacher, especially in small communities, should bear in mind the various talents of the students and their particular interests, especially when those students can be easily grouped or directed toward a definite goal. Language study has taken a great spurt in schools where students working for a domestic science degree with emphasis on cooking, dressmaking, or millinery, have been introduced to the French vocabulary in these fields and have been encouraged to read French books, articles, and pamphlets dealing with their special interest.

To be specific, for majors in cooking, French, Italian, or Spanish menus can be mimeographed and lists drawn up containing technical words such as *soufflé, fondue, pièce de résistance, filet, pâtisserie, pâté, ragoût, sauté, brioche, croissant, cave,* and any others that are useful in translating the recipes to be found in the many cookbooks now published in French. Particularly attractive recipes that the girls might use in their cooking class or at home may be mimeographed and distributed to the students for their cooking notebooks. The same method can be used in an Italian class in high school so that students will become familiar with such words as *antipasto, minestrone, ravioli, risotto, pizza, cacciatora, scaloppine,* and *zabaione.*

The same adaptation of courses to specific needs has been applied in the study of German in many technical schools, and the gain for the student in this direct preparation for a career has been invaluable. In commercial schools, particularly those which emphasize foreign banking or foreign trade and which require contacts with foreign countries, such as those of South and Central America, the vocabulary in Spanish and Portuguese and the work in composition should be modified to prepare the students for communication with these lands. Reading material that is chosen from magazines, newspapers, trade journals, and even novels and short stories should help prepare them more directly for their future work in a foreign country. The conversation work in these classes might well include training in long-distance telephone calls, and the simulation of situations likely to occur in doing business abroad, for the pupils should acquire a knowledge of the special vocabulary needed for such communications. The social life and any peculiarities in doing business in a foreign country should be a subject of study so that a student may develop a sympathetic understanding of the people with whom he will have to deal, before actual contact takes place. The most practical preparation here is to dictate typical dialogues or conversations and have the students act them out. The instructor may also pretend to be a foreigner and improvise questions which will require spontaneous use of the specialized vocabulary by the students. A variation of this technique is to have the students act out a scene in which they use the dialogues they have learned or similar dialogues they invent to suit the situation. Dialogues may be suggested by a comic strip shown to the class.

In military and naval academies and schools that offer training in international relations and diplomacy, the course of study is now particularly adapted to the needs of the students. This direct approach to a specific language problem eliminates waste of time in this preparatory period of their careers. The adaptation of courses and even of methodology to the specific needs of schools and students can be greatly developed. To date, little of a really constructive nature has been done in this field. If enough students with special interests could be grouped in one class or school and material suited to their needs could be prepared for them, they would benefit greatly thereby, and the practical value of language study would be proved once more.

On the level of higher education, technological schools, particularly the Massachusetts Institute of Technology, have tried to meet these needs. The Latin-American Institute, the Department of State Language Institute, the Army and Navy Intelligence Schools, and the Institute of Languages and Linguistics of Georgetown University, directed by Professor L. E. Dostert, have made this their particular concern. On the high-school level, where students have to meet state or municipal academic requirements to obtain a diploma, it has been harder to change the language syllabus completely. Textile high schools, however, have drawn up special vocabularies like those suggested above for majors in dressmaking and costume designing. For students planning to become buyers for importing houses or department stores, conversational and composition topics can easily be adapted in line with these interests. It must not be forgotten that the United States will need more and more translators, interpreters, and secretaries for diplomats and international bankers and businessmen; and that publishing houses, radio and television companies, and the foreign service—to say nothing of the F.B.I., social service, and libraries—also need linguists.

An example of what has been done is the fact that after 2 years of high-school German some engineering schools require their students to take specialized language courses in which all the reading material is taken from articles on engineering. The translation of articles from technical journals, German patents, trade catalogues, and engineering equipment advertisements is emphasized. In some schools of business the reading material for required courses in Spanish and French is taken from Spanish and French business and economic periodicals; these courses also stress commercial correspondence in the foreign language in place of the usual composition assignments. Although a few scientific, chemistry, and economics textbooks have been published for special students in Spanish,

German, and French, the very rapid scientific advances[1] and the changes in economic theory and business management have made current periodicals in these fields more practical for class and library use. When students have been unable to subscribe to these periodicals because of financial reasons, excerpts from them have been mimeographed and distributed to the class daily or weekly.

Since so little material for such courses long remains up to date, the teacher may find it necessary to mimeograph his own lessons, prepare his own audio-visual materials such as posters and other illustrative materials, and watch his students' progress that results from his own initiative and enthusiasm. If his efforts are successful, he will inspire others and see his ideas spreading in a relatively new field of language teaching. However, to avoid the possibility of errors, a young teacher should have the material he prepares checked carefully by an experienced teacher or an educated native.

---

[1] We are only now becoming aware of the importance of the Russian language in the scientific field, particularly chemistry.

* 8 *

TEACHING PRONUNCIATION

For success in teaching pronunciation a definite effort must be made at the beginning to familiarize the pupil with all the new sounds and to make sure that he realizes that a very high degree of perfection—if not perfection itself—is essential in reproducing the sounds characteristic of the particular language. Although he must be able to hear and reproduce each individual sound, at every stage of learning a language correct phrasing should be emphasized, for language is made up of connected, not unconnected, sounds. It is syllabification, stress, and intonation that give meaning to words which are composed of sounds.

In the usual method of teaching pronunciation, the instructor makes the sounds and the pupil repeats them—in his reading, his recitation of verb forms, or perhaps even his translation of sentences from English. Usually, however, this is not adequate to fix the correct sound in his mind to any permanent extent.

Recordings are invaluable teachings aids because they supplement the initial presentation with oral and aural practice. For that reason passages in the foreign language should be recorded and listened to and imitated by students as part of their homework; this can be done in the language laboratory. This study and frequent repetition of recorded material makes correct pronunciation become a subconscious process.

The magnetic tape recorder is a great improvement over earlier methods of recording. It is really practical, for a wire or tape can be demagnetized—in other words, the recorded matter is erased—and used hundreds of times. Paper or plastic tape is more suitable for school use because, although more expensive than wire, it is not affected by these erasures. The Instructional Material Office of the Division of Curriculum Development of the New York City High School System is improving these recorders for use in language instruction. The objective of every language teacher should always be to make the correct pronunciation of every sound automatic.

Many supervisors and educators advocate the use of phonetic symbols. For the instructor who believes that the phonetic alphabet will aid him in this task, a great number of charts are available. These charts help the student associate a sound with each symbol. The symbols should be learned essentially for recognition purposes. In using phonetic symbols, the teacher should give at least a 5-minute drill on the pronunciation of each new sound, together with a review drill on the sounds learned previously, until all have been mastered. Transcribing the foreign language into phonetic symbols and the symbols into the language is a good exercise for advanced classes. But except in advanced work in phonetics, the students should not be expected to write phonetic symbols or to read aloud a text written in them. For the teacher who wishes to drill on isolated sounds, very simple phonetic dictations are sometimes helpful. A physiological explanation of each sound should always be given when symbols are used, and all the sounds and symbols should be learned in words and related to spelling as soon as the students see the printed word.

If the instructor finds phonetic symbols too difficult for his class, he should keep the aim of acquiring perfect pronunciation before his students by showing them pronunciation charts giving the characteristic vowel and consonant sounds, their various spellings in the foreign language, and the equivalent English sound if there is any. Lists of words containing these sounds should also be displayed. To train the students in these sounds, each sound should be shown, preferably in alphabetical order, pronounced, repeated over and over by the class, and finally used in as many words as possible until the students appear to have mastered the sound. These sounds will not be retained by most students unless they have been repeated over and over at spaced intervals in every class session for a period of a year or two. It is therefore helpful to have additional flash cards or charts always available as a means of recalling the correct pronunciation whenever a pupil makes an error.

The teacher who cannot obtain charts must correct errors in pronunciation by writing the correct sound or the symbol for it on the board. Many teachers prefer this method because it is a more personal approach to pronunciation correction; but in a large class, especially in high school, the flash-card or chart technique is very effective. The students should always be on the alert for errors made by the other students, and should be encouraged to correct them. It is true that the use of flash cards often interrupts oral reading or a recitation, but pronunciation is such an essential part of the teaching process that this additional drill is never time lost.

The most important element in teaching pronunciation is the teacher's constant awareness, during the 2 or 3 years of language instruction, of any neglect of pronunciation on the part of his students, and his constant insistence on correct pronunciation as an essential part of each day's lesson. Otherwise, the student will make little if any progress; and frequently he is less capable of pronouncing accurately at the end of the third year of study than in the early lessons when the stress was on pronunciation.

In recent years most publishing houses have prepared phonograph records to accompany their elementary grammars. Students should be encouraged to use these records as part of their homework or laboratory work, outside of the regular classroom drill. This additional practice is valuable at all levels of language learning. It is sometimes difficult to supervise and check on this additional work, but the progress of the students is usually evidence of their diligence and their intelligent use of these records.

As a form of drill, other than reading phonetic transcriptions of individual sounds and words in which these sounds occur and listening to records, the singing of songs, every word of which has been carefully pronounced beforehand, can be of value. Most students enjoy learning the words in order to sing. The students should be required to enunciate very carefully. When singing is done by the class, it is imperative that the aim be to have no errors in pronunciation; perfection should always be the goal. This also applies in general to unison reading and choral reading by the class. Great care should be taken to detect the slightest variation from correct pronunciation. The finest training of this sort is found in choral recitation, in which a poem or bit of prose is rehearsed by the class until it is brought to the point of absolute perfection.

For choral recitation, perhaps the most effective technique is to read and reread carefully the chosen poem or selection to the class and then explain the meaning; this should be done before pronouncing slowly and in unison each difficult word and phrase, until every detail has been mastered. If the class is large enough to be divided into voice groups, then the tonal quality of the reading can be improved. Interpretation of the meaning through the proper foreign-language rhythm and intonation can be taught in this manner. By setting an almost musical perfection as an objective for the class, very noticeable improvement in individual, as well as group, pronunciation may be obtained.

Another excellent training device, even for beginning classes, is the memorization of a simple poem, particularly one in which different vowels or consonant sounds are repeated. If the poem has been recorded, a phonograph will enable a student to hear a record so frequently that he may be able to imitate it almost perfectly. Most schools that do not have a language laboratory and special recording equipment do have a phonograph. In this case a classroom should be available to which a student may come after class, not only to listen to records but to make records himself. The best results, of course, are obtained when the student listens to his own pronunciation and compares it with that on the record he has tried to imitate and also with earlier records he has made. Intonation is also usually taught effectively by this method.

In place of phonograph records, a language laboratory equipped with the ever-improving tape-recorder is being used more and more frequently. According to Professor William

Locke, some 260 colleges and the same number of high schools in the United States were equipped with language laboratories by 1960. Testing techniques that could not be applied before are now being used to improve pronunciation. Intonation patterns can now be repeated over and over, and the student's pronunciation can be compared with the model simply by replaying the tape. Distinctions between utterances that are similar in sound but different in meaning can be noted and, if not distinguished at first, replayed until the difference in sound is caught. In the laboratory each individual can learn at his own pace, and he can come far nearer to mastering each sound than he would if he were in a group. Furthermore, he can hear his own utterance on the tape far more accurately than in a classroom.

Turntables equipped with earphones have been found practical in some schools. As was said above, many schools use the convenient and economical tape recorder. This means that after class a student can not only listen to the recordings of other voices but hear his own recording, compare his voice and pronunciation with those of the model, practice corrections, make another recording, and note improvements.

In obtaining a high degree of perfection in pronunciation the importance of a great deal of supplementary work outside of class cannot be overemphasized. If little or no stress is placed on pronunciation as an essential part of the course, the students will almost always tend to neglect it. They should be led to believe from the beginning that perfection in this phase of oral work is necessary for a passing mark for the course.

If the grammar used has a number of conversational phrases, these phrases can be used by the instructor as an exercise at the beginning of every hour. In this case the students learn the intonation of the language at the same time as the pronunciation of individual words. Since a language is spoken in groups of words and expressions rather than as single words, this method stresses this phase of language learning. In languages in which one word is linked to another, a certain sign, such as a movement of the teacher's finger, can become a signal when a student fails to recognize the linking of two words.

In junior high school and the first year of senior high, some instructors have obtained records made by foreigners in English. If the speaker has a marked foreign accent, his pronunciation and intonation are carefully analyzed and even imitated by the teacher to stress the difference, for example, between vowel sounds in the foreign language and in English. The students often enjoy this type of analysis and learn a great deal from it.

There is a growing tendency to approach sound and pronunciation more scientifically than before. The phoneme, which normally represents approximately the same sound to the ear, is being broken down by many teachers into its several phonetic sounds—with variations in stress, pitch, and transition depending upon whether it is an initial, medial, or final sound. Grasping the distinctions between the phones of one language and another, which are never exactly alike, is being stressed by these teachers to help the student attain a perfect imitation of the native speech with all the natural variations found in the land of its origin. By using native speech on the tape in place of the often less perfect pronunciation of the classroom teacher, the student's ear can be trained to discern such distinctions as *leaf* and *leave* or the difference between the *p* in *pin* and *cap* when pronounced in rapid native speech. From the beginning, sounds can be learned through hearing natural utterances given at the speed of normal native speech. More and more disks and tapes are being prepared with this aim in view. To test proficiency in hearing skill, the Educational Testing Service is preparing tests for teachers as well as for students at the different levels in order to attain, if possible, a higher national standard of foreign-language pronunciation among our students.

There is also a tendency among many instructors to stress phonemic rather than phonetic distinctions, i.e., (1) sounds in which the two languages do not coincide (the French *u* is not found in English, but the French *ou* is), and (2) pairs of sounds in the language which may be confused (the French parler*ai* vs. parler*ais*, and the English *leave* vs. *leaf*).[1]

The important thing is to make students realize that perfect pronunciation of a foreign language should be their goal so that they will strive constantly to attain this perfection.

[1] Bloch and Trager, *Outline of Linguistic Analysis* treats this subject very fully.

* 9 *

TEACHING VOCABULARY

One of the most difficult yet important phases of language teaching is the teaching of vocabulary. Different methods must be employed at various stages of proficiency; but in every case an attempt should be made to <u>facilitate</u> the learning process, for this is always likely to be tedious in learning vocabulary, especially if the student works alone.

It is usually helpful, to both teacher and pupil, to separate the total vocabulary into <u>two groups, active and passive.</u> By active vocabulary is meant the words that the pupil is expected to be able to use in speaking and writing; by passive vocabulary is meant those he should recognize when spoken to or in reading. As he advances in his studies, much of the initially passive vocabulary becomes active until finally only specialized and technical words remain passive.

It must be remembered that for most teachers today the choice of vocabulary is predetermined by the textbook selected. The vocabulary has usually been chosen with great care and after long thought, and hence can be used without question. Such a vocabulary is the most convenient. Even with a textbook vocabulary, however, many of the techniques suggested below may be used to fix the vocabulary in the student's mind, for every word must be mastered accurately from the first if he expects to make any progress in learning the language. Most of the techniques suggested in this chapter can be used effectively to teach words found in reading texts as well as in grammars, words that seem wise additions for an active vocabulary for either oral or written composition.

In elementary classes the use of cognates is often stressed, and in some cases a whole term's work is based largely on words that are identical or nearly so in both English and the foreign language. This technique is particularly applicable in French, for so many words are the same in both languages. Elementary readers in this language have been built upon this principle, and the text of the first lessons in several grammars is made up to a great extent of cognates. These cognates and loan words give an early sense of power, but the vocabulary thus learned leads to stilted, artificial speech and writing. There is also a decided limit to the number of words that can be taught in this manner; furthermore, many of the cognates that are similar in spelling, are very different in meaning, and hence may mislead students who might otherwise be learning more accurately.

As a means of building vocabulary from English words or recognizing the English equivalents of foreign words, certain basic philological rules are sometimes taught which permit students to recognize the changes that must have taken place when, for example, a French or German word became an English word. The following are examples of words that can be compared in this manner: *school*, basically the same as the French *école*; *stable*, the same as *étable*; *mutton*, another form of *mouton*; *crust*, of *croute*; *mustard*, of *moutarde*; *mussel*, of *moule.* In German, *Knabe* has an English form, *knave;* compare *Hund* and *hound, Garten* and *garden, Ding* and *thing, Grund* and *ground, Muschel* and *mussel.* The verbs *geben* and *haben* have developed into the English *give* and *have.* Such similarities are found in several of the Romance languages; thus the English *liberty* becomes *liberté* in French, *libertad* in Spanish, and *libertà* in Italian; *generous* becomes the French *généreux,* the Spanish *generoso,* and the Italian *generoso; naturally* has foreign forms as similar as *naturellement* (French), *naturalmente* (Spanish), and *naturalmente* (Italian). If these similarities can be impressed upon the student, he will look for them in his reading and increase his passive vocabulary appreciably with little effort.

In recent years, words have been listed and taught on the basis of <u>frequency,</u> that is, the number of times they appear in the average reading material likely to be used by certain age groups or available in an average number of schools. Many students increase their passive vocabulary by learning these words a few at a time. Learning vocabulary in this manner is very artificial; but since, according to scientific count, these words are likely to appear more frequently than others in reading material, the student who learns the words in such a list may obtain a working vocabulary for reading sooner than if he tried to increase his passive vocabulary by reading alone.

A method which psychologically is more sound and which perhaps permits quicker assimiliation of words than the direct memorization of unrelated words is their grouping into families—for example, fruits, birds, meats, vegetables, members of a family, objects in a living room, bedroom or kitchen or classroom. This method is popular abroad. Unfortunately, such word groups tend to include rare and unnecessary words that end by confusing the student and cluttering his mind with useless knowledge.

Another method of teaching vocabulary that was applied by the followers of the direct method is to bring to class several objects such as flags, pencils, pens, apples, pears, and oranges, and show each in turn to the class and give the direct foreign-language equivalent, thus teaching vocabulary directly rather than in terms of the English equivalent. Unfortunately, there is a limit to the number of objects than can be brought to class, and even though pictures are substituted for the real objects, vocabulary study usually extends beyond these concrete things. Most abstract words must therefore be learned from the English equivalents or in context in extensive reading. The direct method of teaching vocabulary is interesting and holds the attention of students, especially in beginning classes, but it is not feasible to any great extent in later courses without the use of pictures that involve many objects and provide topics for conversation and composition, such as railroad stations, grocery stores, living rooms, etc.

One of the principles used in the reading method of teaching vocabulary was the systematic introduction and repetition of the same word in the reading texts, which were constructed for that purpose. The words were repeated 6 times at spaced intervals within a certain number of pages, the assumption being that the students would retain them if they saw them frequently. This procedure can be applied in the classroom other than by means of reading texts by bringing the words in a prepared vocabulary to the students' attention at definite intervals in various written exercises and in games.

In another method, which has been used extensively in recent years, a vocabulary of new and difficult words is presented at the beginning of a reading lesson, or at the foot of each page, or on the page opposite the reading selection, for involuntary absorption. This method has never been very successful because students seem unable to retain words that they conclude are relatively unimportant since they have not been required to learn them or to look them up in a dictionary. They soon depend on finding a certain number of these key words repeated at the foot of the page or in some other easily accessible place, and hence never make any effort to learn them.

A more concrete and practical method of teaching vocabulary involves requiring students to list words to be used in a future written composition or an oral composition. This not only forces a student to know the meaning of the word because he will use it later in a sentence of his own composition, but tends to fix the word definitely in his mind. This same method can be used with groups of words and idiomatic expressions. From lists of this sort, if accurately prepared and referred to frequently, a student can build up an excellent vocabulary, both active and passive.

Vocabulary can be taught directly by examining the structure of a word in the foreign language, beginning with the verb—the French *danser,* for example—going from it to the corresponding noun—*la danse*—and to as many derived words as possible—*un thé dansant, danseur, le dancing*—nouns, adverbs, adjectives, compounds, etc. Similarly the Spanish *leer* (read) gives *lectura, leyenda; caballo* (horse) gives *caballero, caballería, cabalgar.* This can become a game, with a reward for the one who finds the greatest number of related words.

Words may be learned by the students for the specific purpose of competing in a vocabulary match or a vocabulary game of some kind. This is probably the most effective artificial way of learning vocabulary that can be used in the classroom. If pictures can be obtained that show a large number of different objects, the game can be based on naming the objects as the teacher or a student points to them. Some textbooks have pictures that can be used for this purpose. Students may be encouraged to draw pictures themselves, labeling each object with its foreign name. Pictures may be cut out of newspapers and magazines, and the foreign word placed beneath as a caption. This can be made into a game, pictures of objects labeled in the foreign language being pinned on one bulletin board and another set of pictures containing their opposites being put on another bulletin board. The student or team who finds the greatest number of pairs in a stated time is declared the winner and rewarded in some way.

Students may be asked to list practical English words whose equivalents they would like to know; when the lists have been translated, they can be mimeographed and distributed to the class. The teacher will find that the pupils have learned many of the words while making up the list because they were interested in knowing these particular words.

For every reading lesson, the students may be required to list in a notebook or on cards any new words they find. This helps them build up a personal dictionary, so to speak, that can be used for daily reviews. Such lists can be used by the instructor for quizzing and for periodic tests to see the gain in vocabulary his students have made; however, he should choose words common to all the lists. These lists may be learned by heart, as is so frequently the practice in European schools, to create a large active vocabulary. As reading progresses, the instructor may have his students underline the words he considers most important and then have the pupils write sentences on the board in which these words are used correctly.

Many students enjoy learning words with either their opposites or their synonyms. Words with opposite meanings used in the same sentence often facilitate the retention of vocabulary without the intervention of the native tongue. For instance: L'homme est *grand;* le bébé est *petit.* L'éléphant est *grand;* le chat est *petit.* La dame est *jolie,* elle n'est pas *laide.* L'auto est *neuve,* elle n'est pas *vieille.*

Additional words can be learned if one word or a list of words is written on the blackboard, the students then breaking down each of the longer words into as many smaller words as possible and putting the meaning next to each word:

> *parebrise: pare(r),* to fend off; *brise,* breeze.
> *gardeboue: garde(r),* to keep, protect; *boue,* mud.
> *paraguas: para(r),* to stop; *aguas,* water.
> *après-midi: après,* after; *midi,* noon.

The students may also be asked to see how many words can be formed from each word in these lists; thus:

$$cependant = ce + pendant$$
$$autrefois = autre + fois$$

The competitive nature of this exercise interests the students and they have the added satisfaction of finding out how many words they can recognize.

Parts of the body are often taught on television programs by singing the French-Canadian song "Alouette" substituting *la bouche* for *le bec; le bras* for *la patte;* etc. Many popular French songs available on records also offer a practical vocabulary that students learn more readily as parts of a song than as lists.

Crossword puzzles provide incentives to learning if the puzzles are properly controlled and the meaning of the words is stressed. Girls may be asked to find the names of colors or other foreign words which have been incorporated in English, such as the French words *rouge, beige, champagne, cerise, chartreuse;* the names of many colors have been take over from the French into English. The memorizing of names of colors may be further motivated by asking students to name the colors of the clothes that other students are wearing.

There are endless devices for building up vocabulary. The principle to be stressed, of course, is the value of learning as many words as possible, not restricting these words either to those in the grammar text or to those on some particular list, or to those in the reading lessons that were emphasized as being important. One Spanish teacher had his pupils copy Spanish words in one column on a sheet of paper, and their English equivalents in another column; the paper was then folded once vertically. After studying the Spanish words, turning to the English list to check his knowledge, the student was questioned orally on the list; any Spanish words he missed he had to write four times.

Vocabulary can also be presented in conversational phrases which have the added advantage of being useful and more easily retained because of their practical value.

"Est-ce que vous avez écrit à votre *beau-père,* Jean?"
"Oui, *je viens de* lui écrire *aujourd'hui même.* Je lui ai écrit une très *longue lettre,* mais je ne l'ai pas encore *mise à la poste. La semaine dernière,* il m'a envoyé *une carte postale.* Je l'ai reçue *hier matin de bonne heure.*"

The difference between passive and active vocabulary need never be emphasized except to indicate words which are used most frequently. In teaching vocabulary the main objective of learning a language—mastering it as a living, usable language for all forms of communication—must always be kept in mind. If too much stress is placed on the difference between active and passive vocabulary, some of the student's incentive to increase his vocabulary will be lost. Each student requires the largest possible vocabulary to express himself to his own satisfaction, and nothing should be done to discourage the development of such a vocabulary. Every possible device should be used to encourage building more vocabulary—finding synonyms, antonyms, and onomatopoetic words; guessing at meanings from the context; studying prefixes and suffixes, and analyzing words by this procedure. In all formal vocabulary study the flash-card technique, in high school especially, makes these exercises more stimulating and alive.

I. A. Richards and Christine M. Gibson in collaboration with others have prepared a series of limited vocabulary texts in which words and dialogues are taught directly through pictures. This vocabulary and dialogue can be so organized and used in class that it serves as a basis for understanding normal, native speech in a market, at a dinner table, or in a post office. Once the vocabulary and patterns of speech have been learned from the simple stick figures drawn at the board or projected on the screen, a film in which natives speak in the foreign tongue (one that has a foreign background, depicting a natural, unrehearsed scene at a market, a dinner table, or post office) is shown to the class to test their comprehension of speech in situations a student might experience in a foreign country.

In classes where aural-oral techniques have developed facility of expression, projecting a colored picture on the screen, preferably one containing some actions and objects not hitherto studied, and then discussing it will enable the students to learn new vocabulary in context. Cartoons without conversation but with a sequence of action can also be used to build up new vocabulary as well as review the old in a natural way.

The teacher who uses the foreign language constantly in class helps his students to learn vocabulary painlessly, although it may be largely a passive vocabulary, at first retained by ear and not always too accurately retained; eventually, however, it becomes so familiar that it becomes active without the student realizing it.

* 10 *

TEACHING GRAMMAR

Grammar is the simplest logical way of learning to reconstruct a foreign language. To many students and teachers it seems artificial and often difficult to understand, but it usually provides a short cut to knowledge which otherwise can be obtained only by the long and tedious process of repetition over an extended period of time. It should always be regarded as a short cut, a means to an end, never as an end in itself.

In other words, for the purpose of language teaching, grammar is the codifying or simplifying of the constructions people use to put vocabulary together in an effective way. Syntax varies with different languages, but there are many similarities with the student's native tongue; and if these similarities are emphasized, the foreign language immediately becomes simpler. Care should always be taken, especially at first, to teach only the essentials and to use every possible device for fixing each grammatical idea or fact permanently in the student's mind in order to avoid confusion with the rules he will study later. If emphasis on the unessential, the intricate, the exceptional construction is avoided, grammar will become an aid to language learning rather than an obstacle. In many cases too much time is spent by the inexperienced teacher on points of minor importance because they are challenging. The experienced teacher chooses only the essential, leaving minor points for incidental discussion as they arise in reading texts. Studies of syntax frequency and lists are the wisest and simplest guides to what is more important.

One of the greatest problems in teaching grammar in a foreign language is nomenclature. Careless use of grammatical terms is a fundamental cause of misunderstanding, prolonged confusion, and discouragement on the part of the student. The terminology used in the past 50 years has been borrowed from Latin, from English, and from the various foreign languages themselves. Some of the terms do not always correspond exactly to the tenses or grammatical functions to which they are applied. The average student seldom really understands even the terms he has studied and is using. The only practical solution for the teacher who wants to clarify the teaching of a foreign language by means of grammar is a yearly or perhaps a term-by-term definition or redefinition of the terms as he understands them and intends to use them in class. It should never be assumed that students understand even the simplest grammatical terms without definition, nor should it be assumed that they will retain the explanation they have been given unless it is repeated and tested frequently. This may seem unnecessary to many, but unfortunately it is an essential part of successful modern language teaching today, at all levels of instruction.

The teaching of grammar, like the teaching of vocabulary, is to some degree predetermined by the choice of the elementary textbook, or of the review grammar in advanced classes. Great care should be taken in choosing a basic text to make sure that it fits not only the intellectual level and special interests of the students but the particular abilities of the teacher. This may be difficult in a large school system. Nevertheless, if the textbook assigned does not suit the needs of the particular group or the teacher, the teacher should always feel free to present each lesson in the most practical way, selecting for drill only the exercises he finds valuable. This may entail preparing different or additional exercises to suit the special needs of the class, but the teacher who wishes to secure the best results will be ready to take on this extra task.

In teaching grammar, every effort should be made to present it dramatically and clearly, and to repeat the explanations several times if necessary. The more dramatic the initial presentation of a grammatical fact, the more likely it is to impress itself on the student's mind, particularly a young pupil's mind. There are many devices which will help. Diagrams and symbols which reduce the grammatical fact to its simplest elements are among the most frequent. Sometimes the use of colored chalks on the blackboard will strengthen the impression. The following examples show the use of simple diagrammatic devices.

$$a + le = \text{au}$$
$$de + le = \text{du}$$

Condition	Conclusion
Si nous **partons**	il **partira**.
Si + *present indic.* = conclusion with *future*	
Si nous **partons**	il **partirait**.
Si + *imperfect* = conclusion with *conditional*	

$$in + dem = \text{im}$$
$$an + das = \text{ans}$$

Condition	Conclusion
Wenn er **kommt**	so **werde** ich ihm das Geld **geben.**
Wenn + *present indic.*	= conclusion with *future*
Wenn er hier **wäre**	so **würde** ich ihm das Geld **geben.**
Wenn + *imperfect subj.*	= conclusion with *present conditional*

For many students one of the most interesting ways of presenting grammar is by the inductive method, in which a series of examples are written on the board and the student is led, by means of questions, to discover the rule for himself. However, this requires the teacher to prepare his questions very carefully and select with equal care a number of sentences which illustrate the rule. This participation in discovering or formulating a rule holds the attention of most students and tends to train them to be on the alert for new grammatical constructions that may be encountered in their reading. Another result of this use of the inductive method is that students usually try to reason out new grammatical constructions for themselves instead of waiting for the teacher to explain them. The initial process is time-consuming, but the end result is usually better.

Here is a brief outline of the essential points to be brought out in using the inductive method for teaching the French partitive construction in an affirmative sentence.

The teacher holds up one book and writes on the board:

J'ai *un* livre.

Then he holds up several books and writes:

J'ai *des* livres.

The pupils are led to to the translation:

I have *some books.*

After giving several other examples, the teacher brings out the fact that in French one of the meanings of *des* is *some*. On the basis of their earlier knowledge the students are led to analyze *des* into *de* plus the definite article. The teacher continues by means of other objects or pictures of objects whose names and gender the pupils already know: *le* livre, *les* livres; *la* plume, *les* plumes; *le* crayon, *les* crayons; and such nouns as *l'*eau, *l'*encre, *le* pain, *la* craie, *le* papier, *la* viande.

The teacher should group together the plurals—*les* livres, *les* plumes, *les* crayons; the masculine nouns—*le* papier, *le* pain; the feminine nouns—*la* craie, *la* viande; and the nouns beginning with a vowel—*l'*eau, *l'*encre. On the basis of what the students have already learned about the meaning of *des* in the sentence *J'ai des livres,* they are asked to form and translate similar sentences using *des crayons* and *des plumes.* From this they proceed to making sentences with nouns in which they use *de* and the definite article, translating each sentence Some students will note the similarity and they can be led by careful questioning to the following conclusions: (1) The masculine singular partitive form is *du.* (2) The feminine singular partitive form is *de la.* (3) Both masculine and feminine are *de l'* before a vowel. And (4) the plural partitive form is *des.* This should be followed by drill on the partitive to fix the point in the student's mind. Almost any grammatical rule can be taught effectively by a similar inductive procedure if careful preparation is made beforehand.

Every teacher will be on the alert for an appropriate classroom incident by which to dramatize a point of grammar or important idiom that is being introduced. The late arrival of a student may be the occasion for him to teach or recall the French expression *être en retard;* as John comes in, the teacher says, "Oh! Jean *est en retard*," and spends a minute drilling on the phrase. Or, for dramatic effect he may begin an explanation with a challenge: "This point is really so hard that I don't think many of you will get it." Most of the class will pay attention under these conditions.

To teach *venir de*, the teacher may send John out of the room, saying, as he leaves, "Jean *vient de* sortir" and as he returns, "Jean *vient d'*entrer," then writing *vient de* on the board. For drill purposes the instructor may then give the present indicative of this idiom and ask John, "*Venez*-vous *d'*entrer?" John should answer, "Je *viens* d'entrer." Two students may be sent out of the room, in order to teach the plural of this idiom: "Ils *viennent de* sortir." "Ils *viennent d'*entrer." "*Venez*-vous *d'*entrer?" should this time bring the answer, "Nous *venons d'*entrer," and so forth. Thus the idiom *venir de* has been taught and the present indicative of *venir* reviewed, and several members of the class have engaged in conversation.

On the other hand, the deductive method of teaching grammar often seems both more direct and more rapid. However, it frequently has less permnent results and it demands much repetition because the students themselves participate less directly in the learning process and hence are likely to be less attentive. Although the lesson may be motivated, it is the teacher who presents the rule and then explains it, giving examples to illustrate it. To be really effective, this method of approach requires immediate drill exercises to fix the rule in the students' mind.

As an example of the use of the deductive method we shall use the presentation of the French rule: "The past participle of a verb conjugated with *avoir* agrees with the preceding direct object in number and in gender." This rule may be read in the grammar, be written on the board, or merely stated by the teacher. The teacher should then explain or review:

1. The past participle with examples: *donné, fini, vendu, mangé, vu,* etc.
2. The past indefinite—the past participle with the present indicative of *avoir.*
3. The direct object pronouns *le, la, les.*

Then he may write sentences like the following on the board:

> Masculine singular
>> J'ai donné *le livre* à mon élève.
>> Je *l'*ai donné à mon élève.
>> J'ai fini *le devoir.*
>> Je *l'*ai fini.
>
> Feminine singular
>> J'ai donné *la plume* à mon élève.
>> Je l'ai donn*ée* à mon élève.
>> J'ai fini *ma leçon.*
>> Je l'ai fini*e.*
>
> Masculine plural
>> J'ai donné *mes livres* à l'élève.
>> Je les ai donné*s* à l'élève.
>> J'ai fini *mes devoirs.*
>> Je les ai fini*s.*
>
> Feminine plural
>> J'ai donné *mes plumes* à l'élève.
>> Je les ai donn*ées* à l'élève.
>> J'ai fini *mes leçons.*
>> Je les ai fini*es.*
>> J'ai vendu *les plumes.*
>> Je les ai vendu*es.*

The rules should be repeated often by the students in as simple a form as possible, such as: "The past participle with *avoir* agrees with the preceding direct object." Other examples of it should be suggested by the students and written on the board. Specific words may be given to the class, the students then giving English sentences to be translated:

| *Les robes* (fem. pl.) | I bought them. | Je les ai *achetées.* |
| *Les hommes* (masc. pl.) | I saw them. | Je les ai *vus.* |

This rule may be called the P.D.O. (preceding direct object) rule for convenience. When an error is made in its use, these initials may be used to call it to the student's attention. This device is very effective for encouraging self-correction and it can be applied to most rules. Some teachers prefer numbers which refer to specific rules in the textbook, but numbers are less suggestive and they are likely to be confusing in spite of their convenience. Such abbreviations and numbers are often written on flash cards and shown the class when an error is made. In a large class these cards help to keep all the students alert during a recitation.

One effective but unspectacular method of enabling students to remember a grammatical rule is to have them repeat it, whenever it occurs in reading or translation, until they remember it in spite of themselves. For instance, the Spanish teacher cannot ask his class too often from what the imperfect subjunctive is derived, from what person, number, tense. How much of *hablaron,* for instance, must be dropped before the imperfect subjunctive endings are added? What are they? He treats the formation of the present subjunctive in a similar manner.

In teaching the separable prefix at the end of a clause in

German, either the inductive or the deductive method may be used. If several sentences like the following are put on the board:

> Ich mache die Tür *zu.*
> Ich mache das Fenster *auf.*
> Ich komme Morgen *an.*

the students will notice the position of the prefix and will be able to discover the rule inductively. But the instructor who prefers to state the rule and give examples of it—in other words, present it deductively—may save some time.

Some teachers find that most of their students learn easily when what they are to learn is carefully grouped. Hence they prepare short model sentences that, once memorized, will be retained for a long time. In teaching Spanish, the principal uses of *pensar* and *creer* and their grammatical peculiarities might be shown by the following sentences:

Pienso en mi madre.	I think about my mother.
¿Qué *piensa* Ud. *de* mi escuela?	What do you think of my school?
Creo que *viene.*	I think he is coming.
No *creo* que *venga?*	I do not think he will come.
¿*Cree* Ud. que *venga?*	Do you think he will come?
Pienso quedarme.	I intend to remain.

The various Spanish equivalents of the English *must* may also be grouped:

Tengo que estudiar.	I must study.
Debo estudiar.	I ought to study.
Serán las dos.	It must be two o'clock.
Habrá llegado.	He must have arrived.
Hubiera debido llegar.	I ought to have arrived.

The problem of using the umlaut in German is simplified for some high-school students if the marks are called *ears* (they do resemble donkey's or rabbit's ears):

Ich kann.	Wir können.
Ich muss.	Wir müssen.
Ich darf.	Wir dürfen.

Similar devices to facilitate learning can be invented by a resourceful teacher.

Teaching numerals and the names of the days and months will be more painless if the students are required to write out the complete date on every paper they hand in.

Most elementary Spanish and French grammars now have a short introductory reading passage which covers most of the grammatical points discussed in the lesson. Students may be required to translate this into English in their notebooks, knowing that they will be called on during the next class hour to translate their version back into the foreign language and compare it with the original. If they underline their errors in red and correct them, they will soon realize that this is an excellent means of self-testing and correction to help them master the grammar and vocabulary in each lesson. Another device is to have the pupils cover the model sentences in the grammar, after having gone over them carefully, and then translate the English into the language being studied.

One way to help students remember the 14 French verbs that require the auxiliary *être* is to list them and their opposites:

monter—descendre	entrer—sortir
aller—venir	arriver—partir
naître—mourir	rester—tomber
devenir—retourner	

Another way is to incorporate them in a story about a house, such as the following, the house itself being sketched on the blackboard:

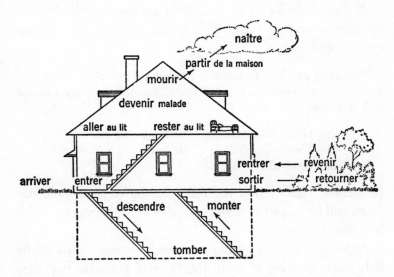

A man *arrives* at his house. He *enters* it through the door, then *goes out* into the garden, *turns around, comes back,* and *reenters* the house. He then *goes down* to the cellar, but *falls down.* He *goes upstairs.* Then he *becomes* ill, *goes* to bed and has to *stay* in bed. Finally he *dies* and his soul *leaves* the house. He *is born* in Heaven as a new soul.

Such a story seems childish but it has helped many high-school boys learn these verbs.

In order to teach the seven French nouns that end in *ou* and form the plural by adding *x*, some teachers use the following paragraph:

Un soir, dans le jardin une dame plante un *chou, à genou.* Tout à coup, elle croit voir un *pou* et à côté, un *bijou,* mais elle se trompe, c'est un *caillou.* Pendant qu'elle regarde, elle entend un *hibou,* elle a peur et elle rentre. Près de la porte elle découvre un *joujou* qu'un de ses enfants a laissé dans le jardin.

A similar device is used to help students recall the five feminine nouns in German that form their plural with an umlaut and *e:*

The *hand* you love to touch is feminine. One *night,* when you are sitting on a *bench* in front of a *wall,* you suddenly see a *mouse* and you scream.

die Hand—die Hände   die Bank—die Bänke
die Wand—die Wände   die Nacht—die Nächte
die Maus—die Mäuse

In German, the verb *to tell* takes the dative case; some students will be helped here by remembering the sentence: "Tell it *to* the Marines!"

Although these and other mnemonic devices undoubtedly help some students to recall the rules of grammar that they need in writing sentences or answering questions on an examination, the number of functional exercises should never be reduced, for they alone will fix these rules in practical form in the students' minds so firmly that their use soon becomes automatic.

A method adopted ever since teachers began to emphasize functional grammar requires the student to learn by heart the model sentence accompanying each rule. Once this is mastered, he can usually construct other sentences based on the same rule; reference to it is also valuable as a means of self-correction. Instilling the habit of self-correction in language students should be one of the constant aims of the teacher. In language study more than in almost any other secondary-school subject the student must make a conscious effort not to repeat his earlier errors that have already been pointed out to him or that he has discovered himself.

Short selections that include the grammatical points discussed in a lesson are to be found in most grammars and may be analyzed by both teacher and pupils. This is a good opportunity for inductive teaching. If the grammar provides no such selections, the teacher may prepare an original passage containing, for instance, a dozen examples of the subjunctive or the agreement of the past participle with *avoir*; he may mimeograph the selection or write it on the blackboard. Sometimes a passage from a newspaper furnishes an excellent example for a grammar lesson; or an advertisement from a foreign periodical will help to bring out a grammatical point which otherwise would be very difficult to explain. Many such advertisements are to be found in easily accessible South American and Mexican newspapers and magazines, and in French, German, and other foreign-language newspapers published in the United States.

Teachers who can draw can explain many grammatical points in pictorial form. These pictures seem to be retained by students indefinitely. Thus two glasses of water being poured into a pitcher will bring out the $de + le = du$ principle graphically.

In teaching the position of the direct and indirect object pronouns in French or Spanish, some teachers have different students carry signs representing the parts of speech—one student is the verb, another the subject, a third the direct object, a fourth the indirect object—and these students are placed in front of the classroom in the proper relationship to each other. The various tenses and their use can be explained by means of questions containing an adverb that indicates the specific tense desired: "Where did you go *yesterday?*" "Where are you going *tomorrow?*" In this way the adverbs themselves are learned almost automatically.

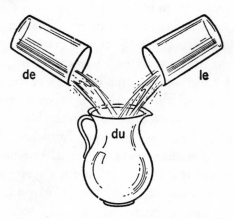

When the textbook presents grammar very clearly, it is sometimes wisest not to depart from the order followed in it, but to explain the grammatical points in much the same manner as it does, so that the students will find it easy to review them in the textbook at home. Before explaining the lesson the teacher should try to anticipate the questions that may arise while the students are reviewing the lesson at home. Students should be encouraged to do as many exercises as possible—as a game rather than a task or a formal assignment, to test their understanding of the points they have studied.

Printed cards containing in tabular form the most important rules, with examples, may be placed on the bulletin board so that the students may become familiar with the rules merely by seeing them frequently. Such cards should be changed frequently, for if left on the board too long they will no longer be noticed. In French, this device is most successful for teaching the position of direct and indirect pronouns, the conjugation of verbs, the agreement of past participles, *if* clauses and conditional sentences, the use of the subjunctive after *il faut,* conjunctions, impersonal expressions, and *il est* and *c'est.* In Spanish it can be used to teach *tener* with a noun, the use of *ser* and *estar,* and verbs that are followed by the subjunctive.

Class dictation based on the points discussed in the day's lesson and written by the students in their notebooks (one pupil may write it on the blackboard, preferably in the back of the room so that it cannot be seen easily by the rest of the class) will test their knowledge of the new material. The notebooks may be corrected by the students from the corrected version on the board, and any errors be explained to the class. Reading lessons often provide examples of the rules under discussion. If the grammar contains sentences illustrating the various rules, they may be used to test their comprehension by the class. When the exercise has been completed, it is probably more effective to have it corrected immediately by the students so that they can eliminate all their errors as soon as possible.

For teaching reflexive verbs and reflexive pronouns Gouin's series method is particularly effective because with it the student's actions may be followed from the time he gets up until he goes to bed again. Tenses can also be taught by this method if the verbs are preceded by the word for "yesterday" for the past tenses and "tomorrow" for the future tenses.

> Je me lève.
> Je me lave la figure et les mains.
> Je me brosse les dents.
> Je m'habille, etc.

Hier je me suis levé.
je me suis lavé la figure.
je me suis brossé les dents.
Je me suis habillé.

Demain je me lèverai à sept heures.
je me laverai la figure, etc.

In classrooms equipped, as most of them are, with projectors, action pictures can now be shown on the screen. Here action verbs can be very effectively taught in the third person. By projecting a series of slides with different actions, several verbs related by meaning or natural sequence can be mastered, somewhat as they are by the Gouin method. From the third person the transfer to the first and second persons is simple. The projected pictures also help to stimulate conversation, first through questions by the teacher and then, once the pattern is established, by an exchange of questions and answers between pupils. Where no projectors are available, stick figures drawn on the board will attain the same result.

The tapes and records accompanying many of our textbooks offer further devices for verb and grammar drill in the classroom. This less spontaneous technique, however, should never be used to replace the live drill offered by the teacher; but it should be encouraged as a required part of home preparation, even in schools where language laboratories are not yet available. The more oral practice required of students, the sooner automatic mastery is attained. Many schemes have been devised to teach irregular verbs, such as the following for the French verbs that require a double *r* in the future:

courrai
enverrai

verrai
acquerrai
mourrai
pourrai

Even though "vamp" has lost its former popularity, the acrostic *ce vamp* in the above list will help students recall these verbs. Similar new devices can be invented to meet the needs of each class. Some of them seem ridiculous but they are effective if they are presented to the class emphatically or strikingly. For instance, the French teacher may say or write on the blackboard, "Don't use *dont* after a preposition." Then he goes on to the example: The man in whose house I met her. Why not *dont* for "whose"? The class should answer, "Because *dont* is not used after a preposition." The repetition of *don't* and *dont* may help the student remember the rule.

The confusion between *vieille*, the French word for "old," and *veille*, meaning "the night before," can be cleared up by having the students spell *vieille* out loud, stressing the two *i*'s loudly, while the teacher writes it on the board.

The Spanish teacher may stress *pairs* of often-made errors or confusions in spelling, such as *perder—pedir* and *ver—venir*, or the preterite of *decir* and *dar*. *Ciudad—cuidado* is a source of common confusion; here he might emphasize that in *ciudad*, the word for "city," the *i* comes first, as it does in city; the other word means "care."

So that the teacher can be sure of having variety in his manner of presentation and can check the effectiveness of the methods he uses, he may find it helpful to list his methods in a notebook and check their success with the different classes he teaches.

Once a grammatical point has been presented, it must always be fixed in some way in the minds of the students. Probly the most effective way of doing this is to give frequent short tests made up of many simple sentences that not only review the particular points in the current lesson but bring in points from earlier lessons so that there will be recall and constant review of material previously discussed. The tests should be given at regular intervals and the teacher should make careful note of the points that the students seem to have most difficulty in retaining over a long period. These points should be explained again and be brought into later tests. Repetition of the same test after it has been corrected is often effective.

Oral drill is usually as helpful as written drill, but it should proceed briskly and quick answers should be required. The sentences may be simple at first; their primary objective should be to fix the rule or pattern in the minds of the students. At first it is the quantity of short drill sentences that produces good retention by students; later on, fewer and more complicated sentences may challenge them more. Oral drills should be motivated in many ways. A grammar or sentence match may be held, the class being divided into two teams. In another simple form of testing, sentences based on grammatical points are typed on cards and translated by students sent to the blackboard. No more than one short sentence should be typed on each card. If the students read the sentences they have put on the board and the class corrects them, the main point in the lesson will usually be mastered by at least a fair percentage of the class in one class hour.

After a grammar lesson has been studied, the teacher may assign the preparation of a dialogue in which the point being learned is repeated frequently. Or he may prepare questions whose answers require the use of the grammar being learned.

Short skits may be written and acted by the students; these, of course, require careful supervision by the teacher to make sure the grammatical point is used frequently in the dialogue. It is often better for the teacher to work with the students from the outset or even to write the skit himself.

To cover the homework assignment, grammar can also be taught by reading each sentence in English to the class, then calling on one student to give his translation, asking a second to correct the first translation, and having a third student repeat the corrected sentence and a fourth write the correct translation on the board. The sentences written on the board should be numbered consecutively and their order should correspond to the homework assignment so that the students may correct their notebooks easily.

When drill exercises are handed in as a written lesson every paper should be checked or at least initialed by the instructor. In a large class this provides a simple way of determining whether or not the students have done their homework. This checking should be done preferably as the students enter the classroom or when the attendance is taken. Although it may be done by the students, the teacher, while checking, can of course determine at a glance the quality of the work handed in. Written exercises are best kept in a notebook. If the instructor wishes to examine the homework each day in detail, every student may be required to have two notebooks, to be handed in on alternate days—one on Mondays and Wednesdays, for example, the other on Tuesdays and Thursdays, etc. A looseleaf notebook is easier to handle from the teacher's point of view, but students frequently lose the pages from these books.

Another method of assuring preparation of written homework is to have the students make a carbon copy of their work, the carbon being put on the teacher's desk at the beginning of the hour.

These measures may seem unnecessary to many. However, since real progress in language study is impossible without regular preparation, and since most classes are so large that it is very difficult for a teacher to be certain of every pupil's preparation, mechanical means of checking such as these become both necessary and practical.

If the class is too large for any of these devices to be used, there is a third method which is usually successful in maintaining regularity in the preparation of written work. Each day the teacher chooses, at random, say ten pupils to hand in their written homework. Since the class does not know which students will be called on, this method should insure regular and careful preparation by everyone in the class. If drill sentences in the grammar are given to test the pupils' knowledge of the grammatical lesson, they may be translated into English by the instructor, the English version then being dictated to the class for translation back into the foreign language for extra practice.

Most modern grammars have many exercises in which the correct word or grammatical form is to be put in a blank space. These exercises may be transferred to flash cards for class drill or to 3″ x 5″ cards for use by students who are sent to the board. Some textbooks contain multiple-choice questions and exercises, but these are usually cumbersome and frequently confusing to both teacher and student. Unfortunately, the incorrect forms so often used in multiple-choice tests tend to remain in the pupil's mind, rather than the correct form. This same criticism holds true of matching exercises in which several forms, some correct and some incorrect, and sometimes even nonexistent forms, are presented. Although frequently very popular among students, all such exercises can be misleading. In spite of their very obvious weaknesses, the objective quality of these tests and the ease of scoring them keep them in continued use.

If student participation in test making is desired, the class may be asked to prepare questions whose answers call for the use of the particular rule under discussion. These may be handed in to the teacher or to a student committee, and the best selected for use in class. Free composition is also helpful in teaching certain points of grammar such as the agreement of the past participle in French, the agreement of adjectives and nouns and of subject and verb, the position of adverbs and of pronoun objects, the causative *faire,* the use of the subjunctive, or, in Spanish, radical-changing verbs and *por* and *para.* If a special review lesson is given on one or two of these points before the assignment and correctness is insisted upon, the students' minds will be focussed on the point being stressed. Sometimes this attention to correct forms persists for a considerable length of time. The substitution of pronouns for nouns and the changing of a whole passage from the present to the past tense or from the affirmative to the negative are means of testing grammar that have proved sound.

It must be remembered that one of the most important things about teaching grammar is to avoid stressing a particular point and then abandoning it once the lesson is completed. It is also essential to review previously learned material in one form or another as frequently as possible. Only in this way will it become a permanent part of a student's knowledge.

When the main objective is approximate comprehension of a reading text, as in the reading method, much less emphasis is placed on the study of grammar. It becomes truly secondary because it is to be used only for recognition purposes. Under these circumstances little if any drill is necessary; the grammar never has to be used in any practical way other than as a tool in comprehending; but verb forms, tenses, and other grammatical peculiarities have to be discussed. This lack of drill is likely to result in considerable inaccuracy, although many students eventually absorb some of the grammatical explanations to which they are exposed through extensive reading. This is particularly true of more mature students.

Up to the present time, few grammars have been constructed on the frequency principle, that is, introducing verbs and grammatical points in the order of their relative frequency in reading, writing, and speaking. As we have seen, the Army and Navy language programs sought to break down the traditional presentation of grammar and to limit the discussion of such material to the essential points. A few very recent grammars have eliminated topics which formed an important part of the older texts, such topics as the past definite and the imperfect subjunctive in French. However, little has as yet been done toward using verb frequency counts and syntax studies in writing grammars. When this technique is introduced, teaching principles of language structure should become more efficient and time spent on unnecessary grammatical points and little-used verbs and verb forms should be greatly reduced.

Growing emphasis on the aural-comprehension approach has also brought new techniques to teaching grammar. One of these, the drill technique, has been used very effectively

in French to teach the relative position of the direct and indirect object pronouns, verb forms, *if* clauses, changes in
adjectival forms due to gender, and the position of adverbs
and adjectives with relation to a verb or noun. Professor
Fernand Marty in his *Language Laboratory Learning* offers
a great number of new and varied techniques which the
student can use in the laboratory to achieve better control of
linguistic structure. Some of these are substitution techniques
whereby the student replaces a verb by one that requires the
subjunctive, or substitutes a subordinate clause for an infinitive
or an infinitive for a subjunctive construction. The student
listens to the original sentence on the tape and then records
the change he believes to be correct. Some tapes give the
correct form after sufficient time has elapsed for the student
to give his version. In that case the student can correct himself if he has made an error. Otherwise the instructor listens
to the student's performance on the tape and later informs
him of his errors, if any. When testing listening comprehension
graphically, the instructor places a choice of four or five printed
answers before the student, who marks the one he believes
to be correct.

Professors Pimsleur and Delattre also offer suggestions for
practical techniques, which have grown out of a series of
careful experiments. For these techniques to be effective and
lead to an automatically correct answer, the correct response
must be repeated 20 times, according to Professor Pimsleur.
For example:

TAPE: Je regarde le livre.
STUDENT: Je le regarde.
TAPE: Je le regarde. (*Correct answer*)
STUDENT: (*Repeats the correct answer*): Je le regarde.

This is followed by 20 similar examples, i.e., *je le vois, je le dis,* etc., to train the student to understand the position of the pronoun object. Other types of pattern drill have been evolved by the linguists Stockwell, Bowen, and Bolinger, as well as by Professor Pimsleur.[1]

1. Response drill
    a. Without hints:
        Jean, est-il ici ou à Paris? Il est à Paris.
        Voulez-vous une pomme ou une orange? Je veux une pomme.
    b. With hints:
        (*samedi*) Quel jour est-il? Il est samedi.
        (*France*) D'où vient-il? Il vient de France.

2. Replacement drill
    De quelle partie des Etats-Unis venez-vous?

———————— nous?	De quelle partie des E.U. venons-nous?
——— sont ———?	De quelle partie des E.U. sont-ils?
——— Floride ———?	De quelle partie de la Floride êtes-vous?
———————— ces enfants?	De quelle partie de la Floride sont ces enfants?

3. Variation drill
    a. Que pensez-vous de ma robe?

(chapeau)	Que pensez-vous de mon chapeau?
(soulier)	Que pensez-vous de mes souliers?
(veste)	Que pensez-vous de ma veste?
(amie)	Que pensez-vous de mon amie?

[1] Paul Pimsleur, "Pattern Drills in French," *French Review* (May, 1960), 570-576.

b. Si elle était plus riche, elle irait en Espagne.

(aller en France)	Si elle était plus riche, **elle irait en France.**
(acheter une auto)	Si elle était plus riche, **elle achèterait une auto.**
(être plus généreuse)	Si elle était plus riche, **elle serait plus généreuse.**

4. Directed dialogue
   a. Dites-moi quel jour nous sommes aujourd'hui.   Nous sommes aujourd'hui **le . . .**

   Dites-lui que vous avez faim.   J'ai faim.

   Demandez-moi où je demeure.   Où demeurez-vous?

5. Singular-plural drill
   Il écrit une lettre.   Ils écrivent une **lettre.**
   Il aime la lecture.   Ils aiment la **lecture.**
   Je danse bien.   Nous dansons bien.

6. Subject change
   Je cherche des livres.
   (il)   Il cherche des **livres.**
   (vous)   Vous cherchez des **livres.**
   (Paul et moi)   Paul et moi, nous **cherchons des** livres.

7. Item substitution
   a. Le magasin est en face.
   (maison)   La maison est en face.
   (église)   L'église est en face.
   b. Je vois une belle maison.
   (grande)   Je vois une grande **maison.**
   (blanche)   Je vois une maison **blanche.**

8. Answer in the negative
   a. Voulez-vous quelque chose?   Non, je ne veux rien.

Voyez-vous quelqu'un?	Non, je ne vois personne.
Avez-vous dit quelque chose?	Non, je n'ai rien dit.

9. Answer in the affirmative

a. Est-ce que ce livre est bon?	Oui, c'est un bon livre.
Est-ce que ce garçon est intelligent?	Oui, ce garçon est intelligent.

10. Ask the question

a. Il regarde la maison.	Qu'est-ce qu'il regarde?
Il y a une chaise près de la table.	Qu'est-ce qu'il y a près de la table?
b. Nous nous asseyons sur le lit.	Sur quoi nous asseyons-nous?
Nous mangeons avec une cuillère.	Avec quoi mangeons-nous?

11. Tense change, with key words

Je lis le livre aujourd'hui.	J'ai lu le livre hier.
Je vois le professeur aujourd'hui.	J'ai vu le professeur hier.

12. Tense recognition with key words

Il donnera le livre à son frère.	Il donnera le livre à son frère demain.
Le train est en retard.	Le train est en retard aujourd'hui.

13. Combine two sentences

a. Jean est ici. Je le sais.	Je sais que Jean est ici.
Elle est arrivée. Je le regrette.	Je regrette qu'elle soit arrivée.
b. Regardez ces livres. Le livre qui est rouge est le mien.	Celui qui est rouge est le mien.
c. Voici trois crayons. Quel crayon voulez-vous?	Lequel voulez-vous?

d. J'ai acheté une auto. | J'ai acheté une auto qui est
Elle est arrivée hier. | arrivée hier.

e. Voici un garçon. Je joue | Voici un garçon avec lequel je
avec le garçon. | joue.

14. Pronoun substitution
   a. Je mange la banane. | Je la mange.
   b. Je donne la lettre à ma | Je lui donne la lettre.
   mère.
   c. Je passe la lait à Jean. | Je le lui passe.
   d. Voici tous les stylos.

   Le stylo à gauche est | Le stylo à gauche est le mien.
   mon stylo.

   Le petit stylo est votre | Le petit stylo est le vôtre.
   stylo.

   Celui qui est rouge | Celui qui est rouge est le sien.
   est son stylo.

Professor Delattre's exercises offer suggestions for verb drill. He advises a 40-minute recitation followed by a 20-minute analysis.

1. Substitute *chercher, écouter, demander*, etc., for *regarder*.

   Dites à Paul de vous re- | Paul, regardez-moi.
   garder.

   Dites à Paul de regarder | Paul, regardez-le.
   Jean.

2. Substitute *plu, souri, menti, parlé*, etc., for *répondu*.

   Est-ce qu'il a répondu à sa | Oui, il lui a répondu.
   mère?

3. Substitute *écouté, demandé, regardé*, and *vu* for *cherché*.
   Substitute *ce qu', lequel, laquelle, lesquels*, and *lesquelles* for *qui*.
   On lui a demandé qui il avait cherché.

4. Substitute *j'ai gardé*, and *j'ai mangé* for *je garde*, etc.
   Substitute *je vais garder*, and *je vais manger* for *je garde*, etc.[2]

   [2] P. Delattre, "Un Cours d'exercices structuraux et de linguistique appliquée," *French Review* (May, 1960), 591-603.

Je garde tout le paquet.	Je le garde tout.
Je mange toute cette tarte.	Je la mange toute.
Je garde tous ces paquets.	Je les garde tous (pronounce the s).
Je mange toutes ces tartes.	Je les mange toutes.

Many similar exercises can be prepared to cover more points of grammar and patterns of speech. Professor Stack offers excellent suggestions.

AUDIO-VISUAL AIDS FOR TEACHING
VERB FORMS

TAPE: Il fera son travail demain. Et vous?
       Je ferai mon travail demain.
TAPE: Marie lira un bon livre. Et nous?
       Nous lirons un bon livre.
TAPE: Je vais au théâtre ce soir. Et Henri?
       Il va au théâtre ce soir.
TAPE: El tiene calor. Y usted?
       Yo tengo calor.
TAPE: Maria va a la casa blanca. Y usted?
       Yo voy a la casa blanca.

Completion exercises for use of prepositions used before infinitives
  Using écrire la leçon
    TAPE: Permettez moi . . .
       Permettez-moi d'écrire la leçon.
    TAPE: Georges finit . . .
       Georges finit d'écrire la leçon.
    TAPE: Henri veut . . .
       Henri veut écrire la leçon.

  Substituting c'est un *or* c'est une
    TAPE: Voilà Henri. Il est médecin.
       C'est un médecin.
    TAPE: Voilà Marie. Elle est infirmière.
       C'est une infirmière.

Using il est *or* elle est
TAPE: Voilà Jane. C'est une Anglaise.
Elle est Anglaise.
TAPE: Voilà Jean. C'est un Parisien.
Il est Parisien.

Teach only one thing at a time.
Keep the utterances short.
Establish and hold a pattern for at least eight utterances.

Combining adjective with noun
TAPE: Voilà une maison. Elle est grande.
Voilà une grande maison.
TAPE: Voilà une femme. Elle est belle.
Voilà une belle femme.

Position and agreement of adjectives
TAPE: Ce monsieur est intelligent. Et cette dame?
Cette dame est intelligente.
TAPE: La mesa es negra. Y el libro?
El libro es negro.

C'est un, c'est une *plus the adjective in a new sentence*
TAPE: Voilà une dame qui est riche.
C'est une dame riche.
TAPE: Je regarde la maison qui est vieille.
C'est une vieille maison.
TAPE: Il touche le livre qui est rouge.
C'est un livre rouge.

Comparing persons and things, using plus . . . que, moins . . .
que, aussi . . . que
TAPE: Paul est grand. Et Robert?
Robert est plus grand que Paul.

Inserting adverbs in their proper place in a given sentence
TAPE: *souvent/* Roger mange au restaurant.
Roger mange souvent au restaurant.
*souvent/*Roger a mangé au restaurant.
Roger a souvent mangé au restaurant.

The negative can be drilled in much the same manner.

TAPE: Je chante.
      Je ne chante pas.
TAPE: J'ai chanté.
      Je n'ai pas chanté.
TAPE: Le professeur me dit de fermer la porte.
      Le professeur me dit de ne pas fermer la porte.
TAPE: Montrez-le-lui.
      Ne le lui montrez pas.

This form of drill is particularly effective to teach pronoun objects.

TAPE: Jean prend le livre.
      Jean le prend.
TAPE: Marie donne le livre à Jean.
      Marie le lui donne.

To furnish drill for the use of the relative pronoun or to convert into a conditional sentence, two short sentences can be given on the tape.

TAPE: Su padre es profesor. Enseña la filosofía.
      Su padre quien es profesor enseña la filosofía.
TAPE: Il fait du soleil. Je vais à la plage.
      S'il fait du soleil, j'irai à la plage.[3]

To teach grammar effectively, especially to a large class, even an experienced teacher should prepare a lesson plan. If possible, a series of plans covering at least a month's work should be completed early in the term. These plans may be modified, shortened, or increased when a class proves to be far above or below the average. The new instructor who hopes to succeed should never begin the term without having on his desk a well-organized plan of work for the months to come.

It will be found helpful to prepare each lesson according to a plan such as the following. Similar plans should be pre-

[3] Edward M. Stack, *The Language Laboratory and Modern Language Teaching,* Oxford University Press, 1960.

pared for reading lessons so that the teacher can see how near to the objectives for the week, the month, or the term he has come. If he finds himself falling behind, he can change his plan and speed up while there is still time. The following plan is typical for practice teachers using the eclectic method.

Class .... Instructor .... Text ....

GRAMMAR LESSON PLAN

GREETING TO CLASS
ROLL CALL

Assignment: Specific pages, lines, or material to be studied written clearly on the board at beginning of the hour.

General aims: To read, speak, write, understand.

Specific aims: To give pupils comprehension of pages in the text. Class drill in use of the present indicative and the formation of the past indefinite.

Visual aids: Letter, penknife, books.

NEW LESSON, OR LESSON FOR THE NEXT DAY

Motivation: Oral questions and answers by teacher and pupils that cover the new work and call for visual materials. For example:

> Instructor: J'ai reçu un livre. Qui a reçu un livre?
> Pupils: Vous avez reçu un livre.

Reading of text: Page 000.

Lines 1–4 read by instructor and the first two rows of students.
Lines 5–8 read by instructor and the next two rows of students.

Vocabulary: Read by instructor. The class will give synonyms or paraphrases.

Grammar: 1. Preparation of short, simple, sentences in present tense: Je donne une lettre à mon frère, etc.

2. Presentation of new tense. Short narrative in past indefinite: Ce matin j'ai donné une lettre à mon frère, etc.

The class is asked questions by the instructor.

3. Comparison and abstraction. One student writes the present tense of *donner* on the board, another the present of *avoir*. The instructor writes the past indefinite of *donner* on the board, the students dictating the forms to him.

Pres.	Pres.	Past Ind.
je donne	j'ai	j'ai donné
tu donnes	tu as	tu as donné
il donne	il a	il a donné
etc.	etc.	etc.

4. Generalization. The students compare the two tenses and formulate the rule for forming the past indefinite, i.e., by using the present indicative of *avoir,* and the past participle.

5. Application. Eight to ten students are given cards prepared in advance, calling for the translation of English to French or French to English sentences to be written on the blackboard. Simultaneously the instructor drills the class in the past indefinite tense. The board work is then corrected by the class, with the teacher as guide.

Explanation of homework. Page ooo. The class turns to this page. The instructor translates a certain sentence. The students read other sentences and try to translate them following directions for the formation of the past indefinite. The class will complete these exercises as homework.

THE LESSON FOR THE DAY

1. The instructor gives the pupils cards containing sentences in the exercise assigned for the day's work, which they are to put on the board. And, simultaneously

2. He drills the class by means of questions and answers on assigned pages in the reading text.

3. The board work is corrected by the instructor in line with the students' suggestions.

4. The students read Exercise oo, one sentence to each student; the instructor asks questions based on the material read.

5. The instructor dictates a short French passage containing the grammatical point of the lesson. One student writes this dictation on the blackboard, preferably on a board in the rear of the room. This is corrected by the teacher and the other students. The students then correct what they have written.

6. If time permits, the class sings an old song or learns a new one.

* 11 *

TEACHING READING

To many people, the most important part of language teaching is the reading lesson. What should be its objectives? The ultimate objective is obviously complete and accurate understanding of the passage that is read. An approximate or superficial understanding is not enough in either a beginning or an advanced class. Complete understanding demands not only mastery of the vocabulary but correct interpretation of the idea and spirit of the passage. If the ability to read the passage orally in the original is necessary for this complete understanding of style and meaning, that, too, must be part of the objective, as must also grammar and syntax when they are essential to thorough understanding. If a text contains allusions to historical or cultural material not clear from the context, thorough understanding of that material must be included in the reading objective. Reading should never be the mere translation of words that may have little or no meaning to the reader or his hearers. Every reading lesson must provide complete comprehension both to the reader and to others, through his exact interpretation of the meaning and spirit of the text. To attain all these aims, great variety in presenting the reading lesson is necessary.

A distinction must be made from the outset between different types of reading, all of which have ultimately the same objective. Intensive reading, for example, is usually based on a relatively short assignment, and every detail essential to complete and accurate understanding of the text must be mastered before the lesson is completed. Extensive or rapid reading for comprehension is less a study of each detail than an instinctive but exact comprehension of the essential ideas expressed by the author. In a novel, reading may be limited to an understanding of the plot, without necessarily involving attention to technical vocabulary or to words that impart local color and descriptive charm or bring out the purely literary quality of the work. Supplementary or outside reading is a form of extensive reading done as a native reads for relaxation or pleasure or to obtain information. In such reading, most of the responsibility for accurate understanding and interpretation rests with the reader, whereas purely extensive reading, although given in larger assignments than intensive reading, is discussed in class with a view to perfect understanding.

There are many ways in which the reading lesson may be treated. If the approach to learning a language has been essentially oral, a story or anecdote based on the vocabulary already learned may be read aloud by the teacher and interpreted by the student either in the original language or in English. In some classes the students read a portion of the text aloud and then explain what they have read in English. Difficult words may be explained in the foreign language by definitions, synonyms, or antonyms. Many recent texts have adopted some of these features and, in addition, the French *explication,* or analysis of the text. In the *explication,* after a paragraph has been read, the student or teacher analyzes not only the author's basic idea but his use of grammar, his style, and the vocabulary he uses. This method of very careful study of reading texts was introduced in this country by the late Osmond Robert of Smith College and the late Albert Cru, formerly of Teachers College, Columbia University.

Oral reading by the students can be treated as an exercise in pronunciation. In this case the teacher must take great care to see that the student pronounces each vowel and consonant accurately. When errors in pronunciation are made, flash cards can be used by the teacher to bring the student's attention to them. A simpler method of correction is to train other students to correct the errors they hear. If the instructor wishes to stress intonation and tonic accent[1] in French, he may ask the students to imitate his pronunciation as they read, after him, one or two sentences at a time.

In classes where the work is not done entirely in the foreign language, a student may read a paragraph and explain the meaning of difficult words in either English or the foreign language. If the instructor feels that a partial translation is necessary to insure complete and accurate comprehension, he may ask the student for such a translation; he may also ask for a summary of what has been read or he may question the student on it in the foreign language.

Some reading lessons, particularly short stories, lend themselves to dramatic treatment. If the short story is largely in dialogue, two or three students may be asked to prepare a scenario of the day's assignment in which they describe the stage setting; the dialogue itself may be read by students playing the role of the characters in the story. This treatment gives a great deal of life to a reading lesson and, in addition, helps

[1] The tonic accent is the accent or stress that comes regularly on the last syllable of a French word and that gives rhythm to French speech.

the students retain the content and, to some degree, most of the phraseology used in the dialogue. If the students are proficient enough and willing to spend the time, they may devise costumes and scenery and perform before other classes.

Another method of conducting a reading lesson requires the students to prepare 10 or 20 questions on the assignment—the questions, of course, in the foreign language—and the following day the teacher chooses among these questions those that he will ask the class to answer. In a variation of this method, the instructor writes the questions himself and gives them to the class; thus the students study the content of the stories through formulating answers to these questions. If the books used for reading contain questions, the students' careful preparation of answers as homework will help train the ear when the teacher reads them, as well as offer practice in speaking the language. To aid in composition, a paraphrase of the assignment will help the student to get the full meaning of what he is reading and to express it in simple terms. This exercise is most profitable as homework but it is also valuable as a classroom exercise.

The language laboratory has inspired an original way of preparing for the reading lesson. It is based upon the practice of simultaneous translation developed at the Foreign Language Institute in Washington. It consists of placing the foreign-language text before the student and letting him hear through earphones a free translation, first of sentences, then of dialogues, then of connected narrative paragraphs, and finally of full pages of text. As the same patterns of speech are repeated in more and more involved contexts, an increasing amount of the foreign language is understood, and eventually comprehension is complete.

The instructor who wishes to emphasize teaching the

vocabulary in the assignment may prepare for dictation a résumé of the assignment that contains most of the difficult words. This can be done only with relatively short assignments. If the teacher has given the class a vocabulary drill and is sure that the students are familiar with the text, he may give them a summary in English for translation into the foreign language.

Another method of conducting a reading lesson is for students or teacher, or both, to list the essential words in any given assignment; these words may be used at the beginning of the next lesson as a vocabulary match or for a short written recognition test. For variety, the teacher may summarize the assignment in the form of incomplete sentences to be completed by the students. A series of true-false questions also tests the student's knowledge of what he has read. In elementary French classes a series of sentences offering various conclusions provides a form of multiple-choice test for the teacher who prefers this type of comprehension test. The following is an example:

Remi est
- un garçon très riche.
- un petit chien.
- un enfant trouvé.

Il croit que Mère Barberin
- est sa mère.
- est sa tante.
- est son ennemie.

Jérôme Barberin
- travaille à Paris.
- est professeur dans un lycée.
- coupe du bois devant la porte.

Un jour Mère Barberin apprend que son mari
- est à l'hôpital.
- est parti pour l'Amérique.
- est millionnaire.

This device provides a test for all the essential points of the day's assignment. These tests should be mimeographed and should be distributed in class only on the day the particular lesson has been assigned.

Some teachers introduce variety by asking a student to summarize what he has read at the beginning of the hour. The instructor may then read the passage sentence by sentence and ask the students to translate orally; the students of course keep their books closed. Or a student may be asked to read the text aloud, after which other students are called upon for oral translations. This method trains the ear to the sound of the foreign language, makes useless the interlinear translations with which some students fill their books, and teaches the pupil to translate quickly without the aid of the printed page. The advantages gained from accurate and spontaneous oral translation certainly equal those obtained from direct rapid reading for comprehension.

With the introduction of listening comprehension as a primary objective, with emphasis on understanding directly and entirely through the foreign language, translation into English, except as a literary exercise for advanced classes, is being stressed less and less. Professor Nelson Brooks advises teachers to abandon, except rarely, all translation into English as well as the use of English in the foreign-language class. With the patterns-of-speech approach to teaching and the totally oral presentation in elementary-school language instruction, this is a very logical and thoroughly practical request to make of teachers. This is also feasible with a completely direct method approach. When reading is begun in such classes, only a foreign-language dictionary should be used.

Translation as a part of language teaching has had a varied

career. At times it has been considered the principal aim of all language study; at others it has been only a method of approach to facile reading; at still others it has been considered the source of most student discouragement and hence a serious obstacle to the language learning process. Whether the student arrives at complete and accurate understanding of a foreign language more quickly and more effectively by a method calling for accurate translation from the beginning or by a process of absorption through direct contact with the language is debatable. To a large degree the nature and temperament of the individual student must be considered. Since the goal of the reading lesson must in the last analysis be complete and accurate understanding of the language, any approach or corrective device that may be used to attain this goal must be used freely and fearlessly.

In classes where translation is used, the teacher should insist on careful translation into the finest possible English. In teaching foreign languages, less emphasis should be placed on the terms *literal* and *free* translation. There are very few difficulties of syntax in most modern foreign languages that require this type of dual translation to clarify the meaning. If this type of translation is necessary, it should be done by the teacher rather than the student. Translation into accurate English is a difficult task that requires careful thought and preparation. This fact cannot be overemphasized. Every effort should be made to keep translation from becoming a purely mechanical exercise that requires little if any preparation or thought on the student's part. Reading may also be taught by reproducing on a tape recorder the English translation of the foreign language text before the student's eyes. With frequent repetition comprehension soon becomes automatic.

Reading matter concerning customs and manners may be supplemented by post cards or photographs, or the showing of motion pictures. Many books used for classroom work—Pagnol's *Topaze,* Loti's *Pêcheur d'Islande,* Dumas' *Les Trois Mousquetaires,* Hugo's *Les Misérables,* Alarcón's *El sombrero de tres picos*—have been made into motion pictures which can be used very effectively.

The reading text may also be used as a means of learning grammar. In this case, verb forms, the agreement of subject and verb and of nouns and adjectives, the use of the various tenses, and the position of adjectives and adverbs may all be explained by examples from the text.

In elementary classes it is helpful to point out the similarity between foreign and English words to encourage the students to read. They will realize that the new language is not as completely foreign as it seems to be. However, as was said earlier, this practice is dangerous because it leads to frequent confusion of words that, although spelled similarly, have totally different meanings. A difficult exercise, but one which should be used from time to time when the students have a good basic vocabulary, is the preparation of simple but comprehensive English sentences which summarize the assignment. These sentences, which will naturally contain much of the vocabulary of the text, can then be translated by the students. This procedure provides a review and vocabulary test as well as an exercise in grammar.

Translating at sight is always an excellent exercise whether the material is a fairly long passage or merely a series of short ones. This tests the student's comprehensive knowledge of the language and also his ingenuity, for it trains him in learning how to interpret an unfamiliar foreign text at first sight.

Akin to this is silent reading, which provides equally fine training. The students are given a book they have not seen previously and are asked to read as rapidly as possible, beginning on a certain page. They may take notes or try to summarize for themselves what they have read. After a set time, the instructor should test comprehension orally and also compare their speed of reading. He may also test comprehension by means of written questions based on the material, completion sentences, oral summaries, or analyses of the passage. Rapid or extensive reading can be encouraged in this manner, after the students realize that it is possible to read and understand a foreign language, once a basic vocabulary of about 1000 words has been mastered, without recourse to a dictionary.

In order further to encourage reading, outside reading may be assigned regularly. This may be in addition to the regular intensive reading assignments, and 1 hour each week may be set aside for discussion of this reading. The outside reading should range from a total of 50 pages the first year to 150 the second year, and to 300 or more the third year. A summary, preferably in the original language, should always be required. For this purpose the instructor should give the students a skeleton outline or a series of questions stressing the essential points. Their answers will show whether they have read and understood the assignment. To train the student in the spoken as well as the written language, the instructor may require him to give an oral report or to answer specific questions. When a written summary is required it is better for the instructor to correct it in conference with the student so that he can point out and explain all the errors; if this is impossible he should put full corrections and explanations on the paper itself. If the same book is to be used another year with another class, it is always wise to collect all student papers at the end of the term so that they cannot be passed on to the students who will be using the book later.

Many foreign-language students complete their course without any confidence in their ability even to read the language, let alone speak it. A teacher can instill this confidence quite early by preparing, for outside reading, lists of books covering a variety of interests, starting from the first year. This will give the students an opportunity to read extensively for pleasure or to broaden their knowledge in a special field of interest.

In the first year the material used for outside reading should be very simple so that the student will not have to refer constantly to a dictionary. First-year students should be encouraged to learn about the country's history and civilization, its customs and manners, by reading about them in English or American novels whose scene is laid in the particular country.

The supplementary reading after the first year can be made attractive by permitting students to choose specific books that they want to read (if a brief outline of each foreign-language book in the library can be provided them) or specific books in their field of interest, such as mathematics, history, or biology, that will not only teach them something about the language but give them a better grasp of the subject that interests them.

Many formal questionnaires have been published for testing outside reading and rapid reading, but it is much better if the instructor prepares such tests himself. They are more personal in nature and seem to be more vital to the students than general exercises taken from a book.

Outside reading assignments should not be chosen hastily by the instructor. He should find out the abilities and particular interests of his students and then allow the class to follow their own inclinations in their choice of reading matter. Some students are interested in learning contemporary expressions, the idiom of the day, and slang; contemporary writers should be read by such students. Students whose main purpose is speed in reading unfamiliar prose can be timed on their ability to cover a certain number of pages in an hour and, as suggested above, tested on their comprehension of the essentials of what they read. Students who are interested in learning more about the country should be directed to historical novels or biographies in the language that will give them information about its history, its art, or its music.

The success of outside reading often depends on the manner in which a choice of books is presented to the students and also on how comprehension is measured. This may be done in several ways, as has been suggested—by a carefully directed report, or by answers to a series of questions covering the characteristics of the book, the questions being given to the class orally or as a written exercise. If enough students are interested in a specific book, an hour may be set aside for questions to be asked the pupil who prepared the report on it.

If other teachers are willing to cooperate, supplementary reading may also be integrated with other subjects and reports on some of it given in other classrooms. Groups of students may work together on a round-table discussion of a subject that is of particular interest to them—some phase of foreign politics; some aspect of living that is peculiar to the country; its scientific, artistic, musical, or commerical development;

its great men; or a literary trend that has influenced writing in our own country. This outside reading can also be used for debates, and for foreign-language club meetings, special assemblies, and other school activities.

Outside reading can be motivated by asking students to help select a play to be given as some form of school activity. Such reading may be assigned as preparation for a special project or a report to be given in class. If a museum is located near the school, outside reading may be suggested as preparation for a visit to it. Thus one day the class may study the characteristic furniture of the country, its architecture, or some phase of its painting. Menus can also be studied in class; but the teacher should at the same time teach the vocabulary that will be needed at a restaurant where such dishes are likely to be served. Outside reading in cookbooks may interest the girls. The teacher should do everything possible to demonstrate the practical value of this supplementary reading.

When reading can be vitalized through the use of foreign films, a scenario of a picture may be obtained and a vocabulary prepared before the film is shown. After the class has seen the film, it should be discussed, and the vocabulary that was not understood should be checked. If the dialogue is available on phonograph records, these records may be played while the class has the text in the scenario before them. This is excellent training in oral comprehension and, if the students attempt to imitate the dialogue, good training in pronunciation.

Reading may also be motivated by stressing the fact that it is preparation for understanding a foreign motion picture to be shown in school or in town, for many pictures today are based on plays or novels that the students may read.

Another way of using the outside reading lesson in more advanced classes is to list all the difficult vocabulary and idiomatic expressions which the student should master. They may be asked to use these words and expressions in sentences which they then translate into English.

A foreign-language newspaper may be used for classroom reading. Many of the items in it can be rewritten by the students for the school foreign-language paper; every school in which a foreign language is taught should have a newspaper to which students of the language are encouraged to contribute.

The aural approach to reading permits, at the higher levels, the introduction of news broadcasts in foreign languages, the schedules of which can be obtained from the foreign embassies in Washington, and in many cases from the consulates; tape recordings of plays by foreign actors; readings of poems or essays by their authors if they are contemporary; political addresses, and broadcasts delivered by news and sports commentators. Most of this material will seem fresh, alive, new, and even exciting to the student.

The vocabulary will appear to be contemporary; yet the same testing techniques can be applied to this form of aural reading. For instance, the teacher can ask students to give a summary, answer questions, substitute a different ending, make a critical analysis, discuss the ideas, or correct false statements and impressions. If the class is well advanced, much new vocabulary and idiomatic expression can be learned. The language laboratory and tape recorder have made it easier to teach reading by using an aural approach. The teacher can read to the class a story or dialogue, made up for the most part of familiar vocabulary, and then ask the students questions which will draw from them the meaning of unfamiliar words. A second or third reading of a new story by the teacher will usually aid the students' comprehension and reduce their need for questioning. Then, once the student has become acquainted with the graphic forms of words, the teacher may prepare and make tape recordings of questions which the student can listen to in the laboratory. The student may record his own answer on the tape, listen for the correct answer which the teacher has recorded, and correct his own mistakes. He may also write what he believes to be the correct answer and check it against four or five printed answers about the story, one of which will be indicated as true.

If phonograph records of the works of the country's composers are available, or, better still, if the class can attend concerts of the composers' works, biographies of the composers and the librettos of operas will make good reading assignments and, in addition, make the concerts more enjoyable.

Thus we see that there are many variations of the reading lesson and the presentation of the subject matter. However, the suggestions made above cover only a few of the many ways in which the classroom hour may be made less monotonous for the student. If the teacher lists all the ways of presenting a reading lesson, he will find that the variety of presentation will serve him well in holding his pupils' interest and making them learn more willingly. What is more important, such variety vitalizes the language, displays its many facets to the students, makes its usefulness clearer, and awakens the enthusiasm that carries the students' work beyond the classroom. No reading lesson should be undertaken, particularly by a new teacher, without a carefully prepared, written plan. The following is only one of many possible such plans.

Class . . . . Instructor . . . . Text . . . .

READING LESSON PLAN

GREETING TO CLASS

ROLL CALL
SONG

Assignment: To read, understand, and be able to answer questions based on pp. oo–oo and written on the board.

General aims: To teach the students to speak, read, write, and understand.

Specific aims: To teach the students to read and understand pp. ooo–ooo.

OLD LESSON

1. Review pp. o–oo, emphasizing thread of plot.
2. Intensive reading, p. oo, paragraph o.
   a. Drill on *salir* and *llegar,* present and future tenses.
   b. Vocabulary building.
      (1) Give synonyms or antonyms.
      (2) Give definitions and paraphrases.
      (3) Give other words in the same family (list the words).
      (4) Use words in the original sentences (give examples).
      (5) Learn, translate, and use in original sentences the words taken from the text (list the words).
3. Extensive reading, pp. oo–oo.
   Teacher: ¿A qué hora llegó Juan a la estación?
   A pupil answers this question.

   Formulation of other model questions to be answered by students. Students then prepare questions for other students to answer.

4. Silent reading, pp. oo–oo.
   a. Students read. Teacher calls on one student to read and on another to explain what was read.
   b. Or the teacher writes questions on the board as the student reads. When the reading is completed, the students answer these questions orally.

New Lesson

1. Explanation of assignment, pp. oo–oo.
   a. Give synonyms, antonyms, or definition of ten words in the text.

   > ventanilla—molestar—la lista—(ten words)

   b. Review the future of six verbs in the test.

   > sentar—beber—traer—(six verbs)

   c. Help students to write three sentences using each of the following:

   > vamos a—tiene razón—tengo hambre

2. First in English, then in Spanish, the instructor tells the story covered by the assignment. Ten questions will be asked, such as the following:
   a. Whom did Maria meet on the boat?
   b. What did he say to her?
   c. What did she answer?

* 12 *

DICTATION AND
AURAL COMPREHENSION

In most languages, dictation is an indispensable teaching device; it is almost a method of teaching, for by means of it so many phases of the language may be taught. This is particularly true today, when so many students are unable to reproduce accurately words they have seen in a book, whether it be in English or a foreign language. Dictation tends to fix their attention on an accurate reproduction of a word they have seen or heard.

Dictation may be used in a number of ways. One of the most effective, from the point of view of learning new vocabulary, is to assign two or three pages to be studied for dictation. From these pages, one paragraph of 10 to 15 lines is chosen the next day and dictated to the class. The students having studied the passage understand it better and hence will not have to try to reproduce words which they have never seen before and which therefore have little or *no* meaning.

In a similar use of prepared dictation the instructor chooses about 20 essential words from the passage he intends to dictate to the class and asks the students to study these words before the dictation. The student, familiar with most of the difficult words, is not confused and discouraged by the dictation but instead gains in aural and written comprehension. To emphasize the study of the future tense, the use of the subjunctive, or the agreement of nouns and adjectives, the teacher may select a passage which contains a great number of any of these grammatical points. In this case the student fixes his attention not only on the correct spelling of individual words but on a grammatical point as well, thus receiving training in specific peculiarities of grammar. Dictation is particularly valuable in a language like French, because of the orthographical difficulties involved in such rules as those for the agreement of the past participle with intransitive verbs of motion, reflexive verbs, and other verbs conjugated with *être.*

When the instructor is reasonably sure that most of his students are accustomed to dictation and can reproduce accurately a sufficiently large vocabulary, it is time to turn to unfamiliar passages for dictation. These passages should, if possible, have unity of thought. If the subject is at all complicated, an English title may be given so that the students will be sure to understand the theme. Thus the class will write fairly accurately and will have at least some idea of what they are writing about, instead of being bewildered from the outset. If the passage is complicated grammatically and contains many new words that are difficult to pronounce, it is sometimes helpful to read them to the class, stressing their pronunciation, before it is dictated. With a really difficult passage, reading it once to the class with their books open may be very helpful. The number of words that the students will recall from their reading should not be a matter of concern in view of the fact that the dictation is given primarily to teach the pronunciation and orthography of the language, rather than as a test.

So that the students will comprehend what they write instead of merely making a transcription of sounds, it is often helpful to require them to translate what they have written at the end of the dictation to see whether it makes sense to them. This will eventually teach them to make an effort to comprehend the dictation as it is read to them.

Dictated passages may be chosen for thought content as well as for training in grammatical accuracy. Thus a painless and convenient way of teaching phases of the history or geography of a country, or the history of its art, is to sum up in a short paragraph for dictation as much information about the particular subject as possible. The concentration required for writing dictation well often fixes facts in the students' minds.

When aural comprehension is to be stressed by means of dictation, a passage is read and questions on the entire passage are asked in the foreign language. The answers must be written in that language. Another similar exercise consists of reading an anecdote or other short passage and asking questions in the language that are to be answered in English. Here the student *must* have understood if he is to answer correctly because he cannot merely reproduce the foreign words he has heard. An answer in the foreign language may at times be a restatement of the question in affirmative form.

In one method of giving dictation that has become fairly standardized, the complete passage is first read at normal speed so that the students will understand what it is about and prepare themselves for the difficult words. Then the passage is actually dictated, the students writing as the instructor dictates. When possible, the passage is read in groups of words containing a single thought which the students can keep in mind until they have finished writing each group. This gradually trains the student in comprehension and also fixes in his subconscious mind certain groups of words which he may use later. The passage is dictated a third time at normal speed to permit the students to fill in words they may have missed and to make any corrections they think are necessary. After this reading, they should translate silently what they have written into English to make sure that everything in it makes sense.

Since dictation is a teaching device more than anything else, it should be used as frequently as possible. A 5-minute dictation each period, based on something taken from the class textbook or the day's reading assignment, is valuable; furthermore, the students can correct their own papers immediately afterward. While the students are correcting their work, it is sometimes helpful to reread the passage to them so that they can see where they missed a word or sound because of the difference in their own pronunciation and the instructor's. Each student may be asked to keep a score of his progress in taking dictation, but in this case emphasis should be placed not on the grades obtained but on the knowledge and improvement resulting from this exercise. In order to check on the accuracy of the corrections, the students should learn to copy accurately and thus discover their own errors by comparing their work with a perfect copy either written on the board or given in the text from which the dictation was taken. It is also advisable for the instructor to correct at least one day's dictation of the class each week and compare the number of errors he has found with the average number found by the student in correcting the other exercises during the week. The dictation may at times be given by a student chosen by the class and approved by the teacher. A certain honor is attached to this because only the best students will be permitted to give the dictation to the class.

Dictation can also be given by means of a phonograph. This enables a student to hear it several times and to use it as an exercise outside of class.

To offset the artificiality of some passages for dictation and aural comprehension, dictation may take the form of conversation, brief sentences taken from everyday life situations and spoken at normal speed. This serves as direct, practical training for work as an interpreter.

For training in aural comprehension a method has been devised similar to that used for dictation, consisting largely of the student's listening to an anecdote and answering in writing questions based on it. The anecdote is first read by the teacher at normal speed, for general comprehension. It is then read a second time so that the student may correct or add anything he missed on the first reading. Each question is then read twice, whereupon the student writes the answer to it. After all the questions have been answered, the entire anecdote and all the questions are read again; during this reading the pupils check and correct their answers. The questions may either be in English or the foreign language; but the answers are to be given in the foreign tongue.

The tape recorder and language laboratory have made possible many new and very effective techniques for dictation and aural comprehension. The student can listen to a taped dictation passage until he recognizes the whole paragraph. With such aural preparation he can write a more intelligent dictation in class. Much of the normal frustration of dictation is thus eliminated.

There are many ways in which the tape can test and train the student's audio-comprehension. He can even train himself to comprehend, before writing, not merely a phrase but a whole sentence, then two sentences, then perhaps even more. He can take notes on a speech or lecture that has been taped and replay the tape to see what he has missed. He can write a summary of what he has heard and answer questions dictated at the conclusion of the lecture. A series of true-false statements may also be printed and distributed to the student to test his comprehension. In short, most of the aural-comprehension techniques used in the classroom can be transferred to the tape, permitting the student more opportunities to perfect his aural-comprehension. In the laboratory, the student can listen to a phrase or sentence as often as he needs to.

The following dictation is suitable for second-year students in French who have been taught the past definite tense:

La mère donna à sa fille une pomme. La jeune fille, après l'avoir prise, pensa que cette pomme ferait plaisir à son frère et la lui porta. Le frère la prit et dit: "Mon père qui travaille là-bas doit être fatigué; je vais lui porter cette pomme délicieuse." Le père prit la pomme à son tour; puis voyant sa femme pas loin de là, il se hâta de venir près d'elle pour la lui offrir. C'est ainsi que la pomme revint dans les mains qui l'avaient donnée; et la mère était très heureuse de voir que tous les membres de sa famille s'aimaient tant.[1]

The following is a typical aural comprehension test of average difficulty for second-year high-school students:

Robert, un jeune garçon d'un petit village avait un jour cassé, en jouant, une fenêtre de l'église. Personne ne savait que c'était

[1] From the New York State Regents examination, June, 1928.

lui qui avait fait cela; cependant, l'enfant tremblait de peur chaque fois que le curé le regardait.

A l'école de dimanche le curé demanda aux élèves:

—Qui a fait le ciel et la terre?

Robert, qui pensait toujours à la fenêtre cassée, répondit:—Ce n'est pas moi, monsieur le curé.

Le curé, tout étonné d'une telle réponse, répondit bien surpris:

—Comment, ce n'est pas toi?

—Eh bien, oui, dit alors le petit en baissant la tête, c'est moi, mais je ne le ferai plus.

Following are the questions on the above passage that are to be answered in French in complete sentences:

1. Quels sont les personnages de l'histoire?
2. Qu'est-ce que l'enfant avait fait en jouant?
3. Que faisait-il chaque fois que le curé le regardait?
4. Qu'est-ce que le curé a demandé aux élèves?
5. Qu'est-ce que Robert a promis?[2]

A typical conversation which might be used either as dictation or for aural comprehension is given below. Similar passages may be prepared by the teacher and read by two pupils who pronounce very well.

—Bonjour, monsieur, je m'excuse de vous déranger mais j'ai perdu ma montre. Pouvez-vous me dire l'heure qu'il est, s'il vous plaît?

—Il est dix heures et demie, monsieur. Allez-vous sortir?

—Je crois que oui. Il fait si beau temps. Il faut en profiter pour faire une promenade. Je voudrais finir par aller dans les grands magasins m'acheter une cravate. Voudriez-vous m'accompagner?

—Non, merci, je le regrette beaucoup mais j'ai rendez-vous à onze heures.

—C'est dommage. Je n'aime pas me promener et surtout faire des achats quand je suis seul.

[2] *Ibid.*, June, 1946.

The 1959 AATF National Contest presented a new type of Aural Comprehension test on the French II level.

AURAL COMPREHENSION

The student is to underline the group of words that complete correctly the statement.

1. Pour manger la soupe, on se sert d'une fourchette, cuillère, . . .
2. A la ferme les machines agricoles ont généralement remplacé les hommes, soldats, . . .
3. Ne répétez pas l'histoire que je viens de vous . . .
4. Soixante-quinze moins cinquante font . . .
5. Il va certainement pleuvoir, n'oubliez pas votre . . .
6. Un synonyme du mot *aussitôt* est . . .
7. Marie ôte son manteau, car elle a . . .
8. Louise va chez le boulanger, sa mère veut . . .
9. La petite fille entre dans l'église et se met à genou pour faire . . .
10. On ne peut pas faire une omelette sans casser des . . .

The student sees only the words needed to complete that part of the sentence which he has heard.

In their report at the Yale-Barnard Conference on March 19, 1952, the Committee on Aims and Tests, Nelson Brooks chairman, proposed a test (see p. 215) of aural comprehension. The test contains neither dictation, anecdotes, English, nor incorrect French.

In 1959 the Modern Language Association working in conjunction with the Educational Testing Service initiated a comprehensive series of tests in French, German, Spanish, Italian and Russian, aimed at the student-teacher and teacher level as well as at two secondary-school levels. Tests have also been prepared for the College Entrance and Advanced Placement levels. In the process, new techniques have been developed and some of the tests revised on the basis of their efficiency and reliability. Many of these tests are still in the making and will not be ready for several years. The aural or listening-comprehension tests remain basically like those on pp. 215-220, except for these variations: (1) a careful gradation in progressive difficulty within a given test, (2) a choice of pictures in place of printed sentences for answers to certain questions, and (3) a reduction in the length of answers wherever possible. Beside these variations, there are two additions to the tests: (1) a two-utterance dialogue, a short advertisement or news item with a choice of printed statements applicable to what has been heard on the tape and only one of which is correct, and (2) the similar use of a telephone conversation (in which the student participates by choosing the correct response) and a short scene from a play in which several persons—male and female, young and old— take part (the student proving his comprehension by his choice of printed true-false statements). These aural tests are delivered at normal speed in the foreign tongue by natives although careful directions in English usually precede each section of these tests. Not only the material but the nature of these tests will have to be changed frequently to insure reliability. Since the new tests are only available on tapes, the following original Yale-Barnard Conference Tests will serve to indicate their general characteristics.

AURAL TEST NO. 1, TEACHER'S COPY

Part I

The student has before him in writing the five statements in each item. One of these statements is read aloud, and the student checks the one he has heard.

1. Voilà ce que nous allions faire.
   Voilà ce que nous avions fait.
   Voilà ce que nous allons faire.
   Voilà ce que nous savons faire.
   Voilà ce que nous savions faire.

2. Le soleil s'est levé lentement.
   Le soleil se levait lentement.
   Le soleil se lève lentement.
   Le soleil s'était levé lentement.
   Le soleil se leva lentement.

3. *Que fait monsieur?*
   Café, monsieur?
   Que faire, monsieur?
   Qu'a fait monseiur?
   Que veut monsieur?

4. Sa femme est pauvre.
   Sa famille pauvre.
   Cent familles pauvres.
   Sans femme et pauvre.
   Sans famille et pauvre.

5. On va à cet hôtel.
   En face de l'autel.
   En face de cet hôtel.
   En face de l'hôtel.
   On voit cet hôtel.

6. Tout est rangé.
   Tout était arrangé.
   Tout est arrangé.
   Tout était à arranger.
   Tout a été rangé.

7. J'entends mon père.
   J'attendrais mon père.
   J'attendrai mon père.

J'entendais mon père.
J'attendais mon père.

8. La guerre a été déclarée.
   La gare était éclairée.
   La guerre était déclarée.
   La gare est éclairée.
   La guerre est déclarée.

9. Ah, vous vendez votre récolte?
   Avez-vous vendu votre récolte?
   Ah, vous vendrez votre récolte?
   Aviez-vous vendu votre récolte?
   Ah, vous vendiez votre récolte?

10. Va-t-il aussi le faire?
    Va-t-il oser le faire?
    Va-t-il hausser le fer?
    Va-t-il aussi les faire?
    Voit-il aussi l'affaire?

11. Vous m'étendrez la main.
    Vous me tendrez la main.
    Vous m'attendrez demain.
    Vous me tendez la main.
    Vous m'étreindrez la main.

12. A-t-elle peur de cela?
    A-t-elle perdu celle-là?
    A-t-elle perdu cela?
    A-t-elle peur de celle-là?
    A-t-elle perdu ceux-là?

13. Il a mis le fusil à l'épaule.
    L'ami mettait le fusil à l'épaule.
    L'ami a-t-il le fusil à l'épaule?
    L'ami a le fusil à l'épaule.
    Il l'aimait le fusil à l'épaule.

14. *La vieille était tombée.*
   La ville était tombée.
   La veille il était tombé.
   La veille elle était tombée.
   La vieille est tombée.

15. Elle s'agenouille sur un coussin.
   Elle a gêné son cousin.
   Elle était à genoux sur un coussin.
   Elle a chatouillé son cousin.
   Elle s'agenouillait sur un coussin.

PART II

The student has before him the five statements in each item, but he does not see the question. He hears the question read aloud and checks the statement that would be a suitable answer.

16. Est-ce qu'elle demeure dans une maison voisine?
   Non, sa mère est malade.
   Oui, elle habite tout près d'ici.
   Non, je ne la connais pas.
   Oui, elle est très gentille.
   Non, il n'y a jamais de bruit ici.

17. Comment trouvez-vous ce café?
   Il est vraiment excellent.
   Seulement un peu de crême.
   Je vais vous l'apporter.
   Mettons-nous à la terrasse.
   Merci, je n'ai pas faim.

18. Est-ce que ce chapeau me va bien?
   A merveille.
   Emporté par le vent.
   Sa santé est bonne.
   A ce soir.
   Très bien, merci.

19. A quoi sert une clef?
    A faire du pain.
    A nettoyer la maison.
    A cueillir des fleurs.
    A faire des statues.
    A ouvrir une serrure.

20. Où se trouve-t-elle à présent?
    Cela coûte trop cher.
    A Noël.
    C'est un cadeau de son père.
    A son anniversaire.
    A Paris.

21. A qui appartient cette montre?
    Au premier étage.
    A moi, monsieur.
    La route de Paris.
    Elle retarde un peu.
    Elle est tombée sur le plancher.

22. Qu'est-ce qu'on achète chez le boulanger?
    De la viande.
    Des bougies.
    Du pain.
    Du charbon.
    Des jouets.

23. Est-ce que votre père s'est mis en colère?
    Non, son veston était noir.
    Oui, il portait une cravate rouge.
    Non, il n'est pas artiste.
    Oui, la peinture était toute fraîche.
    Oui, il était bien fâché.

24. Que se passe-t-il ici?
    Depuis une demi-heure, monsieur.
    Oui, le repas est délicieux.
    Non, monsieur, on dîne à sept heures.

Vous voyez, monsieur, ces garçons se battent.
Oui, monsieur, mais la route est dangereuse.

25. N'a-t-il pas honte de sa conduite?
C'est l'auto de son père.
Il en est très troublé.
Il y avait trop de bruit.
Il n'a pas encore son permis.
Quand il aura seize ans.

26. Va-t-il être absent toute la journée?
Jusqu'à la tombée de la nuit.
Il n'aime pas voyager.
Les nouvelles sont mauvaises.
Cinquante-cinq kilomètres.
Il a perdu son billet.

27. Est-ce que la petite s'est fait mal?
Elle partira demain.
C'est plutôt une valise.
Elle s'est cassé le bras.
En effet, elle est très petite.
Si l'on mange trop.

28. Pourquoi m'en voulez-vous?
Très volontiers.
J'en ai déjà assez, merci.
Il nous en faut un quatrième.
Pour chercher ce qu'il nous faut.
Vous m'avez trahi.

29. Pouvez-vous vous passer d'auto?
J'aurai bientôt mon permis.
Je n'aime pas conduire vite.
Je n'ai jamais eu d'accident.
Je préfère le train.
Je n'en ai vraiment pas besoin.

30. Y êtes-vous arrivé à l'improviste?
    Non, il faisait trop sombre.
    Oui, mon ami était tout à fait surpris.
    Non, le magasin était fermé.
    Oui, maintenant tout est correct.
    Oui, je voulais allumer ma pipe.

PART III

In this part there are four prose passages, each followed by five questions with a choice of answers. The student has before him the five possible answers to each question, but he does not see the passage or the questions. The procedure recommended is as follows: Read the passage once and the questions once while the student listens. Then read the passage once more and the questions once more while he checks the appropriate answers.

A

Le lampion permettait de distinguer une blouse, un pantalon de gros velours déchiré, des pieds nus, et quelque chose qui ressemblait à une mare de sang. Maurice entrevit une tête pâle qui se dressait vers lui et qui lui dit:
—Vous ne me reconnaissez pas?
—Non.
—Angeline.
Maurice se baissa vivement. C'était en effet cette malheureuse enfant. Elle était habillée en homme.
—Comment êtes-vous ici, que faites-vous là?
—Je meurs, lui dit-elle.
Maurice s'écria:
—Vous êtes blessée! Attendez, je vais vous porter dans la maison. Où souffrez-vous? Est-ce grave?
En voulant la soulever dans ses bras il recontra sa main. Elle poussa un cri faible.

—Vous ai-je fait mal? demanda Maurice.

—Un peu.

—Mais je n'ai touché que votre main.

Elle leva sa main vers le regard de Maurice, et il vit au mileu de cette main un trou noir.

—Qu'avez-vous donc à la main? dit-il.

—Elle est percée.

—Percée!

—Oui.

—De quoi?

—D'une balle.

—Comment?

—Avez-vous vu tout à l'heure un fusil qui était dirigé contre vous?

—Oui, et une main qui l'a bouché.

—C'était la mienne.

31. Où cette scéne a-t-elle lieu?
Dans la maison de l'enfant.
Dans la rue.
A l'école.
A l'hôpital.
Dans une voiture.

32. Quelle émotion Maurice manifeste-t-il en parlant à l'enfant?
La sympathie.
La joie.
La peur.
La colère.
La cruauté.

33. Qu'est-ce que cette enfant avait essayé de faire?
Se suicider.
Protéger Maurice.
Faire le coup de feu.
Echapper à Maurice.
Trouver un médecin.

34. Qu'est-ce qui est arrivé à l'enfant?
    Elle est tombée dans la rue.
    Elle a été heurtée par une voiture.
    Elle s'est blessée en jouant avec un fusil.
    Elle a reçu une balle dans la main.
    Elle s'est coupée avec un couteau.

35. Que veut faire Maurice pour aider l'enfant?
    Se sauver aussi vite que possible.
    Retirer le fusil de ses mains.
    La sauver des voleurs.
    L'emmener à sa maison.
    Lui chercher du secours.

B

—Qu'est-ce qui vous prend? Je me demandais où vous me meniez.
Chut! Pas si haut.
—J'ai failli ne pas entrer. Ça nous portera malheur.
—Ne dites pas de bêtises.
Le bas côté nord de l'église était vide. Antoine chercha un endroit obscur, éloigné de toute porte, et d'où pourtant on pût voir venir les gens à quelque distance.
—Asseyez-vous. Nous serons très tranquilles pour causer. Mais arrangez-vous pour parler à voix très basse. Si je vous pousse le coude, c'est qu'il faudra se taire.
—Ils ne vont pas trouver drôle que nous soyons là? Si encore on avait l'air de faire sa prière. Hein?
—Mais non. Ayons l'air tout simplement de gens fatigués. L'essentiel est qu'on n'entende pas que nous parlons. Vous ne savez donc pas chuchoter, sans bruit de voix!
—Non, pas bien. Ça m'embrouille les lèvres. Je ne me reconnais pas dans les mots que je dis.

36. Où se trouvent les deux hommes qui parlent?
    Devant une église.

Dans leur maison.
Sur une tour.
Dans une église.
Dans une cave.

37. Qu'est-ce qu'ils cherchent?
Un endroit pour causer.
De l'argent.
L'entrée de l'église.
Un banc pour se reposer.
La maison d'un ami.

38. Qui les accompagne?
Un autre voyageur.
Un prêtre.
Des gens fatigués.
Les habitants du village.
Personne.

39. Comment doivent-ils parler?
A haute voix.
Rapidement.
A voix basse.
Très distinctement.
En criant.

40. Quel sentiment expriment-ils par les paroles qu'ils échangent?
Le plaisir qu'ils éprouvent à se retrouver.
Une peur d'être entendus par hasard.
La haine de l'un pour autre.
Leur désir de se confesser.
Leur empressement d'en avoir vite fini.

C

Le souper fini et les quatre convives revenus de la table à la cheminée, ma mère se jetait, en soupirant, dans son vieux fauteuil; on mettait devant elle un guéridon avec une bougie. Je m'asseyais auprès du feu avec ma sœur; les domestiques enlevaient le couvert et se retiraient. Mon père commençait alors une promenade qui ne cessait qu'à l'heure de son coucher. Il était vêtu d'une espèce de manteau blanc que je n'ai jamais vu qu'à lui. Sa tête, demi-chauve, était couverte d'un grand bonnet blanc qui se tenait tout droit. Lorsqu'en se promenant il s'éloignait du foyer, la vaste salle était si peu éclairée par une seule bougie qu'on ne le voyait plus; on l'entendait seulement marcher dans les ténèbres; puis il revenait lentement vers la lumière et émergeait peu à peu de l'obscurité, comme un spectre, avec sa robe blanche, son bonnet blanc, sa figure longue et pâle. Ma sœur et moi nous échangions quelques mots à voix basse quand il était à l'autre bout de la salle, mais nous nous taisions quand il se rapprochait de nous. Il nous disait en passant: "De quoi parliez-vous?" Saisis de terreur, nous ne répondions rien; il continuait sa marche. Le reste de la soirée, l'oreille n'était plus frappée que du bruit mesuré de ses pas, des soupirs de ma mère, et du murmure du vent.

41. Qu'est-ce qu'on décrit dans ce passage?
　　Une vaste salle de classe.
　　La nef d'une cathédrale.
　　Le foyer d'un théâtre.
　　La salle à manger d'un grand hôtel.
　　L'intérieur d'une grande maison.

42. Pourquoi le père avait-il l'air d'un spectre?
　　Parce qu'il était mort.
　　Parce qu'il était vêtu tout en blanc.
　　Parce qu'il demeurait dans une maison hantée.
　　Parce qu'il portait une bougie à la main.
　　Parce qu'il voulait effrayer les enfants.

43. Que faisaient les enfants après dîner?
　　Ils se disputaient constamment entre eux.
　　Ils causaient avec leur mère.
　　Ils répondaient brièvement aux questions de leur père.
　　Ils échangeaient quelques paroles.
　　Ils ne disaient rien du tout.

44. Comment le père passait-il la soirée?
    A marcher de long en large.
    A causer avec sa famille.
    A faire la lecture à haute voix.
    A se promener dans la campagne.
    A gronder ses enfants.

45. Quel air tous ces personnages avaient-ils?
    Malades.
    Gais.
    Ennuyés.
    Très pauvres.
    Très fâchés.

D

—Mioche, es-tu un homme? demanda Rimailles.

—Qu'est-ce qu'il vous faut, répondit le gamin, avec dédain.

—Grimper par ce tuyau, puis nouer cette corde à la fenêtre. Il y a un homme là-haut que tu sauveras.

Le garçon examina la corde, le tuyau, le mur, les fenêtres, puis, sans mot dire, il ôta ses souliers.

Rimailles le saisit d'un bras, le posa sur le toit de la baraque, et lui remit la corde. Le gamin se dirigea vers le tuyau où il était facile d'entrer grâce à une large crevasse qui touchait au toit. Au moment où il allait monter, le vieux prisonnier, qui voyait le salut et la vie s'approcher, se pencha au bord du mur. La première lueur du jour blanchissait son front, ses pommettes livides, son nez effilé, et sa barbe grise.

—Tiens! dit le garçon, c'est un grand-père. Mais cela n'empêche pas.

Et prenant la corde dans ses dents, il commença résolument l'escalade. Il parvint au haut de la masure, enfourcha le vieux mur comme un cheval, et noua solidement la corde à la traverse supérieure de la fenêtre.

Un moment après, le prisonnier était dans la rue.

46. A quelle heure de la journée cet incident a-t-il lieu?
    À midi.
    A l'heure du dîner.
    A minuit.
    De bonne heure le matin.
    Dans l'après-midi.

47. Qu'est-ce que Rimailles demande au garçon de faire?
    De couper la corde.
    D'aller chercher la police.
    De casser la fenêtre.
    D'aider le vieillard à s'échapper.
    De monter à cheval.

48. Comment le garçon réussit-il à monter?
    Il est aidé par le prisonnier.
    A l'aide d'une corde.
    Il est aidé par Rimailles.
    Il agit tout seul.
    Avec l'aide d'un agent de police.

49. De quoi ce garçon a-t-il peur?
    De tomber.
    D'être vu par la police.
    D'effrayer le vieillard.
    De faire du bruit.
    De rien.

50. Quel sentiment le vieillard devait-il éprouver en voyant le garçon s'approcher?
    La crainte.
    La rage.
    Le remords.
    La joie.
    Le dédain.

AURAL TEST NO. 2

This is the teacher's copy, with the correct answers indicated. The student's copy should contain only the item numbers, the parentheses, and the five possible answers in each item.

PART I

After giving the item number, read the statement that is checked and repeat it once (only). The student selects the statement he has heard by putting a check mark in the parenthesis that precedes it.

1. ( ) Ils amuseraient.
   ( ) Ils s'amuseraient.
   (x) Ils amusaient.
   ( ) Ils les amusaient.
   ( ) Ils l'amusaient.

2. ( ) Ses cent francs.
   (x) Seize cents francs.
   ( ) Est-ce cent francs?
   ( ) Six cents francs.
   ( ) Sept cents francs.

3. ( ) Qui est-ce qui l'a?
   ( ) Qu'est-ce qu'il y a?
   ( ) Qu'est-ce qu'elle a?
   ( ) Qu'est-ce que cela?
   (x) Qu'est-ce qu'il a?

4. ( ) Elle quitta la cuisine.
   ( ) Elle quitta la cousine.
   ( ) Elle a quitté la cuisine.
   (x) Elle quittait la cuisine.
   ( ) Elle quitta la cousine.

5. ( ) Il leva les épaules.
   ( ) Levez les épaules.
   (x) Il levait les épaules.

   ( ) Il lève les épaules.
   ( ) Lève les épaules.

6. ( ) Pourquoi est-il parti?
   (x) Pourquoi es-tu parti?
   ( ) Pourquoi était-il parti?
   ( ) Pourquoi êtes-vous parti?
   ( ) Pourquoi être parti?

7. (x) J'ai travaillé.
   ( ) Ai-je travaillé?
   ( ) Je travaillai.
   ( ) Et je travaillais.
   ( ) Je travaillerai.

8. ( ) Est-ce qu'ils en avaient?
   ( ) Est-ce qu'ils en auraient?
   ( ) Est ce qu'ils s'en allaient?
   (x) Est-ce qu'ils s'en iraient?
   ( ) Est-ce qu'ils s'ennuyaient?

9. ( ) J'attends sa réponse.   10. ( ) Il se lève lentement.
   ( ) J'entends ta réponse.   ( ) Il se lave les mains.
   ( ) J'attends ta réponse.   (x) Il se lèvera demain.
   ( ) J'entends la réponse.   ( ) Il se lavait les mains.
   (x) J'entends sa réponse.   ( ) Il se laverait les mains.

PART II

Read each question and repeat it once, while the student checks
the statement that would be a suitable answer.

11. Où va-t-on pour prendre un train?
    ( ) En voiture.
    ( ) Au guichet.
    (x) A la gare.
    ( ) En chemin de fer.
    ( ) A la guerre.

12. Que mettez-vous dans votre café?
    ( ) Une tasse.
    ( ) Le garçon.
    ( ) Le pourboire.
    (x) De la crème.
    ( ) L'addition.

13. Que dit-on à une jeune fille à qui on vient d'être présenté?
    ( ) Merci, mademoiselle.
    ( ) S'il vous plaît, mademoiselle.
    ( ) Pardon, mademoiselle.
    (x) Enchanté, mademoiselle.
    ( ) Au revoir, mademoiselle.

14. Avec quoi s'essuie-t-on les lèvres et les doigts à table?
    ( ) Une toilette.
    ( ) Un couvert.
    ( ) Le vestiaire.
    ( ) La nappe.
    (x) La serviette.

15. Qu'est-ce qui sert à allumer une cigarette?
    ( ) Un cendrier.
    (x) Un briquet.
    ( ) Un fumoir.
    ( ) Un porte-cigarette.
    ( ) Une cheminée.

16. Vous n'avez rien entendu?
    ( ) Non, je n'ai rien.
    ( ) Si, j'ai quelque chose.
    (x) Rien du tout.
    ( ) J'attends depuis longtemps.
    ( ) Voici tout ce que j'ai.

17. Qu'est-ce qu'on achète à la boulangerie?
    ( ) Du vin.
    ( ) Du beurre.
    ( ) Des vêtements.
    ( ) De la viande.
    (x) Du pain.

18. Avec quoi assaisonne-t-on un œuf?
    ( ) Au printemps.
    ( ) Avec du sucre.
    ( ) A la coque.
    (x) Avec du sel.
    ( ) Avec une fourchette.

19. Quelle partie d'un grand magasin se trouve en dessous du rez-de-chaussée?
    (x) Le sous-sol.
    ( ) Le premier étage.
    ( ) L'entre-sol.
    ( ) Les étages supérieurs.
    ( ) Les vitrines.

20. Que porte-t-on sur soi pour savoir l'heure?
    ( ) Une pendule.
    (x) Une montre.

( ) Une cloche.
( ) Un horloger.
( ) Un horaire.

Part III

Read each sentence and repeat it once, with a pause or gesture to replace the missing word or expression, while the student checks the word or expression that would complete the sentence suitably.

21. Pour payer le journal, Jacques met . . . sur le comptoir.
    ( ) Le coin.
    ( ) L'argenterie.
    ( ) Le change.
    ( ) Le compte.
    (x) L'argent.

22. Le garçon jette l'assiette par terre et la . . . en mille morceaux.
    ( ) Fond.
    ( ) Cache.
    ( ) Braque.
    (x) Brise.
    ( ) Brille.

23. On met des caoutchoucs et un imperméable quand . . .
    (x) Il pleut.
    ( ) Il fait beau.
    ( ) Il fait noir.
    ( ) Il fait chaud.
    ( ) Il gèle.

24. Si l'on commence à travailler à onze heures et demie, à deux heures on travaille depuis . . .
    ( ) Une demi-heure.
    ( ) Midi.
    ( ) Une heure.
    ( ) Une heure et demie.
    (x) Deux heures et demie.

25. Le bateau se trouvait . . . , prêt à partir.
   ( ) A la queue.
   ( ) Au pire.
   (x) Au quai.
   ( ) Sous l'eau.
   ( ) A toute vapeur.

26. Lorsque je descends en ville, je vais dans les grands magasins faire des . . .
   ( ) Marches.
   ( ) Cours.
   ( ) Marques.
   (x) Emplettes.
   ( ) Marchands.

27. Pour monter à ma chambre, qui se trouve au quatrième, je prends . . .
   ( ) Le lever.
   ( ) L'omnibus.
   ( ) Un taxi.
   ( ) L'élevage.
   (x) L'ascenseur.

28. Le malade va bien mieux; il sera bientôt . . .
   ( ) Béni.
   (x) Guéri.
   ( ) Curé.
   ( ) Soigné.
   ( ) Remédié.

29. La maison était pleine de vieux meubles, de la cave . . .
   (x) Au grenier.
   ( ) Aux fenêtres.
   ( ) Au parquet.
   ( ) Aux cheminées.
   ( ) A la façade.

30. S'il pleut à verse, il nous faudra chercher . . .
    ( ) Un couvercle.
    (x) Un abri.
    ( ) Une échelle.
    ( ) Une couverture.
    ( ) Un protégé.

Part IV

In this part there are three prose passages, each followed by several questions with a choice of answers. Read each passage once, and the questions following it once, while the student listens. Then read the passage once more, and the questions once more, while the student checks the suitable answers.

A

Or, un matin, comme il achevait de déjeuner, M. Thérive entendit tout à coup un grand bruit dans la cuisine. Il y courut. Son domestique, Jean, se débattait, saisi par deux gendarmes. Le brigadier prenait gravement des notes sur un carnet.

Dès qu'il aperçut son maître, Jean se mit à sangloter, criant:

—Vous m'avez dénoncé, monsieur, ce n'est pas bien, après ce que vous m'aviez promis. Vous manquez à votre parole, monsieur Thérive, ce n'est pas bien!

M. Thérive, stupéfait et désolé d'être soupçonné, leva la main:

—Je te jure devant Dieu, mon garçon, je ne t'ai pas dénoncé. J'ignore absolument pourquoi messieurs les gendarmes sont venus ici.

Le brigadier articula sévèrement:

—Monsieur Thérive, je suis chargé d'arrêter votre domestique pour vol de deux canards enlevés chez monsieur Duhamel votre voisin, pour lesquels il y a des témoins. Je vous demande pardon, monsieur Thérive.

Et, se tournant vers ses hommes, il commanda:

—Allons, en route!

31. Pourquoi M. Thérive court-il à la cuisine?
( ) Pour achever son déjeuner.
( ) Pour battre son domestique.
( ) Pour parler aux gendarmes.
( ) Pour recevoir son voisin.
(x) Pour voir ce qui se passe.

32. Quelle émotion M. Thérive doit-il éprouver en trouvant les gendarmes dans sa cuisine?
( ) La honte.
( ) La peur.
( ) La satisfaction.
(x) La surprise.
( ) Le plaisir.

33. Que fait le brigadier au moment où M. Thérive entre dans la cuisine?
( ) Il accuse M. Thérive de vol.
(x) Il écrit sur un petit livre.
( ) Il aide les gendarmes à tenir le domestique.
( ) Il dénonce M. Thérive.
( ) Il rend à M. Thérive ce qu'on lui avait volé.

34. De quoi Jean accuse-t-il son maître?
( ) De l'avoir volé.
( ) D'avoir volé deux canards.
(x) De l'avoir dénoncé.
( ) De l'avoir battu.
( ) De ne pas avoir payé ce qu'il avait promis.

35. Pourquoi les gendarmes sont-ils venus?
( ) Parce que M. Thérive a dénoncé son domestique.
(x) Parce que les témoins avaient accusé Jean de vol.
( ) Parce que M. Thérive a manqué à sa parole.
( ) Parce que Jean a volé l'argent de son maître.
( ) Parce que M. Thérive a été dénoncé par son voisin.

B

Sans attendre qu'on lui dît d'entrer, la jeune fille entra résolûment dans l'appartement. Elle avait les pieds nus et le jupon déchiré. Elle tenait une lettre à la main, qu'elle présenta à François. En ouvrant la lettre, François remarqua que le pain à cacheter était encore mouillé. Le message ne pouvait venir de bien loin. Il lut:

"Mon aimable voisin, jeune homme!

"J'ai appris vos bontés pour moi, que vous avez payé mon terme il y a six mois. Je vous bénis. Ma fille aînée vous dira que nous sommes sans un morceau de pain depuis deux jours. Quatre personnes, et mon épouse malade. Si je ne suis pas déçu dans ma pensée, je crois devoir espérer que votre cœur généreux s'humanisera à cet exposé, et que vous daignerez me prodiguer un léger bienfait.

"Je suis, avec la considération distinguée qu'on doit aux bienfaiteurs de l'humanité,

Marivaux."

36. Qui est-ce qui apporte la lettre?
    ( ) Celui qui l'a écrit.
    ( ) La femme de Marivaux.
    ( ) Le facteur.
    (x) La fille aînée de Marivaux.
    ( ) Une jeune fille bien habillée.

37. Qui a dû écrire cette lettre?
    ( ) Un homme assez riche.
    (x) Un père de famille très pauvre.
    ( ) Un homme malade.
    ( ) Un homme ingrat.
    ( ) Quelqu'un qui ne connaît pas François.

38. Pourquoi a-t-on écrit la lettre?
    (x) Pour demander de l'argent.
    ( ) Pour offrir de l'aide au jeune homme.

( ) Pour répondre à la demande du jeune homme.
( ) Pour demander plus de temps pour payer ce qu'on doit.
( ) Pour demander la permission de faire une visite.

39. Qu'est-ce qui indique nettement que Marivaux dit la vérité?
    (x) L'aspect misérable de sa fille.
    ( ) La maladie de sa femme.
    ( ) Le style de la lettre.
    ( ) Sa reconnaissance.
    ( ) Le pain à cacheter que porte la lettre.

40. Comment sait-on que François est en effet un homme généreux?
    ( ) Il donne de l'argent à la jeune fille.
    (x) Il a déjà aidé Marivaux.
    ( ) Il donne à manger à la jeune fille avant d'ouvrir la lettre.
    ( ) Il envoie du pain à Marivaux.
    ( ) Il dit à la jeune fille de prendre du pain.

C

On célébrait une noce dans une métairie. Les mariés avaient déjà reçu les compliments de leurs amis, et l'on allait se mettre à table sous un grand figuier devant la porte de la maison. Tout à coup parut un homme à cheval, sortant d'un bois à portée de pistolet des invités. L'inconnu sauta lestement à terre, salua les convives de la main, et conduisit son cheval à l'écurie. Pendant qu'on se demandait tout bas quel était cet étranger, le vieux notaire, qui assistait à la noce, était devenu pâle comme la mort. Enfin un des convives s'approcha de la mariée et dit: C'est José Maria. Je me trompe fort, ou il vient ici pour faire quelque malheur. C'est au notaire qu'il en veut. Mais que faire? On délibérait encore quand l'inconnu reparut suivi du marié. Il jeta un coup d'œil de tigre au notaire, qui se mit à trembler comme s'il avait la fièvre, puis s'assit sans façon à côté de la mariée, entre elle et le notaire. On commença à manger. Lorsqu'on servit du vin, la mariée, prenant un verre de montilla, le toucha de ses lèvres et le présenta ensuite au bandit. C'est une politesse que l'on fait à table aux personnes que l'on estime. José Maria prit le verre, remercia avec effusion et déclara à la mariée qu'il ferait avec joie tout ce qu'elle voudrait lui commander.

—Oubliez, dit-elle, se penchant à son oreille, les mauvais vouloirs que vous avez peut-être apportés ici. Promettez-moi qu'il n'y aura pas de scandale à ma noce.

—Notaire, dit José, se tournant vers l'homme de loi tremblant, remerciez madame. Sans elle, je vous aurais tué avant que vous eussiez digéré votre dîner.

41. Où cette scène a-t-elle lieu?
    ( ) Devant une église.
    (x) Dans la campagne.
    ( ) Au centre d'un village.
    ( ) A la plage.
    ( ) Dans une grande ville.

42. Qu'est-ce qui se passe au moment où arrive le bandit?
    ( ) Le notaire va commencer la cérémonie.
    ( ) La procession se met en route pour l'église .
    ( ) Les invités sortent de l'église.
    (x) On va manger.
    ( ) On achève de dîner.

43. A qui le bandit semble-t-il en vouloir?
    ( ) A personne.
    ( ) Au marié.
    ( ) A la mariée.
    (x) Au notaire.
    ( ) A toute la compagnie.

44. Quelle émotion éprouve le notaire en voyant le bandit?
    ( ) Il est reconnaissant.
    ( ) Il est parfaitement calme.

(x) Il est effrayé.

( ) Il est amusé.

( ) Il est enragé.

45. Pourquoi le bandit vient-il à la fête?

    ( ) Il a perdu son chemin.

    ( ) Il veut enlever la mariée.

    ( ) Il veut demander de l'argent.

    (x) Il veut tuer quelqu'un.

    ( ) Il apporte un cadeau pour les mariés.

46. Qui est le premier à reconnaître le bandit?

    (x) Le notaire.

    ( ) Le marié.

    ( ) La mariée.

    ( ) Le convive qui parle à la mariée.

    ( ) Celui qui sert le vin

47. Que fait le bandit quand il s'approche de la mariée?

    ( ) Il lui baise la main.

    ( ) Il lui fait ses compliments.

    ( ) Il lui offre ses excuses.

    (x) Il s'assied auprès d'elle.

    ( ) Il lui donne un cadeau.

48. Qui est-ce qui offre un verre de vin au bandit?

    ( ) Un des invités.

    ( ) Un domestique.

    ( ) Le marié.

    ( ) Le notaire.

    (x) La mariée.

49. A quel moment le bandit renonce-t-il à ses projets de meurtre?

    ( ) Quand il descend de cheval.

    (x) Quand il entend la demande de la mariée.

    ( ) Quand il cause avec le marié.

    ( ) Quand il se met à table.

    ( ) Quand il remarque la peur du notaire.

50. De quelle qualité le bandit fait-il preuve à la fin du récit?
    - (x) De générosité.
    - ( ) De faiblesse.
    - ( ) De traîtrise.
    - ( ) De curiosité.
    - ( ) D'orgueil.

* 13 *

TEACHING CONVERSATION

To the average person, the primary form of communication is oral and the ability to speak a foreign language correctly and without accent constitutes real knowledge of it. The ability to read and write a language well, although in most cases far more difficult to attain, is generally not so regarded. Reading ability can be interpreted in so many ways and the amount of comprehension expected varies so widely that to most people this ability comes easily. Oddly enough, until very recently, only occasionally has conversational ability been made the primary objective in language teaching, and then for the most part only in private language schools and the armed forces. There has been much experimentation with the teaching of conversation but it is still one of the most difficult and elusive phases of instruction for a young teacher to master. Many teaching techniques have been devised and progress in the early stages of instruction is often very encouraging, but after this initial spurt most students advance no further unless the teacher makes a conscious effort to build up an active vocabulary, vary the phraseology, and increase each student's facility in speaking. Teaching techniques should be based on the proficiency of the students.

The teacher may base elementary work in conversation, whenever he can, first on objects in the classroom, by showing an object to the class, giving the foreign name for it, using the word in a sentence, asking a question, and having a student answer it. As soon as the entire class seems to have mastered its pronunciation, the word may be written on the blackboard or shown on a flash card so that each student may fix it in his mind visually as well as orally. Conversations of this type need not be limited, however, to classroom objects alone; they may deal with articles of clothing or anything the students have been asked to bring to class to serve as a basis for discussion. An effort should be made to have these discussions natural and spontaneous. Everyone should be allowed to participate and, particularly in the beginning, nothing should be done that will discourage the students' attempts to express themselves. One of the most important aspects in teaching conversation is to stimulate students and break down their self-consciousness and natural reticence. Once they have learned a little vocabulary, students enjoy asking questions of their instructors and classmates. This procedure affords a variation of the more formal pattern in which the instructor always asks the questions. In elementary courses the students must make their questions very simple and clear. They should be ready with an answer to any of their questions, in case none of the other students can answer them.

Another method of teaching conversation is to dictate, write on the board, or distribute in mimeographed form short practical conversations which may contain a series of questions and answers or a dialogue between two persons in a store, for example, or between two friends meeting in the street or going to school together. Conversation between two people at a base-ball or football game, or at dinner, or in any other situation that forms a regular part of the student's life may also be used. These conversations are most successfully taught if read first by the teacher and then in unison several times by both teacher and class to assure correct pronunciation and intona-tion, and a natural manner of saying each sentence. The teacher should be sure that the meaning of every word is clear to the students. Then the class should read the sen-tences alone. The teacher may then ask individual students to read the material and act out the scene it suggests. After this, volunteers may be invited to act out the scene from memory, trying to repeat as much of the actual con-versation as they can remember. If they cannot remember all of it, they should be encouraged to improvise so that, should they ever find themselves in a similar situation, they will be able to make themselves understood.

To provide variation of subject matter and make it more in-teresting to the students, the teacher may choose situations characteristic not of their own lives or of life in this country but of the land whose language they are studying, situations they might meet if they were traveling. The teacher should always describe the scene, using motion pictures or slides, if possible, before the conversation is given to the students. This will make these situations stand out as truly different from those encountered in this country. There should be a great deal of freedom in creating these scenes. For example, the students should be allowed to use simple props that will give the illusion of the actual scene.

Students may be asked to pantomime a scene and then describe it. They may also choose words or a sentence to be acted out like a charade. When the word or sentence has been guessed, the entire class should discuss the way it was presented. Conversation may also be based on a map of the country, on pictures, a comic strip, a drawing on the board, on post cards. There are endless possible variations for a conversation lesson. The most important thing is to give the students the feeling of being uninhibited so that they will express themselves as freely as possible.

This has been done very successfully by projecting a series of cartoons that depict a popular comic-strip personality on a screen, with conversation and captions omitted. Answering questions asked by the teacher or by a student, developing the theme of the pictures, putting words into the characters' mouths, and connecting the action of this comic strip with that of previous drawings will make a lively class. Also, limiting light to that projected on the screen seems to reduce inhibitions and encourage freer speech.

A kodachrome or action picture showing a foreign marketplace, a European schoolroom or schoolyard, children playing games in the Tuileries Gardens, or people riding on streetcars or trains in Spain and Italy will furnish a basis for good conversation and comments on foreign life.

A story may be started on a tape or by the teacher and left unfinished so that the students can conclude it in their own way. The story may then be continued to its end, after which the several conclusions can be discussed and compared. The tape may also be used to describe a familiar foreign picture, church, public building, or famous man, all of which the students may then identify and discuss. An imaginative teacher may also prepare a tape containing a series of patterns of speech that are typical of conversation at a restaurant, bank, railroad station, or grocery store; the student can learn these as part of his laboratory homework and thus facilitate his natural conversation in class.

Marjorie Johnston[1] found those high schools in which the language laboratory has been introduced have noticed a marked improvement in the oral-aural abilities of their classes, particularly with regard to the students' ability to give automatic responses and to think in the foreign language.

For another lesson, the instructor may dictate or distribute a series of questions, for which oral answers are to be prepared at home. This method brings better results if the questions are based on a grammar lesson which has already been taught and hence requires the use of previously learned vocabulary. They may also be based on the reading assignment, thus giving the students an opportunity to learn the reading vocabulary more thoroughly.

As has been suggested, conversational subjects based on familiar experiences prove most successful. They are endless in number—meals, football and baseball games, swimming, sailing, a picnic, a visit to an exhibition, an evening at the theater or the movies, a concert, a railroad or boat trip, a day at the beach, a dance, sleigh ride, a skiing party, a card game. The vocabulary in these fields is retained very easily because it grows out of the students' own experiences; but to facilitate conversation, some teachers prefer to write on the board or to mimeograph a list of words and expressions centering around each topic. The length of such a list depends on the capacity of the class to learn and use this vocabulary and its enthusiasm for this type of exercise in conversation. These lists should be given to the class the day before the lesson so that the students

[1] Marjorie Johnston, *op cit.*, p. 77.

will have time to familiarize themselves with the vocabulary.

One of the reading texts may contain a play with scenes that the students can learn by heart and give in class. The students may also introduce variations of the scenes with suitable dialogues. This same procedure may be applied to passages in stories and novels that contain good dialogues. These dialogues may be paraphrased and made into little scenes that are acted out or read in class by the students; any other treatment that stimulates conversation is also applicable.

To secure sustained speech in the language, the instructor may begin to tell or read a story which he thinks will interest the students, and then call on one of them to complete it. He may call for half a dozen different endings and ask the class which one it thinks is best. In a variation of this method, the classroom may be set up as an imitation radio or television studio, with members of the class speaking over microphones as if they were actually broadcasting. A class period of conversation may take the form of a quiz program, one student being Mr. Quiz and the instructor being a member of the audience; questioning him usually provides a certain amount of amusement to the pupils. An "Information Please" program can also be simulated, especially if the class is permitted to elect a "committee of experts" who will try to answer the students' questions in as interesting and spontaneous a way as possible. A "Double or Nothing" program may also be used as a means of stimulating conversation.

In one interesting variation, which has an entirely natural basis, the instructor acts the part of a native shopkeeper, for example, or a hotel clerk, policeman, or important personage to be interviewed, and the students themselves play the parts of purchasers, tourists, reporters, etc. The students should be told that the goal here is comprehensibility, not perfection in the choice of vocabulary or in sentence construction. The instructor can prepare them for this in advance by explaining the situation in which they will find themselves. He must take the part of a native who knows absolutely no English. This is likely to create very amusing situations.

To bring the student into contact with persons other than the teacher, a native may be invited to talk informally to the class. This is a variation of the informant technique used by the Army. Phonograph records of conversations may also be played for the students, and specially prepared dialogue films like *La Famille Martin* or one of the British Information Service Films may be shown. These are particularly well adapted to conversation.

The retelling of a previously read anecdote, short story, article, or item from the newspaper will give a student self-confidence and facility of expression. Progress in oral work can be made only by increasing his opportunities to express himself in as many different situations, simulated or real, as possible. At first he may speak from notes, then from a carefully prepared outline, and finally without either. The instructor should note on paper all the errors in wording and pronunciation made by each student and discuss them with the class at the end of each recitation.

When an *explication de texte* technique is used—with its repeated questions and answers based on the reading, plus explanations of vocabulary, cultural references, etc.—the teacher has less difficulty in developing uninhibited conversational ability in his students.

Professor Ruth Wasley sums up the objectives of the conversation course and gives servicable materials, successful techniques, and a helpful bibliography. She also describes in detail a very interesting French Assembly Program prepared to a large degree by the students in the conversation course.[2]

If freedom and ease in speech are one of the teacher's goals, as they should be, errors in pronunciation and language use should be corrected at the end of the period, rather than as they occur, in order not to interrupt the natural flow of speech. The teacher can make a list of errors as each pupil recites and discuss them in conference with the student or with the class as a whole.

[2] Ruth Wasley, "Course of Study for Conversation," *Modern Language Journal*, vol. 30, no. 7 (Nov., 1946).

* 14 *

TEACHING COMPOSITION

A written composition lesson may be one of the most effective methods of teaching a foreign language because what the student gains in expressing himself in writing may be carried over into oral work as well. By composition is meant free composition, i.e., writing created by the student. It is an excellent way for the teacher to detect errors that are peculiar to each student and that are seldom detected in translation exercises.

In order to make the teaching of composition more concrete, it is wise to prepare a plan of procedure in advance. A list of idiomatic expressions may provide the basis for a composition on a particular subject. A number of conversation and composition books have been published which contain subjects suitable for oral or written compositions and also good lists of the words and idioms connected with these subjects. In French, a typical list of idiomatic expressions that might be used is as follows:

1. Comme-ci comme-ça	6. En attendant
2. Au lieu de	7. Avoir du mal à
3. C'est mal	8. Se décider à
4. Comme résultat	9. En pleine campagne
5. Faire un compromis	10. S'avancer

Such a list in Spanish might include:

1. Tener ganas	7. Tener suerte
2. Encanter a alguien	8. Eso es que
3. Deber de	9. Cuanto màs . . . tanto
4. Equivocarse	menos
5. Ponerse a	10. Echar algo de memos
6. Valer la pena	

Composition can also be used as a device for correcting general errors which students make and particularly for directing their attention to certain typical errors and insisting on their correction before the composition is handed in. For example, before a student hands in his paper he may be told to underline every noun or pronoun subject once and every verb twice, to make sure that the agreement of subject and verb is correct. In French, where the past participle may agree with either the direct object or the subject, the pronoun object may be underlined once, the subject twice, and the past participle three times. Similarly, in the agreement of adjectives and nouns, the noun may be underlined once and the adjective twice. In the use of relative pronouns, it is particularly worth while to have the student underline each relative pronoun once and the word it represents twice, so that he will be sure he is using the correct relative and referring to the proper antecedent. This seems to be one of the most effective ways of eliminating errors and its use may make composition writing a means of learning how to write without error, or at least without the most common ones. Any device that attracts the student's attention to an error that he is likely to make frequently can be used profitably. In most classes, certain errors tend to become general, and these errors lend themselves to this sort of self-correction.

Once the students have become accustomed to writing in the language (composition should preferably be begun early in the first year of study, but certainly at the beginning of the second year), subjects of a general nature may be used as topics—what they have done at home, what they intend to do during the summer, a motion picture they have seen, a conversation during a meal or in a store. Any subject is suitable that will require them to use some of the vocabulary from their grammar or their reading text. Any practical words from the reading vocabulary should become part of the student's active vocabulary. If the instructor assigns a particular story for a composition, he may if necessary put on the board the words the students are most likely to need in writing it.

Compositions are better when prepared according to a very definite plan, especially in more advanced classes. A general outline of the subject may be prepared in the language and dictated to the students. For example, if they are to write about a great painter, the divisions of the composition might be as follows: (1) His life, with such subdivisions as date and place of birth, family, education, and general appearance; (2) his qualities as an artist, the highest achievements of the school to which he belonged, what characterizes his painting, his masterpieces and their particular value; and (3) why the student likes the painter, the impressions his paintings have made on him, the painter's influence on his ideas.

Other subjects which may be treated in the same way are the school day; school life; skating; the student's home town; a favorite friend; how the student wants to earn his living; a trip by train, automobile, boat, or airplane; a camping trip; what the student would do if he had a large sum of money to spend. If the student's vocabulary is likely to be insufficient, the instructor can supply additional terms so that the composition lesson will be helpful and instructive.

An outline like the following should be given the pupil, preferably in the language being taught:

A DAY IN THE COUNTRY

1. Preparation for departure.
   a. Preparation of lunch.
      Bread—Ham—Cheese—Butter—Fruit, etc.
   b. Trip.
   c. Arrival; description of picnic grounds.
2. Picnic.
   a. Amusements before luncheon.
      Swimming—Boating—Walking, etc.
   b. Luncheon.
   c. Amusements after luncheon.
      Tennis—Baseball, etc.
3. The trip home.
   a. Conversation on the way.
   b. Comments on the scenery.

For elementary classes it is often helpful to prepare a series of incomplete sentences and ask the students to complete them; in this way they produce a complete composition. This gives them the habit of thinking in the language, but it is not as good an exercise as straight free composition; it will, however, limit the number of errors. Moreover, it will encourage students at this level, and give them more confidence. This same idea may be used in preparing multiple-choice beginnings or endings to sentences which make up a composition. Such devices, of course, are less valuable in developing student ability because the creative element is lost either wholly or in part; but they are usually considered a game and the pupils retain some of the correct phraseology that has been used.

In the first reading assignments given in elementary classes, a student often gains a great deal if he is permitted to paraphrase the day's assignment by incorporating parts of sentences from it in his own version of the story. Using the reading text as a basis for composition helps the students learn to spell new words correctly and also fixes in their minds, often subconsciously, a new grammatical rule which they were forced to use several times. Perhaps it is only a verb or an idiom that the student thus comes to understand and use naturally, but it is an important gain for a beginner. The use of the future can be taught in this way, as can also the subjunctive, the imperfect, and difficult constructions like the causative *faire* in French, to say nothing of new vocabulary. There are, of course, many errors due to ignorance which creep into this paraphrasing but the exercises offer so much of positive value that they are truly worth while.

In more advanced courses the students may dramatize the story they are reading if it lends itself to dramatization. If their written versions are acted out in class, both the enthusiasm for writing and the impression on the class are greater. In very advanced classes where writing style is under consideration, imitating a paragraph by a great writer is a valuable exercise. Here the most natural procedure is to analyze the author's sentence structure and paragraph organization, and his vocabulary and the manner in which he achieves his effect. After a thorough analysis has been made of his general topic, his sentence structure, and his choice of idiomatic words and expressions, a similar topic may be assigned to the students; in developing it they must try to imitate the author's style. Loti, Gide, and Maupassant are excellent models in French, as are Bécquer, Alarcón, and Unamuno in Spanish. This is frequently an effective way of developing writing style in more advanced classes and teaching students to appreciate the qualities that constitute greatness or success in writing. This is especially valuable because few students recognize qualities of style in a foreign language.

The application of the pattern-of-speech technique to teach better composition writing to advanced classes stimulates interest and brings worthwhile results. At the third-year level, in addition to reviewing grammar and verb forms through pattern questions and answers, it is possible to choose characteristic idioms, phrases, and even linguistic mannerisms from selected paragraphs in reading texts, which not only reveal the author's way of thinking but indicate the way in which a Frenchman or Spaniard expresses himself. These may be incorporated into pattern questions and answers until the student has become familiar with them. If the student is allowed to concentrate on one paragraph that has a unity in itself, pattern exercises will help him adapt these turns of phrase for his own use in an original free composition.

The following passage from Gide's *La Symphonie Pastorale* was read aloud by the teacher who then asked pattern questions and dictated the most difficult phrases for reference since the students had no books. The drill, which lasted 25 or 30 minutes was followed by writing the composition. The whole lesson totaled 50 minutes.

Un des premiers jours d'août il y a à peine un peu plus de six mois de cela, n'ayant point trouvé chez elle une pauvre veuve à qui j'allais porter quelque consolation, je revins pour prendre Gertrude à l'église où je l'avais laissée; elle ne m'attendait point si tôt et je fus extrêmement surpris de trouver Jacques auprès d'elle. Ni l'un ni l'autre ne m'avaient entendu entrer, car le peu de bruit que je fis fut couvert par les sons de l'orgue. Il n'est point dans mon naturel d'épier, mais tout ce qui touche à Gertrude me tient à cœur; amortissant donc le bruit de mes pas, je gravis furtivement les quelques marches de l'escalier qui mène à la tribune; excellent poste d'observation.

Pattern commands and questions such as the following will not only drill the student in various verb forms but also familiarize him with natural French word order and characteristic French phrasing:

1. Dites que vous auriez été extrêmement surpris de trouver Jacques auprès d'elle.
2. Dites que vous avez gravi furtivement les quelques marches de l'escalier
3. N'est-il point dans votre naturel d'épier?
4. Est-ce que tout ce qui touche à Gertrude vous tient à cœur?

These are but a few of the many characteristically French phrases which can be repeated in slightly varied pattern forms until they are mastered. Then it is time to suggest parallel subjects for free composition, such as:

1. Une surprise visite à la maison d'un ami
2. Une surprise visite à bord le yacht d'un ami
3. Une surprise visite chez soi après une absence de quelques jours

Students seem to enjoy this type of free composition. The patterns they have learned and used give a native flavor to the language used in their compositions, and at the same time they can use their imagination to create a new theme suggested by the original paragraph.[1]

If poetry is being discussed, the paraphrasing of a simple poem into prose will often help the student to distinguish between poetical language and prose. It will also enable him to understand more easily the content of the poem, for otherwise he might fail to analyze it carefully enough.

Composition can also be based on an illustration from a newspaper or a book. In this case, it is always well to list on the board the foreign words for most of the objects in the picture, as well as a few helpful associated expressions.

Many teachers have found that projecting a picture or a series of pictures is an interesting device for stimulating student imagination in writing compositions. If requested by students, essential vocabulary or idioms may be given, either through discussing the picture in the foreign language or directly by the teacher when he deems it wise.

An anecdote which the students have never heard before may be told by the teacher, and a student may be sent to the board afterward to write any new words he remembers from it. If the anecdote is to be retold by the students, an outline of it may be worked out with them so they will learn how to organize their thoughts before they begin to write. If the vocabulary in it is too difficult, the teacher may write appropriate words and expressions on the board as soon as the outline has been completed. Compositions may retell the story of songs that the class has learned, or songs can be played on a phonograph several times while the students take notes on the

[1] Edmond A. Méras, "The Pattern-of-Speech Technique in Third Year French," *French Review* (April, 1959), 465-467.

words. Songs that suggest or tell a definite story are best for this purpose.

A composition may be based on work done in another class —for example, a class in the history of English literature, or music, or science. This constitutes a form of integration and shows how the various studies in the curriculum can be inter-related.

In order to increase writing facility as well as build vocabulary, another procedure for composition in more advanced classes is to permit free use of the dictionary, as is done in Europe. This offers the added advantage of teaching the intelligent use of the dictionary.

For many years, foreign-language textbooks and examinations used the term *composition* to describe the translation, into the foreign language, of a connected passage in English. Sometimes this passage for so-called composition merely contained a number of difficult grammatical points in concentrated form. This must be distinguished from the free composition discussed above, for this is really the translation of consecutive sentences, usually but not necessarily having a connected thought. This, the so-called formal composition, has the misfortune of not developing creative ability or creating much confidence in one's ability to use the language. Relatively little is retained by the student from such an exercise except a little grammatical accuracy and some vocabulary. If this type of translation is used in elementary and intermediate classes, it is helpful to give the student a passage in the foreign language to use as a basis for study before he is given a corresponding and similar passage in English to translate. Many textbooks in composition are built on this principle. Endless variations of this method can be devised, depending on the instructor's imagination and what he hopes to achieve with his class. In very advanced courses, however, once a student is proficient, translation is the most effective way of teaching the delicate shadings of meaning and the subtle differences which must be considered in transposing an idea from one language to another. It is excellent training for professional translators, for it encourages increased care in understanding accurately and gives training in precision in expressing ideas.

One of the greatest values of written free composition is that it can be so easily transformed into oral composition. As a preparatory step to oral composition, a written composition or outline on the subject gives substance to the oral exercise and develops clear, accurate, logical thinking as well as expression.

It is difficult to overemphasize the importance of free composition, both written and oral, as a practical aid in language teaching. Most teachers are discouraged by the mass of errors in their students' free compositions and by the difficulties of evaluating these errors and marking the papers fairly. If a triple grade is used—one for grammatical errors, the second for manner of expression and comparative length, and the third for content—these difficulties can to some extent be overcome. From the point of view of success in language teaching, it is very unfortunate that free oral and written composition has not been used more generally.

* 15 *

TEACHING CULTURE AND CIVILIZATION IN CLASSROOM AND LANGUAGE CLUB

To many educators the most valuable result to be obtained from the teaching of any foreign language is the awakening of a sympathy for and an understanding of the people of the country. Some language courses have been centered exclusively on this cultural objective, but this is far from general. Even when teaching culture is a secondary objective, there are definite teaching procedures which may help students to realize that there are great nations other than our own, whose manner of life differs from ours. In most cases it can be shown that their customs, though different, are as interesting and as practical as our own. Thus tolerance and understanding of others can be taught. This is probably one of the most valuable secondary objectives of all language teaching.

One of the simplest ways of teaching another country's cultural achievements is to organize a class project in which the students cooperate in studying that country's music, poetry, art, architecture, or manners and customs. Thus each

student can choose a composer, for example, and prepare a
talk on him and his work. A student who is talented may be
encouraged to perform some of the musician's compositions
to illustrate his talk.

When films are available, an excellent means of making a
foreign civilization real to the students is to show a film depicting life there and to discuss it with the students as soon as it
is finished. If no films are available, postcards, photographs,
and Kodachromes may be thrown on a screen, or exhibitions
of posters and other material illustrative of the country may be
put on the bulletin board. Many countries publish bulletins,
posters, graphs, and circulars that are available to teachers.

The bulletin board display is excellent for giving students a
relatively clear and concrete idea of any phase of civilization
that can be described by pictures or printed material. Such an
exhibit may include, in addition to pictures, examples of the
country's publicity, comic strips clipped from its newspapers,
and covers of such products as toothpaste and soap that are
produced there exclusively. Such displays are usually of great
interest to students. Not only will the students learn a certain
amount about a foreign civilization in this manner, but they
will gain a practical vocabulary.

Restaurant menus, wine labels if the country is noted for its
wines, the various coins and paper money used in it, postage
stamps, university bulletins, passports and identity cards,
money-order blanks, telegram blanks, and newspaper clippings
or copies of its papers and magazines are also valuable means
of bringing a country closer to the members of the class.
Pictures of costumes of different periods, photographs of the
work of the country's great painters and sculptors, theatrical
posters and programs, and pictures of the interiors of schools,

business offices, department stores, and historical monuments are more than good teaching devices, they are inspirational.

Students can be given responsibility for changing the exhibits on the bulletin boards and preparing information about the material in the display that will make these exhibits more interesting to the class.

Some of the bulletin board exhibits may center about a specific subject, such as the history of contemporary painting or contemporary furniture, or contemporary architecture. Photographs of writers prominent in the country today may be put up and, if possible, copies of their principal works or the dust jackets exhibited in showcases. Copies of finely bound editions of books published in the country may also be made available, either through private collections or from the library.

Students may work on specific projects, such as making a map of the capital of the foreign country. Each student can be made responsible for making a model, in soap or some other suitable material, of an outstanding monument or statue which will be put in place on the map. A map of the entire country may be made, with university centers or principal cities or famous cathedrals or castles or any other feature of special interest indicated in some striking way.

An English book dealing with civilization and history may be read in class. This information about the country may be supplemented by the teacher to make it more vital. In some languages there are easy books on culture for beginning students that can also be used as a basis for discussing the customs and manners of the country.

Some of the most popular recent books in the field of French for secondary schools and colleges are: B. Bart, *La France,*

Carrefour des Civilisations (Harcourt, Brace); C. Bagley and G. E. Diller, *La France d'autrefois et d'aujourd'hui* (Appleton-Century-Crofts); G. Chinard, *Scènes de la Vie française* (Ginn); A. and P. Langellier, *Ces Gens qui passent* (Holt); M. Reboussin, *Les grandes Epoques culturelles de la France* (Ronald); P. Brodin and F. Ernst, *La France et les Français* (Holt). Many other books, some of them easy and others more advanced, have been published in the field of French, Spanish, German, and Italian culture, both in English and the foreign language. Students may be assigned topics, material for which may be found in these books or in history books or encyclopedias, to be discussed in class.

Many libraries have established a language corner or table, on which current magazines, foreign-language periodicals, and newspapers can be displayed and read at will. Some schools have reserved a foreign-language room, which has display showcases as well as a collection of periodicals from abroad. The modern-language department corridor is an excellent place for such displays and such a cultural center. Some teachers prefer to have their own collection of foreign periodicals, which students are permitted to glance over or read before or after the period begins or during free periods. It is astonishing what interest secondary-school students have in the articles, advertisements, and pictures shown in these periodicals.

Local, foreign, or school newspapers that are published in the language can be used in class, if special emphasis is placed on articles that deal with life in the country concerned. If the school is near a foreign center, such as the French, Italian, and Spanish Cultural or Tourist Offices in New York, Boston, and Chicago, the class can visit these centers. The students may also dine in foreign restaurants and visit bookshops that specialize in the publications of a particular country; this invariably awakens an enthusiasm in students that is often transferred to their studies.

In order to stimulate more interest in a country and the desire to obtain information about it after a visit to an exhibition or museum, an "Information Please" or question and answer hour can be arranged, with a long series of questions and answers. Every pupil should be required to submit a question and be able to answer it. To make the competition keener, a prize may be offered for the highest score and the class formed into two or three teams.

None of these programs should ever be impromptu; they should be carefully prepared beforehand by the students under the teacher's guidance so that they will provide really valuable information for the class. If this information is entered in notebooks, it will increase the students' knowledge of the country and its people.

In most cases the regular reading text can serve as a basis for comment by the teacher and offer an opportunity to give information about the country. The instructor who has visited the country and knows it well can enliven the text by accounts of his experiences there. If he has photographs, slides, or motion pictures he should use them to illustrate his talks. Any such display of interest on the teacher's part will bring a reward in increased enthusiasm at least from some students. In some high schools, where it is impossible to show slides or motion pictures to a small class group, arrangements have been made to set aside 1 hour a week in which all classes studying the same language text will meet to be shown this material. This should, of course, be followed by a discussion in the next class hour. Sometimes material can be presented more attractively if the class is temporarily converted into a language club. The discussion then becomes less formal and the students usually enjoy it more and retain more because it seems less artificial.

The danger in this phase of language teaching is that it may become so interesting that it will tend to take the place of language study itself. There is no question of the vital importance of the cultural aspect in teaching foreign languages, but the teacher should always emphasize its value as a means of making possible intelligent communication between Americans and foreign people.

The Northeast Conference on the Teaching of Modern Languages (1960) invited both linguists and anthropologists to offer their respective definitions of culture and the role it should play in teaching languages. Their suggestions will without question cause many language teachers to reappraise what they have been teaching as culture and extend it beyond mere factual data.

The word 'culture' as it is used in anthropology does not, of course, refer exclusively to the arts and the humanities. Men of 'culture' are not, in our sense of the word, that small group in any society which appreciates man's finer achievements in literature, music and painting. For our discipline, every man participates in some regularly patterned ways of life characteristic of his society. Such regularly patterned objects, habits, manners, actions, values and ideas comprise roughly what, taken as a whole in any one society, anthropologists mean by that society's 'culture.'

Although the language teachers at the Conference did not subscribe entirely to this definition they did say that "culture as it is used in this study refers to the sum total of patterned manners, customs, norms and values which are characteristic of a society. Language is in this sense inseparable from culture, and we as language teachers deal every day with a highly cultural phenomenon which we alone are equipped to discuss."[1]

These interpretations of culture fortify the linguistic scientists' emphasis upon the student's most meticulous imitation of the native's speech, including his inflections, natural speed of delivery, and gestures. The teacher's task, then, is to go beyond mere facts about the foreign country and to explain the spirit of the country and the people whose language he teaches, as well as the traditional and psychological factors that make them what they are and which have helped them to create a distinctive civilization. Teaching culture, like teaching a language, is a broad and all-inclusive task.

For many years, when culture was taught only incidentally, the Language Club was often the main source of information about a foreign country. Through this club contacts were made with centers of foreign culture in this country. In schools where language clubs continue to fill this important role in teaching foreign languages, many of the above suggestions can be applied to the club programs. Materials for club meetings can be obtained from most of the modern-language associations and from the cultural branches of the various embassies, as well as from tourist bureaus. By carefully choosing from the mass of available material, great variety in programs can be obtained and language study can be made a vital part of the whole educational program. Whenever the club meeting replaces a class hour, the same suggestions apply.

[1] Northeast Conference on the Teaching of Modern Languages, "Culture in Language Learning, (foreword,) *Northeast Conference Reports,* 1960.

In large communities, consolidating language clubs of several schools is advisable, at least for a few meetings, so that dinners may be held to which a member of the consulate or a popular lecturer or foreign actor or singer may be invited. Such meetings also make possible the presentation of foreign movies and professional entertainment to a larger audience. Several clubs may join together to organize a dance or some other form of entertainment. They may organize a bazaar to aid foreign school children or to raise funds for a scholarship for an outstanding language student in one of their own schools. Such bazaars are usually very popular with the students both during the period of preparation and while the sale is being held. Furthermore, they arouse wide interest in the community if merchants and parents are invited to participate by donating food or gifts to be sold in the various booths.

The ingenuity of the teacher must be exercised constantly if the Language Club is to be a success. Not all localities offer the same opportunities for diversified and interesting programs, not all student bodies are interested in purely cultural information. But by careful and intelligent organization, by feeling out the students' interests and guiding their program choices, and by taking a personal interest in the students themselves, a teacher can develop in most of them a natural enthusiasm for language study.

* 16 *

TEACHING LITERATURE IN THE SECONDARY SCHOOL

It is difficult to teach foreign literature and achieve real appreciation of it before a student has had at least 3 years of normal language study, unless he is very exceptional. As foreign languages are generally taught today, most students do not have sufficient command of one before the third year to be able to appreciate differences in style. Although they may have had some experience in judging English literature they are too apt to apply English standards of criticism and taste to foreign books, whereas the foreign literature usually stems from a different tradition. In many cases students are intolerant of anything that is unfamiliar and they pass judgment on the literature too hastily and without sufficient understanding. In the average secondary school there is not enough time to provide the background necessary for real appreciation.

There is, however, a great deal of necessary literary groundwork that can be covered in the secondary school and that should form part of every high-school language course. Students *can* become thoroughly familiar with the great names in the literature. They *can* learn, at least in outline form or in abridged versions, the stories of the leading plays and novels, although many can and do read them in the original. They can learn short poems by heart. This will improve their pronunciation, as well as familiarize them with new vocabulary. If they are observant and properly guided, it should also acquaint them with a manner of writing, thinking, or wording ideas in the foreign language.

When extensive reading is assigned for outside work, specific questions aimed at facilitating a better literary analysis of the book may be dictated or distributed to the class to be answered by the students. The class can also prepare an outline or a good summary of the book. Instead of merely summarizing a novel or play, the students may be asked to list its outstanding qualities or defects. Such a searching study often demands more complete comprehension than writing a simple summary of the action or plot will give. If a novel is read in class, its construction can sometimes be studied. However, most of the novels now used are so abridged that they are poor examples of their authors' writing. Plays are usually less abridged and can be treated similarly. Here, as was suggested in Chapter 10, to bring out the particularly dramatic qualities of a play, students with exceptional dramatic ability may be asked to act out parts in it. Just as actors make clear the meaning of a play on the stage, so are many students able to see the real meaning of the lines if they are given an opportunity to act under supervision.

Sometimes the teacher can take his class to a nearby college whose Language Club or Dramatic Association is giving a contemporary play such as Pagnol's *Topaze,* Rostand's *Cyrano de Bergerac,* Werfel's *Jacobowski und der Oberst,* or a play by Anouilh, Benavente, Romains, or Pirandello. The class can be taken to see a foreign motion picture; as was said earlier, the teacher may be able to arrange with the local theater owner to show such a film, guaranteeing him a definite attendance. In the big cities this problem is simpler, for there is always some foreign film or play on the boards, either in the original or in translation.

On the secondary-school level care must be taken to choose novels and plays that are within the experience of the majority of the students. Teachers who are preparing for a degree from a graduate school while teaching in a secondary school must guard against the danger of forgetting the immaturity of their pupils and expecting them to have an ability to analyze that is beyond their years. They must remember that while these boys and girls can usually understand the personality of the characters in a novel, this sort of analysis is frequently quite limited. Students at this level can rarely be expected to understand a philosophical idea that may be the basis of the novel or play being read. The main difficulty, however, as was said above, is to make them comprehend the subtleties of style in a foreign language. For most students of high-school age, then, emphasis should be placed on learning the characteristics of great literary movements and the great names in the country's literature.

Literary movements may be studied by centuries or by types of literature, such as the novel, the theater, or poetry. The influence of a foreign country's literature on American or English literature, particularly that of our own time, interests most students even at the secondary-school level. Therefore the teacher should bring out differences and similarities.

Projects can be centered around the great literary names. For example, the class can be taken to a library to make a list of the foreign authors and acquaint themselves with some of their books, either in the original or in translation. A literary chart can be made by a student or the entire class, on which are marked the birthplaces of the leading writers or the regions most commonly written about by outstanding authors. This serves as excellent motivation for a lesson on the geography of the country. The preparation of notebooks containing information about authors and their ideas, and also about literary movements, should be encouraged so that this material may be used for further class discussion about the novel or play. Encyclopedias or histories of literature frequently are also good and easily available sources of information.

With the average high-school class, any very deep study of literature in a foreign language should be avoided for the group as a whole, except where students are preparing for Advanced Placement. To compete satisfactorily such students should have completed in secondary school the equivalent of 5 years of study in a foreign language. Furthermore, the students chosen for Advanced Placement must have superior ability and be mature in their judgment. When possible, these students should be sectioned apart from the rest of the students and prepared for this final objective from the tenth grade on. Advanced Placement Tests demand not only proof of high proficiency in mastering the language but a broad knowledge of literature, such as one normally finds in a college survey course. For example, not only should the student be familiar with the main currents of French Literature, but he should also have a knowledge of the representative works within each field. Candidates for this test must be able to analyze such works critically and be sensitive to shades of meaning, structure, and rhythm and music in prose as well as in poetry. Where registration is small this work can be accomplished with exceptional students in private conferences with the student—a modification of the tutorial system.

Very successful results have also been obtained with high-school students who have done voluntary but supervised reading on such topics as the novels of Balzac, the history of the French novel, and the main currents of seventeenth-century French literature. In each case the extensive reading done by the student was followed by a pupil-teacher discussion of the book read. Such a course represents the most advanced study of literature that should be attempted in a foreign language on the secondary-school level and it should be limited to non-advanced placement students, who have been well prepared however, and who are truly enthusiastic. Unless the high school is very large, this type of teaching, although very rewarding to the teacher, must be voluntary and carried in addition to his regular teaching program.

* 17 *

AUDIO-VISUAL AIDS IN LANGUAGE TEACHING

Since audio-visual aids[1] have of necessity been discussed as part of almost every phase of language teaching, the present chapter can be little more than a repetition or summary of what has already been said. This accessory to modern teaching has become so important, however, that it seems wise to review the possibilities of using these materials and to offer a comprehensive bibliography of commercially available materials as well as suggestions for obtaining them from foreign agencies in the United States.

Audio-visual aids generally include such materials as objects, pictures, slides, records, tapes, or motion pictures that are supplementary to actual textbooks. In teaching languages such aids often do more to interest and inspire students to further study than the actual classroom instruction and textbook assignments; hence their importance cannot be overemphasized. Much of this material can be exhibited by the teacher

[1] With the extended use of the phonograph, radio, projector, motion-picture machine, and television for the classroom, the term *audio-visual aids* has to some extent replaced the earlier term *realia*.

or displayed on tables or in exhibition cases in the classroom, the library, or the halls. Pictures, menus, tickets, programs, clippings, and the like may be tacked to bulletin boards.

In the majority of schools the use of audio-visual aids has become an essential part of every language program; for it is through them that an attempt is made to create the atmosphere of a foreign country in the classroom. Included in this category are maps and pictures of the country, its products, railroads, highways, rivers, valleys, mountains, industries, and monuments—anything that will help the student picture in his mind the country whose language he is learning. Materials obtained from travel agencies, from the offices of cultural attachés, and from consulates and embassies come under this heading, as do also photographs, Kodachromes, post cards, tickets of all kinds, costumes, money-order blanks, hotel bills, airline calendars, timetables, menus, theater programs, book and other catalogues, flags, stamps, coins, pottery, models of monuments—in short, every type of souvenir.

Many games offer students cultural material and fun at the same time; many such games can be obtained from shops and from publishers who specialize in audio-visual aids for the classroom. However, building a vocabulary around a picture of "The House," "The Store," or "The Station" gives facts in an atmosphere of play.

Ruth E. Wasley, of New York State College for Teachers, in Albany, New York, has successfully adapted many popular games to suit the purposes of language teaching. She uses bingo for teaching numbers and their pronunciation, and "Who am I?" "What is it?" and "Where is it?" for identifying through pictures the names or descriptions of foreign buildings, cities, rivers, and so forth. Teams are organized, and the members of each team guess names of objects and places from their opponents' descriptions. Points are given for each correct answer. The location of places in "Where is it?" is organized like a relay race; opposing teams run to a map until the place is discovered.[2] Football, baseball, and bowling have been used as a framework for learning vocabulary and reviewing verb forms and cultural material. For playing "baseball," two teams are chosen and a word is given in English; incorrect spelling or no answer constitutes a "strike," and the next student on the team answers. An error in accent, gender, or pronunciation counts as a "foul," and the word is passed to the next student on the same team. A "hit" is a correct answer, and four "hits" make a "run." Three "strikes" constitute an "out." After every "out," the opponents are called "to bat," and the final score is tabulated as in baseball.[3]

The use of scrambled words or letters which when put in their proper order give the name of a city, an author, a historical event, or even a verb or a noun makes learning words and facts less monotonous to young people. Breaking down one long word into many short ones is very instructive; cards, each of which contains one long word, can be prepared for this game. "Information Please" and other similar programs can make use of illustrative material to inject more fun in any fact-finding exercise.

Visual aids, of course, include artistic or decorative material such as famous buildings modeled from soap or plasticine. These may be placed around the classroom or put in the proper

[2] Ruth Wasley, "A Junior High School Exploratory Course in Modern Languages," *Modern Language Journal*, vol. 39, no. 4 (April, 1955).
[3] Ruth Wasley, "Laugh and Learn in Language," *Casdaids*, vol. 5, no. 2 (Winter, 1953-1954).

place on a large table map. When this map with its famous monuments is spread out on the table, the city or country takes on life to many students. To familiarize the class with the names and faces of the country's great men, pictures of outstanding people can be displayed in the classroom or corridor. Universities often display reproductions of famous paintings in the corridors, classrooms, or exhibition rooms of a language department, thus eventually giving students a comprehensive view of the art of that particular country. Reproductions of contemporary paintings and photographs of contemporary sculpture and architecture will acquaint students with the modern artistic achievements of the country. Railroad, steamship, and airplane posters also provide excellent scenes of foreign lands. Foreign costumes, usually peasant or regional, make very picturesque displays if means of exhibiting them are available; if not, students can wear them to language club meetings and entertainments to provide local color. Dolls dressed in the characteristic brilliant provincial costumes can be purchased and displayed in departmental showcases. An integrated project with the sewing department might provide such dolls for the language departments.

Illustrated books and magazines which give the atmosphere of the land whose language they are studying, e.g., children's books and cook books, may be left handy for the pupils or distributed to give them a more intimate picture of foreign life. Bulletin board exhibits of photographs and advertisements from the *National Geographic, Life, The Saturday Evening Post,* and *Look,* and from the magazine sections of newspapers and similar publications that feature foreign countries always create considerable interest on the part of students. If magazines can be obtained directly from the various foreign countries, they will invariably provide great pleasure for the class not only in examining them but in reading the articles which seem much more interesting than similar articles in American magazines. *Realités, Match, France-Illustration, Hoy, Mundo, Hispanico, Hispanoamericano,* and *Frankfurter Illustrierte* are among the most popular. Foreign newspapers are also of definite cultural value, for students enjoy them and furthermore they learn to read the language with a much more spontaneous and natural interest because of the wide variety of material discussed.

Marjorie Johnston suggests using a news question box from which students draw and answer questions dealing with current events but written in the foreign language. She also suggests putting a news headline in the foreign language on the blackboard, with five or six key words to help tell the story.[4]

Recently, through the cultural branches of the various embassies, many visual aids have been made generally available to teachers of foreign languages. Most embassies now have large libraries of motion pictures, some dealing with the industries, others with the activities of the people, and still others being mere travelogues showing the more picturesque spots. A few films have been prepared showing the outstanding arts and crafts of European nations. There are also available films of purely artistic or literary value which help give students a complete and realistic understanding of the country. The dialogue in these films is in the foreign language, with English subtitles. Hence, if students can study the script and dialogue before seeing a picture, they can usually learn something of the intonation and pronunciation of the lan-

[4] Marjorie Johnston, *The Bulletin,* vol. 40 (December, 1956), 79.

guage and the natives' everyday speech and vocabulary.

The phonograph makes available interesting collections of recordings of stories and plays. Records of the most dramatic scenes in the great classical plays and of well-known poems can be procured. Some famous speeches have also been recorded. Records of foreign music, both classical and popular, are available. Some of the songs, sung by popular singers of today, are particularly attractive to young students. Folk songs, operas, operettas, and even church services have been beautifully recorded in some languages. Most textbooks are now accompanied by specially prepared records or tapes of the reading selections and conversational units.

The extensive use of audio-visual aids in the A.S.T.P. courses during World War II both modernized and improved much of the old materials. For example, foreign-language records and tapes were made with pauses so that students could repeat sentences after they were said. New and better language records, with more practical and up-to-date dialogues, were also produced. Magnetic tape recorders and wire recorders have been perfected, and less expensive projectors which could be used for both silent films and slides have been devised.

Tape recordings are particularly valuable aids because they can present a great number of voices, and a greater variety of them, than the classroom offers. If space is left on the tape for student imitation of a native model, he can compare his speech with that of the native and improve it more effectively than he could with less frequent classroom imitation.

Radio programs in foreign languages are now broadcast from several university centers—from the Connecticut College for Women, the University of Wisconsin, and Ohio State

University, to mention only a few—and television programs from educational networks. Some of the recordings of these foreign-language programs have been released by foreign-language publishing houses.

The Pan-American Student Forum, sponsored by the Good Neighbor Commission of Texas, offers programs in which Spanish departments may participate. Similarly, through Le Monde Bilingue in Paris, French students in cities affiliated with a city in France can participate in the activities of people in both countries.

For students who want to make personal contact with people in foreign countries and who would like to extend their knowledge of the language by using it practically abroad there are a number of excellent opportunities offered. The following organizations stress learning through service: Experiment in International Living (Putney, Vt.); American Friends Service Committee (Philadelphia, Pa.); Brethren Service Commission (New Windsor, Md.); Girl Scouts of U.S.A.; International Division (New York City); American Youth Hostels (New York City); American Field Service International Scholarships (New York City); Kiwanis International (Washington, D.C.); New York Herald Tribune Forum for High School Exchanges, sponsored by local chapters of the Lions and Rotary Clubs; and the U.S. Junior Chamber of Commerce.

As a result of the experience of the A.S.T.P. and through more extensive use of audio-visual aids, certain helpful techniques for effective teaching have been developed. Both song records and films can now be used in preparing a lesson for which a suitable atmosphere is desired—they can, for example, provide background for a story about the South of France, Brittany, Barcelona, Mexico City, Venice, or Heidelberg. Such material arouses the students' curiosity and makes their understanding of the text far more real than do the teacher's comments. As has been indicated, such material can be used with excellent results in cultural courses; historical films like *La Marseillaise* are particularly valuable in this connection. The use of audio-visual aids should be followed by a question-and-answer period or a test covering what the class has learned from them. This need not be a formal examination; it can grow out of an informal discussion of what the class has heard or seen. But unless some effort is made to fix the knowledge thus acquired, the audio-visual materials may become mere entertainment.

A short list of sources of audio-visual materials for French, German, and Spanish is given below. Unfortunately, such lists become outmoded, but most of the sources listed are permanent. Invaluable new sources are the Office of the Voice of America and the Foreign Country Cultural Information Offices of the United States, Department of State, Washington, D.C.

REALIA AVAILABLE AT THE AATF BUREAU[5]

FILM STRIPS

Films on:
1. Every French province, the various regions of France, and the main river valleys.
2. The history of France: origins, Middle Ages, society in the

[5] Dr. Armand Bégué, Brooklyn College, Brooklyn 10, N.Y.

Middle Ages, Renaissance, Reformation, absolute monarchy, XVIIth and XVIIIth centuries, revolution and empire.
3. Roman art (in several provinces) and Gothic art (Notre Dame de Paris, Cathedral of Chartres, Cathedral of Strasbourg).
4. Great figures: Saint Vincent de Paul, Louis XIV, Napoléon, Jeanne D'Arc, Molière, Pasteur, Hugo, Vigny, Delacroix, Lamartine.

> Each film, black and white, sells at $2.00. Some have 22 pictures, some up to 52. Some have captions printed above the picture, others are accompanied by an 8-page descriptive pamphlet.

5. Paris: Paris (general); Paris, rive droite; Paris, rive gauche ouest; Paris, rive gauche est; Paris, le marais; Paris, le coeur de Paris.

> Special price for five of this last series on Paris: $8.00.

POSTCARDS

Artistic water-color postcards (made in France)
1. Le Folklore de France, provincial costumes; 20 different folders, 10 cards each; each folder: $1.25.

> Bretagne, 5; Provence, 2; Pyrénées, 3; Normandie, 2; Limousin; Auvergne; Bourgogne; Alsace; Alpes; Savoie; Flandre; Pays basque.

2. Children's costumes of the provinces; 40 cards: Ten cents each.
3. French fashion through the ages; one folder, 16 cards: $2.10.
4. Paris through the centuries; one folder, 16 cards: $2.10.
5. Le Vieux Paris pittoresque; one folder, 16 cards: $2.10.
6. La Parisienne from the fifteenth to the nineteenth century; five folders: $2.10 each.
7. Coat of arms, French cities and provinces; one folder, 25 cards: $3.10.
8. Santons de la crèche provençale, one folder, 25 cards: $3.10.

All these attractive cards can help decorate classroom walls, bulletin boards, etc.

Color Photographs of France (5¾" by 4", Yvon and Draeger)

The following sets are now available:

1. *Châteaux de la Loire:* 25 pictures, including Chambord, Chenonceaux, Chinon, Blois, Azay-le-Rideau, Amboise, etc.: $2.50 for set of 25 cards.

2. *Provence:* 30 pictures including Tarascon, Saint-Trophime, les Alyscamps, the Palace of the Popes in Avignon, the "pont d'Avignon," Saint Rémy, les Baux, Daudet's windmill, the Saintes-Maries-de-la-mer, the arenas and the "Maison Carrée" at Nimes, Aix-en-Provence, Aigues-Mortes, etc.: $3.00 for set of 30 cards.

3. *Bretagne* I: 25 pictures including Ploumenach, Brehat (the port and church), Perros Guirec, Saint Thegonnec (calvary and church), Pointe du Raz, Concarneau, etc.: $2.50 for set of 25 cards.

4. *Alpes:* 30 pictures including several views of Annecy and its lake, Evian, and Lake Leman, the "needles" in the Mount Blanc region, Mount Blanc seen from different angles, the "Mer de Glace," the Lautaret pass, etc.: $3.00 for set of 30 cards.

> Printed by the same firm, a set including eight photographs of the famous dolls by Peynet, representing modern French characters: the painter and the dancer, the student, the gardener, the flower-girl, the "midinette," etc.: $1.00 for set of 8 cards.

Recordings

Cut to order on 33 r.p.m., 10-inch discs, 15-minute reading on each record, any material student read in class. $2.50 each record. Two series of 33 r.p.m. recordings (cut):

1. Based on the Cleveland Juvenile French Course of Study I and II. For elementary-school level.

2. Well-known passages from French authors (Hugo, Daudet, etc.) For second-year French students. $2.00 each record.
3. *Les Albums de l'Oncle Max* (Folkways), Frances Patterson; two 10-inch 33 r.p.m. recordings, and books: $13.00 (see 1 and 2).
4. 22 *Children's songs for teaching French* (with booklet), two 10-inch 33 r.p.m. recordings: $7.25.
5. Mauger's Français élémentaire, (see 1 and 2); two sets of two 10-inch 33 r.p.m. recordings: $15.00 each set.
6. Short popular songs recorded on large postcards from Paris; "Cartes-postales-disques," "Sous les toits de Paris," "La Seine," etc.: 60 cents each.
7. *Sonorama*, sound magazine; monthly: $2.00 a copy.
8. Livre-disques: five different "Babar" records; *Voyage de Babar, Le Roi Babar, Histoire de Babar, Babar en famille, Babar et le Père Noël*: $3.00 each.
9. *Intonation du français* (Didier) and *Prononciation du français*, two 10-inch 45 r.p.m. recordings. Both have been out of print for several months but are expected any day.
10. 12 *Fables de La Fontaine* (spoken by Robert Hirsch): $4.25.
11. *Speak and Read French*: Part I, grammar, three 12-inch 33 r.p.m. recordings: $16.00; Part II, conversation, two 12-inch 33 r.p.m. recordings: $12.00; Part III, readings from literature, two 12-inch 33 r.p.m. recordings: $12.00.

There is no longer a tape-recording service at the NIB. Please write to:

French Cultural Services
972 Fifth Avenue
New York 21, New York

GEOGRAPHY

Notebook-size maps: (1) France (villes principales, cours d'eau); (2) anciennes provinces; (3) départements; (4) agriculture; (5) industries; (6) chemins de fer; (7) monuments; (8) villes historiques et artistiques; (9) ville d'eau plages, tourisme; (10) carte muette; (11) Paris; (12) la langue française dans le monde.

Michelin maps: Grandes routes, toute la France. Most of the 60 well mounted for classroom display.

Guidebooks: Château de la Loire, Bretagne, Dauphiné, Vosges-Jura, Côte d'Azur, Provence, Jura, Savoie. $1.30 each. Hachette: *Guides Bleus. Bords de la Loire.* Paris. $3.00.

Terre et hommes de France. A splendid collection of photographs —portraits, scenes and scenery—with brief texts. $2.25.

1. *La Vie Française à travers les âges.* A beautiful publication of the Documentation française. 164 illustrations. $2.25.

2. *Plan de Paris à vol d'oiseau* (Blondel la Rougery), 20″ by 42″ (to be folded only); $1.85.

3. *Map of regional costumes and coifs,* 23″ by 27″, in 5 colors: $2.25. Also in black and white: $1.25.

4. Booklets and "Aide-Mémoire":

5. *mementos USEL,* made for French students; clear, handy guides and charts, 7-12 pages, cardboard folders, 8″ by 5″. The following titles sell for 65 cents each:

Orthographe; grammaire française; composition française; lecture expliquée; rhétorique; français correct (dites . . . , ne dites pas . . .).

The following titles sell for 75 cents each:

Littérature française; histoire (France et Europe); histoire (Révolution et Empire); géographie générale (ou par régions physiques et économiques).

COSTUMES

Watercolor post cards: (1) 18 folders of 10 different provincial costume cards, $1.00 each folder; (2) one folder of 24 cards: coats of arms, cities, and provinces, $3.00. (3) cards representing children in the costumes of their provinces, sold in groups of three to a province, $0.30; (4) French fashion through the ages, a dozen cards, $1.80. French costume cards, to be colored: two sets of five, $0.20.

Songs

1. *Chantons la France,* 53 songs, 112 pages: $1.25.
2. Fifteen sheets with words and music: $0.02 a sheet.

   "Mon père m'a donné un mari," "Ne pleure pas Jeannette," and "Trois jeunes tambours"; "A la claire fontaine" and "Chevaliers de la table ronde"; "La vigne au vin" and "Qu'est-ce qui passe ici si tard"; "J'ai perdu le do de ma clarinette," "En passant par la Lorraine," "Ma Normandie," and "Les filles de la Rochelle"; "Le temps des cerises," "Le chant de la Libération," "Fleur de Paris," "La Gauloise," "C'est la France de demain," "Voici nos amis," and "Auprès de ma blonde."
3. *Dix chants de Nöel,* Presses d'Ile de France: $0.40.
4. *Jouons, dansons, chantons,* Ed. Arma (Bloud et Gay): $1.85.

Science

French Science and its Principal Discoveries since the 17th Century. M. Caullery. $.50.

Art

Cent Chefs d'Oeuvre de l'art français. Beautiful art prints 20″ x 25″. One print $.35; 25, $5.50.

French commemorative stamp enlargements. Black and white prints. 11″ x 16½″. 53 prints. $5.00.

Books

1. *Les Albums de l'Oncle Max,* Frances Patterson. An introduction to reading for children in the primary grades, containing (1) "Nos amis les Animaux," (2) Jeannot Lapin," and (3) "Paul et Paulette": $0.50 each.
2. *Andromaque,* Brunsvick and Ginestier (Didier). Complete, well-illustrated text, with explanations in the "1300 words": $.75.

3. *Audio-Visual Aids and Techniques*, 1955, 120 pages.
4. *Beginning French in Grade III*, MLA Teacher's Guides: $2.75 each. Comes with notebook-size copies of five different pictures illustrating French scenes, ten copies to packet: $0.50.
5. *Couleurs de l'Histoire* (Didier), 4" by 6", 60 pages; half text, half photographs and reproductions. First book of French history for primary grades: $1.50.
6. *Dictionnaire Fondamental*, Gougenheim (Didier), first year: $1.60.
7. *Dictionnaire Francais-Anglais et Anglais-Francais*, Larousse: $1.75 (hard cover).
8. *Dictionnaire en Images*, Fourre (Didier), 255 pages: $1.85.
9. "Education in France," Yale French Studies, no. 22: $1.00.
10. *Effective Methods for Teaching Modern Languages*, T. Huebener, New York University Press, Fall, 1959: $3.00.
11. *Les Femmes Savantes*, Brunsvick and Ginestier (Didier). Complete, well-illustrated text, with explanations in the "1300 words": $0.75.
12. *Foreign Language Laboratory in Schools and Colleges*, Johnson and Seerly, U.S. Department of Education, 1958, 166 pages: $1.00.
13. *Le Français Elémentaire* (Hachette) Mauger and Gougenheim, two booklets, 122 pages each: $1.25 each. See also *Recordings*.
14. *Français Fondamental du 1er Degré*. Available here late this spring.
15. *La France* (documentation française), 280 pages. In English, illustrated and well documented on the social, economic, intellectual, and artistic life of France (1958): $1.25.
16. *French Science and Its Discoveries Since the 17th Century*, Caullery, 230 pages: $0.50.
17. *Introducing France*, 3" by 4", 250 pages with maps and illustrations. Compact and well done, in English: $0.80.
18. *Langue et Civilisation françaises*, Mauger (Hachette). Vol. I, 230 pages; $2.35; vol. II, 280 pages (36 photographs): $3.00; vol. III: $3.00; vol. IV, 522 pages: $3.00.

19. *Materials List*, MLA publication, September, 1959. To be used by teachers: $0.70.

20. *Modern Foreign Languages in High Schools*, 1958, 166 pages: $1.00.

21. *Modern Languages and Latin*, New York City Board of Education, May, 1959. Regents course of study and syllabus materials for grades 8 to 12: $1.00 plus $0.15 postage.

22. *Opportunities for Foreign Language*, Huebener, 86 pages: $1.65.

23. *Poèmes d'aujourd'hui pour les enfants de maintenant*, Ouvrières (ed.), 1958, 145 pages. Delightfully illustrated, with more than 120 poems by Eluard, Fombeure, Desnos, Prévert, Claude Roy, Appolinaire, etc.: $2.25.

24. *Précis de littérature française*, Professor Launay, (ed.), prepared by the French faculty at McGill University. For high-school and college freshmen: $2.00.

25. Readers, Didier (ed.). Written for grades 8, 9, and 10, in the "1300 or 3000 words." Titles are: "Médecin sous les tropiques," "La maison d'autrefois," "Pionniers des grands lacs," "Images de Jean Mermoz," "M. et Mme. Curie" (in 3000 words), and "Marie Claire" (cut from Marg. Audoux): $0.75.

26. *Speak and Read French, II*, Begué (Folkways). Has a topical vocabulary of 3000 words: $1.50. See also *Recordings*.

27. *Terres and Villages de France* (documentation française). Contains photographs, scenes and portraits, and brief texts: $2.25.

28. *Vers La France*, Brunsvick and Ginestier (Didier), first year: $1.60.

29. *The Young Face of France* (documentaire française), 8″ by 8″, 62 pages. A good English presentation of the France of today: $0.60.

REPRINTS

1. "Common mistakes in grammar," H. Harvitt: $0.10 a copy, or 20 for $1.00.

2. "Common mistakes in pronunciation," L. Gaudin: $0.10 a copy, or 20 for $1.00.
3. "Dynamic French culture," Eli Blum. Prescription for a successful Assembly Quiz program: $0.06 a copy.
4. "Foreign Languages and job opportunities," L. Gaudin: $0.10 a copy, or 20 for $1.00.
5. "French in the elementary school," L. Johnson's committee, 1957. A bibliography of FLES materials: $0.10, 15 copies for $1.00.
6. "Languages for life," M. Pei: $0.06 a copy.
7. "On French Science," L. Sas. A short bibliography: $0.06 a copy.
8. "Teaching modern France to the American students," O. Andrews, Jr.: $0.10, or 20 copies for $1.00.
9. "What is your Realia Quotient?" M. Robinove: $0.06 a copy.

SUBSCRIPTIONS TO MAGAZINES

1. *La Documentation Française Illustrée:* $4.00. Samples ("le fromage français," "le palais de la Découverte," "l'aménagement de la région parisienne," "Soieries et Tissus de Lyon," "le Sahara," and "le palais du Louvre et son musée") are available at $.35 each.
2. *La Documentation-Française Photographique:* $8.50. A few samples are available at $1.00 each.
3. *France-Amérique:* $4.00 for 10 months. Send orders directly to:
   France-Amérique
   127 East 81st Street
   New York City
4. *The French Review:* $4.00.
5. *Revue de la Pensée Française:* $5.00.
6. *Sonorama:* $15.00, $2.00 a copy. A magazine of sound, comes out monthly.

MISCELLANEOUS

1. 1962 calendar. Should be sold out by April 15th.
2. French commemorative stamp enlargements. Write to:
   D. Girard
   Teacher's College
   Columbia University
   New York 27, New York
3. French flag, 40" by 60": $2.45.
4. Medals for official school awards:
   a. the New York Chapter Memorial Medal: $2.50
   b. AATF Shield: $1.00
   c. Fleur-de-Lys pin, marked or unmarked, for junior high school: $1.00.
   d. "La Minerve, de Brenet" 41 mm. and "Les Armes de Paris" 32 mm., new from the Paris Mint: $2.50 each.

GOOD ADDRESSES TO KNOW

AATF Placement Bureau: R. Poggenburg, Carleton College, Northfield, Minn. Correspondance Scolaire: François Guille, College of Wooster, Wooster, Ohio; or, for the metropolitan chapter, write: Sylvester Berger, James Monroe High School, 172 Boynton Avenue, Bronx 59, N.Y. Please send in $.20 per name.

National French Contest: J. Glennen, University of North Dakota, Grand Forks, N.D.

Société Honoraire de Français: Helen Bridey (president), Brookline High School, Brookline 46, Mass.

The French Cultural Services, 972 Fifth Avenue, New York 21.

SOURCES OF MISCELLANEOUS AUDIO-VISUAL MATERIALS

FRENCH, SPANISH

Banks, Upshaw & Co., 707 Browder St., Dallas, Texas.
The Gessler Publishing Co., Hasting-on-Hudson, N.Y.
Mme. Hilde K. Held, Cold Hill, Granby, Mass.

The Service Bureau, Kansas State Teachers College, Emporia, Kansas.

GERMAN

Frederick Ungar Publishing Co., 105 E. 24th St., New York City 10.

SPANISH

Hispanic Society of America, 156th St. and Broadway, New York City.

Pan-American Union, Washington, D.C.

FRENCH

French Embassy, 972 Fifth Ave., New York City 21.

PICTURES, PRINTS

FRENCH, SPANISH, GERMAN

Artex Prints, Westport, Conn.

Metropolitan Museum of Art, 82nd St. and Fifth Ave., New York City.

National Geographic, 16th and M Sts., N.W., Washington, D.C.

Perry Pictures Co., Malden, Mass.

University Prints, 11 Boyd St., Newton, Mass.

FRENCH, SPANISH

Brown, Robertson Co. Art Education, 35 W. 34th St., New York City.

FILMS AND SLIDES

American Council on Education, 1785 Massachusetts Ave., N.W., Washington, D.C.

American Library Association, 50 E. Huron St., Chicago, Ill.

Belgian Government Information Center, 639 Fifth Ave., New York City.

Canadian Information Service, 400 W. Madison St., Chicago, Ill.

National Broadcasting Co., Radio and Television, R.C.A. Building, Radio City, New York City.

National Film Board of Canada, 400 W. Madison St., Chicago, Ill.

National Travel Office, 30 Rockefeller Plaza, New York City.

New York Times, Office of Educational Activities, 229 W. 43rd St., New York City.

New York University Film Library, Distribution Dept., 26 Washington Place, New York City.

U.S. Office of Education, Federal Security Agency, Washington, D.C.

Ohio State University, Bureau of Education Research, College of Education, Columbus, Ohio.

Pan-American Union, Organization of American States, Div. of Labor and Social Affairs, Washington, D.C.

Pan-American World Airways System, 28-19 Bridge Plaza North, Long Island City, New York.

Pennsylvania State College, Audio-Visual Aids Library, State College, Pa.

Princeton Film Center, Princeton, N.J.

RCA Manufacturing Dept., Educational Dept., Camden, N.J.

RKO Radio Pictures, Inc., 1270 Ave. of the Americas, New York City.

Southern California, University of, Audio-Visual Service Dept., Los Angeles, Calif.

Teaching Aids Exchange, Post Office Box 1127, Modesto, Calif.

United Nations, Dept. of Public Information, Film and Visual Information Div., Room 6300 C, Empire State Bldg., 350 Fifth Ave., New York City.

United World Films, 1445 Park Ave., New York City.

FILMS

FRENCH, GERMAN, SPANISH

Brandon Films, Inc., 1700 Broadway, New York City.

Ideal Pictures Corporation, 28-34 E. 8th St., Chicago, Ill.

International Film Bureau, 57 Jackson Blvd., Chicago, Ill.

Slides

FRENCH, GERMAN, SPANISH

Charles Beseler Company, 60 Badger Ave., Newark, N.J.
Chicago Art Institute, Chicago, Ill.
Society for Visual Education, 100 E. Ohio St., Chicago, Ill.

Maps

FRENCH, GERMAN, SPANISH

Denoyer-Geppert Company, 5235 Ravenswood Ave., Chicago, Ill.
A. J. Nystrom, 3333 Elston Ave., Chicago, Ill.
Rand, McNally & Co., 536 S. Clark St., Chicago, Ill.
The Thrift Press, 317 College Ave., Ithaca, N.Y.

Recorders

DISK RECORDERS

Lafayette-Concord Radio, 100 Ave. of the Americas, New York City.

TAPE RECORDERS

Amplifier Corp. of America, 396 Broadway, New York City.
Bell Sound Systems, 555 Marion Rd., Columbus, Ohio.

WIRE RECORDERS

Radio Corporation of America, Camden, N.J.

Records

Chicago Board of Education, 228 N. LaSalle St., Chicago, Ill.
Educational Services, 1702 K St., N.W., Washington, D.C.
Federal Radio Education Committee, Script and Transcription Exchange, Office of Education, Federal Security Agency, Washington, D.C.

Funk & Wagnalls Co., Dept. of Foreign Languages, 354-360 Fourth Ave., New York City.

Harry S. Goodman, Radio Productions, 19 E. 53rd St., New York City.

Ohio State University, Office of Radio Education, Columbus, Ohio.

Radio Specialty Co., 829 N. Broadway, Milwaukee, Wis.

FRENCH, GERMAN, SPANISH

The Gramaphone Shop, 18 E. 48th St., New York City.

Linguaphone Conversational Records, Linguaphone Institute, 30 Rockefeller Center, New York City.

FRENCH, SPANISH

Holt, Rinehart & Winston, 383 Madison Ave., New York City.

NEWSPAPERS

SPANISH

El Eco—Odyssey Press, 386 Fourth Ave., New York City 16.

La Luz—Banks, Upshaw & Co., 707 Browder St., Dallas, Texas.

La Prensa—245 Canal St., New York City.

FRENCH

Le Petit Journal—Odyssey Press, 386 Fourth Ave., New York City 16.

La Presse—7 rue Saint Jacques, Ouest, Montreal, Canada.

La Vie—Banks, Upshaw & Co., 707 Browder St., Dallas, Texas.

GERMAN

Jugendpost—237-239 Andrews Ave., Rochester 4, N.Y.

RADIO PROGRAMS

FRENCH, SPANISH

Columbia Broadcasting System, 485 Madison Ave., New York City.

National Broadcasting Co., R.C.A. Building, Radio City, New York City.
Worldwide Broadcasting Foundation, 598 Madison Ave., New York City.

FRENCH, GERMAN, SPANISH

Ohio State University, Columbus, Ohio.
Wisconsin, University of, Madison, Wis.

Songs

FRENCH, GERMAN, SPANISH

Edward B. Marks Corp., R.C.A. Building, Radio City, New York City.
G. Schirmer, Inc., 3 E. 43rd St., New York City 17.
The Thrift Press, 317 College Ave., Ithaca, N.Y.

SPANISH

Banks, Upshaw & Co., 707 Browder St., Dallas, Texas.
Silver Burdett Co., 221 E. 20th St., Chicago, Ill.

FRENCH, SPANISH

D. C. Heath & Co., 1815 Prairie Ave., Chicago, Ill.

GERMAN

Holt, Rinehart & Winston, 383 Madison Ave., New York City.
Theodore Presser Co., 1712 Chestnut St., Philadelphia, Pa.

Student Correspondence Service

FRENCH, SPANISH

National Bureau of Educational Correspondence, George Peabody College for Teachers, Nashville, Tenn.

* 18 *

THE LANGUAGE TEACHER
AND THE COMMUNITY

In the last few decades teachers in different parts of the country, especially in small towns, have done a great deal to stimulate interest in language study in the community as a whole and to make students and parents alike feel that it is not a useless part of the curriculum. In the classroom, of course, the best way to make any subject vital is to teach it well, but this is not enough where the community is concerned. The teacher, particularly in a small town, must know the people's needs and interests and must try to present his material in such a way that it will seem practical to the average person.

Within a very short time after his arrival, especially in a small place, the teacher should get to know his students well, and if possible their families, so that he can find out as soon as possible what the community as a whole expects of him. If it has no discernible interests or needs he may be able to discover or create them. Most really modern schools try to adapt their programs so they will fit the special needs of their students. But too many modern-language programs lag in this respect. In a French-Canadian community, for example, instead of drawing on the natural enthusiasm of his bilingual students and building his course around their previous knowledge, however faulty, the French teacher too often discourages them—and even arouses antagonism—by stressing the difference between the French they speak at home and that spoken in France. He will obtain better results, and his students will gain in fluency and correctness in using French, if he encourages them to read French books and newspapers in addition to their regular textbooks.

In communities where the usual academic program is not popular, the teacher's first effort should be to organize the classroom work so that it will seem practical and purposeful to both the students and their parents. The classroom should be active and alive. For example, an otherwise dull and tiresome hour can be made very interesting by duplicating as many real-life situations as possible and keeping the pupils active. The teacher, not the class, should be the spectator. Under such circumstances the time will pass quickly and the pupils will gain a great deal. Impromptu or prepared conversations or dramatizations based on the lesson are one of the many devices that can be used. The important point, however, is that the work must not drag.

If the community is centered around a definite, specific interest such as mining, farming, or a particular branch of manufacturing, or if it has a large foreign population, the teacher should do all in his power to see that the foreign-language courses, including even the vocabulary and reading material, are connected with this interest as closely as possible. If he has to make curriculum changes, it may be advisable for him to ask parent-teacher groups and committees of parents to work with him. Talks with them will often indicate new opportunities for stimulating his students and giving to the work what the parents consider a practical turn.

In communities whose large foreign populations still celebrate their national festivals, the teacher can make these festivals a subject for class study. Their origin and purpose can be explained, and their beauty and their value as a source of community enjoyment can be emphasized and made the basis of a lesson in tolerance and appreciation of other peoples and their distinctive customs. If the teacher himself can take part in such festivals he will make many friends who can help make his teaching task easier.

In schools where either no foreign language is taught, or at least not the one that the community would like to have offered, language instruction can be made available by means of voluntary classes after school or in the evening, or broadcasts over the local radio. Such instruction, if it is successful and hence awakens interest in the language, may lead to the inclusion of a regular course in the curriculum.

But for the community at large, it is not always enough to awaken enthusiam in language courses and to teach them realistically. It is also necessary to convince both students and parents that language study can lead to many and varied opportunities for successful careers. The following statement by Professor Mario A. Pei of Columbia University, regarding positions which have been filled by his own students, gives the sort of information that is both convincing and inspirational.[1] A teacher who has enthusiasm and imagination can easily

[1] Paper read at the Twenty-fifth Anniversary Meeting of the American Association of Teachers of French, December, 1952.

make his students and their parents see the practical opportunities that are open to able linguists.

I am always skeptical when people remark that the study of languages is "of no practical value" to the majority of our young people, who will have to make their way in an English-speaking country like America and never set foot abroad.

Is earning a living practical? Then let us cast a glance at the many in our midst who earn their living by foreign languages.

People have always known that there are certain occupations in which one or more foreign languages are indispensable—foreign language teaching, diplomacy, the operatic and concert stage, the import and export trade, foreign banking. People know, or should know, that there are numerous other occupations in which foreign languages play an important even if not paramount role. Such are the varied branches of science, medicine and technology. One can conceivably dispense with Latin, Greek, German and French in these fields, but at what additional cost of time, labor and memory! Newspaper and magazine editing, the publishing trade, lexicography, the compiling of encyclopedias are other professions in which one can perhaps get along without foreign languages, but only at the cost of precision and accuracy. There are other traditional occupations, such as the running of travel and tourist agencies and the U.S. Immigration and Naturalization Bureau, in which a knowledge of languages is useful and generally recognized as such.

But twentieth-century civilization has expanded the possibility of earning a livelihood with languages far beyond the wildest dreams of the cultural and cultured language lovers of the past. I know that this flat assertion runs squarely into the objections of many advocates of bread-and-butter education. Permit me, therefore, to refer to my own experience and that of many of my former students to substantiate my statement.

When I was attending high school, I found it necessary to seek gainful employment during the summer vacations. I spent one

summer in a law office, another in a bank, a third in a Fifth
Avenue jewelry shop. In each case, the fact that I knew some
foreign languages was decisive in my getting the job. Later, when
I found myself temporarily unemployed by reason of returning
from a European trip too late to secure a teaching post, I had no
difficulty getting a temporary position as section manager in
Macy's—because I knew some languages and could assist foreign
customers.

After this, I went in for language teaching on a permanent
basis and became, like you, a living monument to the proposition
that you can earn your living with languages. But by the same
token I severed my connections with the outside world, so here is
where the people I trained in languages take up the story.

Half a dozen of them turned up during the war with well-paid
posts in censorship. Others were radio monitors for the State Department. Some were in OWI. One was director of the translation
bureau of the War Department.

But, some say, these were war jobs. What of normal, peace-
time occupations?

We might reply that the Cold War is still with us, that the
OWI has been replaced by the semi-permanent Voice of America,
that the State and War Departments still need translators, interpreters, radio monitors and other language experts in ever-increas-
ing numbers, that so long as the United Nations continues to
function language experts will be in demand (one of my former
graduate students, as a matter of fact, is a highly paid UN
secretary).

But let us go on to occupations that have no possible connection
with war, hot or cold, or with official international relations. Here
is a former student who is a radio announcer on an Italian-
language station; there are many like him. Here is another who
makes her living by translating French and Italian books for
American publishers; with the craving for European literature
that has recently developed in America, the good literary translator is much in demand. A third former student has become a
language-and-accent expert for the Hollywood movies, and from

him I learn that there is a sizable demand for people who can direct extras in films made abroad. A fourth student, before being promoted to the post of City Magistrate, was in the District Attorney's office, where cases involving speakers of foreign languages were regularly turned over to him. Two of my students earn a living censoring foreign-language films for the State of New York. Then there is the one, for whom I really cannot claim credit, who went into the F.B.I. and became their specialist in Slavic languages. I must not forget, either, the one who went into foreign advertising for Coca-Cola and devised the hundreds of equivalents for "Have a Coke" in the major tongues of the world.

My course in the World's Chief Languages at Columbia is primarily a course in recognition and identification of tongues. It served its war purpose for the military and the government bureaus, and with the close of the war it was confidently predicted that it would wither away. Instead, it continued to attract students in large numbers. Today, a good half of its enrollment comes from our School of Library Service. Librarians, who must handle books in many tongues, find that an elementary acquaintance with those tongues is indispensable in their work.

Examples of the bread-and-butter value of foreign languages in our present-day world can be multiplied. One newspaper item informs us that many airlines require of all their employees and stewardesses the ability to converse in one or more foreign languages. Another tells us that New York department stores employ polyglot "personal shoppers" to escort their foreign-speaking customers from Europe and Latin America, and that leading hotels in our big cities make it a point to have on hand one or more clerks acquainted with foreign languages. The National Academy of Broadcasting urges all radio announcers to become familiar with at least two foreign tongues for the sake of exactness in the pronunciation of musical, geographical and proper names. The Arabian-American Oil Company sets up a school to teach Arabic to its employees who must work abroad, and American oil concerns in Venezuela and Mexico do as much for their employees in Spanish-speaking lands. The American Society of Metals publishes a multi-language journal whose editors must be polyglots as well as technicians, and the American Type Founders employ at their Chicago exhibit guides who are competent in a dozen foreign tongues.

Insofar as politicians may be said to earn a living, some of them do it with the aid of languages. Mayors LaGuardia, O'Dwyer and Impellitteri of New York and the Lodges of Massachusetts and Connecticut all managed to win votes with assorted addresses in Spanish, French, Italian, and even Serbo-Croatian.

To return for an instant to the business of war, let us not forget Eisenhower's order to all American officers concerned with the NATO forces in Europe to acquire some knowledge of French, or the Army Language School at Monterrey and the Air Force School at Syracuse, where languages are imparted in large doses to our future officers and fliers. They, too, while serving their country, earn a living.

So far we have been crassly utilitarian, for that was our assignment—to demonstrate that languages can be of use in the everyday task of earning a living, here and now.

But in closing, let me recount an episode or two of the kind that warms the heart and makes the whole world kin. Languages are not only for use abroad, by tourists. They can serve us here, in America, to help our fellow man and be helped by him.

One day, standing on a New York street corner, I was approached by a Puerto Rican woman who knew no English. She wanted to be directed to an extremely complicated destination. Sign-language would not have served in her case. But since Spanish is one of my better languages, I was able to direct her with absolute assurance and understanding.

On another occasion, in a New York subway station, I ran across an old Palestinian Jew who spoke only Hebrew and Arabic. With my very scanty knowledge of these two tongues I finally made out that he was trying to reach a Hebrew hospital in the section of the city to which I was going. I took him most of the way, then entrusted him to a woman passenger who was going the rest of the way to his destination. Boy scout good deed for the day? Yes, thanks to languages.

Bread cast upon the waters—Driving on a lonely Jersey road, I had a flat. While struggling with inadequate tools and an even more inadequate mechanical ability, a police sergeant came along. We exchanged a few words. His accent told me he was a native Hungarian. A few phrases in his native Magyar, a few glowing remarks about pre-war Budapest, and the sergeant not only put his own excellent jack and wrench at my disposal, but shifted the tire for me. My investment in Hungarian had paid off.

So, pay no attention to those who tell you that language study is not a "practical" subject, that it is not for the multitudes who have to earn their living, that it is not for domestic use. Its usefulness ranges all the way from earning a highly satisfactory living, right here on U.S. soil, to giving and receiving aid, directions and comfort, with all the joy of human coöperation and human friendliness involved. Language study is fruitful, helpful, broadening to the highest degree, both spiritually and materially. It is the one subject that is superlatively worthy of the well-rounded human being.

In the classroom and outside, the teacher in every community—large or small—should be on the alert to use every possible technique to awaken interest and enthusiasm in his students and the members of the community. Many of the following suggestions have been made in earlier chapters, but since they are so effective in building up language interest in both home and community they are repeated here.

The teacher of French, Spanish, or particularly German, can give his pupils opportunities to correspond with boys and girls in other countries. Young people enjoy corresponding with others of their own age in foreign countries, and lifelong friendships frequently are formed. Apart from its linguistic value, the importance of such correspondence in developing a spirit of understanding between the youth of different nations is inestimable. Many questions that arise from this exchange of ideas can be answered by showing pertinent foreign films. American films showing life in foreign countries can also be used. The teacher will find that the student who has a foreign correspondent is far more interested in foreign films and foreign-language records and radio programs. Short-wave radio programs in French, German, Spanish and Portuguese will also interest students and their parents.

If a convenient time can be found, much good will for foreign-language study in large cities can be created by organizing visits to museums and exhibits featuring the work of outstanding foreign artists. Adults find such trips especially helpful if they go in groups of three or four and if the work of the artists is explained in understandable terms. Visits to foreign consulates and embassies that can be arranged for the parents and adult friends of students often sow the seed of better international understanding and impart besides a sounder appreciation of some of the broader aspects of the language the children are studying.

In school, special exhibitions concerned with foreign civilizations and having general interest can be organized. These should be opened to the public with a special ceremony. A resourceful and imaginative teacher will find innumerable subjects for such exhibits, as well as original ways of publicizing them and of calling on both students and parents for help so that they will feel they are sharing in the activity. Suggested topics for such exhibits include stamps, medals, prints, Kodachromes, book bindings, paintings, magazines, newspapers, foreign-made articles, costumes, photographs of eminent foreigners, foreign interiors, peasant types, and characteristic means of earning a livelihood.

In places where it has been impossible to introduce foreign-language courses but where some members of the community are interested in international affairs or in a particular country whose language is generally popular, it is often feasible to establish a club—a Spanish-American or Franco-American club, for example—in which the members can learn about the life, business opportunities, culture, and civilization of the country without necessarily studying the language. In large communities these clubs can publish a newspaper in English containing information about the particular country and its activities in the United States. Such a newspaper not only is interesting but it makes members of the community aware of how important the influence of other nations is on our own civilization in the past and today.

An enterprising language teacher will make his school a center in which clubs interested in foreign languages and civilization can meet, in which language competitions—both school and community—can be held, in which concerts of foreign music can be given, and in which entertainments by both amateurs and professionals can be presented. If lecture programs for adults are popular, the teacher can suggest subjects —the accomplishments of foreign scientists, the role of other nations in international affairs, etc. A travel film showing motion pictures, in color, of foreign countries is usually stimulating and instructive and helps awaken interest in language study among parents.

Undoubtedly there are many more things that a language teacher can do to bring his subject out from its dreary place in the curriculum. His ingenuity and enthusiasm and the needs of the community should inspire him; but anything he does that shows that both he and his subject are alive and vital and are available to serve its members, both old and young, will bring him ever greater satisfaction.

VOCATIONAL OPPORTUNITIES

Americans at Work Abroad, The Maxwell Graduate School of Citizenship and Public Affairs, Syracuse University, 1957, 28 pages.

"Careers in Languages," *The Bilingual Secretary,* Latin American Institute, 2 West 45th St., New York 36, N.Y., 12 pages.

The Foreign Service of the United States, pub. 6608, June, 1958, Department of State, Washington 25, D.C.

"Jobs for Language Majors," *Mademoiselle Magazine,* Careers and College Department, 230 North Michigan Ave., Chicago, Ill.; and 575 Madison Ave., New York, N.Y., February, 1956.

Occupational Information Bulletin No. 1, "Sources of Employment for Foreign Language Majors and Minors," revised June, 1959; Career Counseling Unit, Bureau of Appointments and Occupational Information, 3528 Administration Bldg., University of Michigan, Ann Arbor, Mich.

A COMPILATION OF THE MOST USEFUL INFORMATION ON THIS SUBJECT

Occupational Opportunities for Students Majoring in Spanish and Portuguese, bulletin no. 1, 1958; available free from the Pan American Union, 19th and Constitution Ave., N.W., Washington 6, D.C.

Teaching Opportunities, U.S. Department of Health, Education, and Welfare (office of Education Circular No. 589), Washington 25, D.C., 1959, 39 pages.

* 19 *

TESTS AND EXAMINATIONS

Although tests and examinations have already been discussed in various portions of this book, they are so important, not only in modern teaching but as measures of student achievement, that it has been thought advisable to briefly summarize the most popular techniques in this chapter. A few examples of comprehensive examinations are also presented to serve young teachers as patterns in constructing examinations that will conform with a general nationwide standard.

Language tests are most valuable when used as a teaching device; they should occur frequently and be short. Most students show far more interest in errors in grammar, spelling, or translation when they are brought to their attention by means of a test. When tests are used as a teaching device rather than a means of determining a grade, they can stress one or several grammatical points or aid in building vocabulary.

The purpose of the short test is not to worry the students but to help them and stimulate them to review a series of lessons. The short test, given frequently, tends to decrease student nervousness during examinations, serves as a drill, enables the teacher to discover typical errors before they become a habit, and is less tiring to correct. It is really as much a teaching device as a measure of proficiency.

An examination, on the other hand, is long and comprehensive; every attempt should be made to have it touch as many phases of the language as possible so that students who are visual-minded may not have an advantage over those who are essentially oral-minded. Therefore the oral ability of a modern-language pupil should be tested as well as his ability to handle the written language.

An examination on language comprehension should seek to evaluate the following abilities: (1) pronunciation, by recording while the student reads in the language; (2) comprehension, determined either by an oral test, in which a passage is read in the language and the student answers questions based on it, or by a dictated passage (if there is time, both types of tests may be given); (3) use of the language as a means of communication, that is, in free composition; (4) translation of the language into idiomatic English that conveys the exact meaning of the original; (5) translation from English into the foreign language that tests ability in correct use of grammar and knowledge of vocabulary. However, this last type of test is more practical if the passage used for translation expresses a connected thought. Detached sentences seldom demand more than mere mastery of the mechanics of grammar.

The Committee on Language Competences Through Testing (Nelson Brooks, chairman) of the 1959 Northeast Conference, has offered new recommendations, which are slowly replacing many earlier ideas for testing. It has set forth some basic principles of test construction which are at present influencing the preparation of tests at all levels. Among these principles are the following:

1. Prepare more material than is needed and discard what is less satisfactory.
2. Try out the directions and items of the test on others whose advice will be useful.
3. Pretest if possible, and on the basis of results recast.
4. After testing, discard material that is less satisfactory for measurement and reuse the good.
5. Tests should be made in terms of what the student *should* know.
6. Answers should be in the foreign language exclusively.
7. All directions should be in English and examples should be given to clarify procedure.
8. Responses required should be within limits of normal language behaviour or expected knowledge at the given level.
9. All skills should be tested.
10. No incorrect forms should be presented.
11. Translation should not be used to test comprehension, but only as a literary exercise at advanced college levels.

Professor Brooks offers further valuable suggestions:

1. Announce test and define and specify its scope so that the student can concentrate on his preparation.
2. Test only one item at a time.
3. Test vocabulary only in context.
4. Test what you have announced you would test.
5. Test through normal speech patterns and normal situations.
6. When writing is required, indicate the number of words to be used in the answer.[1]

There are many ways to test a student's knowledge of grammar. His knowledge of verb forms can be determined by

[1] Nelson Brooks, *Language and Language Teaching,* Harcourt Brace, 1960, chapter 12.

sentences requiring him to substitute the correct verb form for the infinitive. The correct use of pronouns can also be tested by substitution. The position of adverbs and adjectives, the agreement of subject and verb, the proper sequence of tenses—all these can be tested by a fill-in type of examination. Vocabulary knowledge can be tested by offering a number of synonyms or antonyms for a word, in either English or the foreign language, and requiring the student to make what he thinks is the proper choice. He may be given sentences to be completed by words chosen from a given vocabulary. Vocabulary building can be tested by asking him to name as many parts of speech as possible that stem from a single noun or verb.

Tests may be divided into several groups on the basis of the material to be tested. Oral proficiency may be tested by having the student record his imitation of a reading or recitation recorded earlier by the instructor, recite a memorized passage of prose or verse, read a passage from a book or from a phonetic transcript, write a passage from dictation, answer questions orally, name objects that are shown to him, or hold an impromptu conversation based on vocabulary that has been previously studied.

Reading comprehension may be tested by a passage which is to be translated into good English, or by questions based on the content of a passage. In this case the passage is not translated, since the questions are being asked in the foreign language and the student is answering in English. True-false questions based on a given passage are becoming increasingly popular as an objective reading test. Comprehension can also be tested by multiple-choice statements, completion statements, and the summarizing of a passage, either in English or in the foreign language. If an extensive reading of a novel or play is to be tested, the student may be required to identify scenes, characters, and special incidents, to name the author and the location of the story, and even to spot lines and paragraphs.

Vocabulary proficiency may be tested in any of the following ways: (1) By asking for a synonym or antonym in the foreign language for each word in a list of foreign words; (2) by listing several synonyms or antonyms from which the one nearest in meaning is to be chosen for each word; (3) by asking the students to choose several possible derivatives from a list of words; (4) by listing several foreign words, one of which is an adequate translation of a given English word, and having the students underline the nearest equivalent; (5) by listing several English words, one of which is to be chosen as the best translation of a given foreign word; (6) by having the students regroup general lists of words into specific categories such as flowers, food, clothing, and give their English equivalents.

A grammar test may consist of a dictated passage that contains many examples of a grammatical point—for example, in French the agreement of adjectives with the nouns they modify. The test may also call for the translation of sentences in the foreign language into English or of English into the foreign language, the insertion of the correct foreign word in sentences that contain a blank space or an English word, or the substitution of one from among several correct forms for a blank space in sentences in the foreign language. A written free composition that calls for the use of a particular tense or the application of a grammatical rule can serve as a test of a sort, since the repetition fixes the usage in the student's mind.

When the students are trained to check and recheck for errors as soon as the composition is completed, the results are better than when the teacher makes the corrections and the student merely looks them over; for the first method develops reliability and encourages confidence. Such devices as substituting nouns for pronouns, changing adjectives to adverbs, changing the tense in a series of sentences, and rewriting a sentence in the plural instead of the singular, or in the third person instead of the first, all provide drill as well as a test of the students' knowledge.

Civilization or culture can be tested by asking the student to show on an outline map the country's rivers, mountains, towns, industries, or monuments. The use of true-false and multiple-choice statements about historical or literary or general cultural material has already been mentioned. The essay type of test is still found. However, matching the names of authors with the names of their plays, novels, or poems; of painters with their paintings; of composers with their works; and identifying monuments, cities, famous people, and objects of historical or cultural importance are more objective and more definite tests of knowledge. This identification can also be made by means of slides or moving pictures.

For occasional simple grammar and translation tests, correction by the instructor of exercises written on the board by a few students, with the other students grading their own papers, is of value; however, it is fairer if the grades are not counted. Under such conditions the student is more at ease when he takes the test, and if he is conscientious he will find out for himself what mistakes he has made.

Following are examples of types of tests that are, or have been, popular; in some cases examples from several languages are given. Items involving incorrect forms are likely to confuse the student, although some experts apparently think that they have merit. Although some of the tests included in this chapter are being discarded for new and more reliable testing techniques, many are still being used, and national examination boards continue to offer them with modifications, pending the testing and perfecting of the more modern comprehensive examinations.

Professor Brooks, one of the leading experts in the field of testing, suggests three basic types of tests: (1) Prognosis tests for aural-oral skills, (2) tests that will determine what success a student has attained by a particular learning process, and (3) tests that measure general language proficiency in the broadest sense. These last two have now become essential, since students who learn language by the aural-oral approach —although highly proficient in those skills—do not necessarily show similar proficiency in the graphic form of the language. Other students trained to translate and to read the printed page may show no audio-comprehension or oral skill at all.

Tests, such as those suggested by Professor Brooks, are in the making; but time is needed to prepare, experiment with, and rewrite them so that their effectiveness will be assured. The wide adoption of the tape and tape recorder has, however, given teachers a means of testing skills and knowledge which used to be very difficult to evaluate. The student's ability to reproduce sound, stress, and inflection can now be tested very easily; so can his skill in distinguishing between words and phrases that sound alike but have different meanings. Administering an individual listening-comprehension test to a large group is now possible in the language laboratory. The reaction of each student can be independent—free from any possible influence by the instructor or a fellow student that might occur in the classroom. Listening comprehension and the ability to recognize variations in structure can be very accurately measured. Using the tape recorder also facilitates a more accurate testing of the relationship between listening comprehension and the printed page.[2]

From 1959 to 1962 the Modern Language Association and the Educational Testing Service worked together and prepared two series of proficiency tests, one under the general direction of Professor Wilmarth H. Starr, the other under that of Professor Brooks. They incorporated most of the latter's ideas as outlined above. These tests cover all the principal languages taught in our schools and colleges, including Russian, and test the following skills: (1) listening comprehension, (2) speaking, (3) reading comprehension, and (4) writing.

These tests have been planned for at least two secondary-school levels below the advanced placement tests by Professor Brooks' committee. Tests have also been prepared for teachers in training as well as for teachers. The listening comprehension tests are very similar to Professor Brooks' aural tests outlined in Chapter 12. They are carefully graded within each level, moving from a choice of one of five written statements or pictures identifying a simple statement heard on the tape, to a short dramatic scene or dialogue involving several people. A series of true-false statements, usually applicable to what has been heard, are given to the student. Only one of these statements is correct, the others being merely distractors. The student chooses the statement he believes to be correct; his choice determines the extent of his comprehension. Other items in

[2] *Ibid.*

the test may be a two-utterance dialogue, a short advertisement, a news item, or a telephone conversation, the latter requiring the participation of the student by letting him choose the correct responses to the utterances heard.

The speaking tests require the student to have an ability to repeat what he has heard on the tape, to answer questions or make statements according to some verbal or other pattern suggested, to read a passage printed in the foreign language, and to answer questions about himself.

Reading tests, except at a very advanced level, avoid using translation to determine comprehension; and writing tests, except on a high-level control composition, require only the completion of unfinished words or sentences—even paragraphs. Sentences or paragraphs may be restated with changes in tense, a regrouping of patterns, or even rephrasing in order to express a new, indicated point of view.

A teacher preparing such a test, of which the following is only one possible item, would, after checking the vocabulary, verb forms, etc. with which his students should be familiar, read onto the tape with two others the following dialogue. The student should be told where the conversation is supposed to take place. When the examination begins he hears these lines played on the tape recorder:

Man A.: Voici notre menu, madame.
Man B.: Que désirez-vous, Marie? Il y a un bon choix, aujourd'hui.
Woman A.: Je choisirai du rosbif au jus et des petits pois, Henri.
Man B.: Bon! Je commanderai le même.
Man A.: C'est otut, monsieur?
Man B.: Pour le moment, oui, merci.

The student has before him a printed sheet with the following three statements about the conversation. He must choose the one he thinks applies.

1. Le menu offre très peu de choix.
2. Le client commande immédiatement un dîner avec café et dessert.
3. La dame ne prend que du boeuf et un légume.

To test comprehension the statements should avoid using the same words as the dictated dialogue. This type of test is far more realistic than the old fashioned oral comprehension tests.

The Advanced Placement Examination is 3 hours long and tests (1) listening comprehension; (2) speaking ability; (3) reading comprehension; (4) composition; (5) translation into English. The listening-comprehension test is also patterned on the aural-comprehension tests prepared by Professor Brooks. Reading comprehension tests the student's ability to read with understanding and answer searching questions on the passage read. To test the student's knowledge of literature, he is asked to identify ten quotations from authors dating from the Middle Ages to contemporary times, and to write a critical essay in English built around a series of quotations, either from the author under discussion or from one particular work. In addition, a few specific questions in grammar, vocabulary, or linguistic structure are to be answered. The type of question varies from year to year and from language to language, but the general categories remain much the same.

The reading lists offered in French and Spanish are more specific than those in German, but include between 50 and 100 literary works. The Spanish list covers the field of

Spanish-American as well as continental Spanish literature. German alone offers two levels; Intermediate, considered more advanced that what is expected of most third-year secondary-school courses, and Advanced, somewhat beyond 4 years of secondary-school German.

Following are some of the most widely used testing methods, past as well as present.

MULTIPLE CHOICE

1. Choose the proper idiom for the English words in the following sentences:

avoir envie de	se décider à
avoir froid	venir de
penser à	entrer dans

1. *I want to* lire un roman.
2. *He has just* manger sa soupe.
3. *We decided to* faire faire un complet.
4. *You will be cold* si vous ne vous couvrez pas.
5. *Let us enter* la salle de classe.
6. *They thought of* cette pauvre petite fille.

2. Put a cross next to the correct form for the English sentence: *We fear he will be late.*
   1. Nous craignons qu'il soit en retard.   ( )
   2. Nous craignons qu'il sera en retard.   ( )
   3. Nous craignons qu'il ne soit en retard.   ( )

3. Underline the correct translation:
   bon: bone   friend   good   handsome
   lápiz: jewel   rabbit   pen   pencil

4. Choose the nearest synonym:
   chapeau: château   bonnet   enfant
   pièce: chambre   paix   prix

alfombra: caja   cama   tapiz
camino: árbol   calle   río
Zimmer: Stube   Stab   Schwester

5. Choose the nearest antonym:
grand: énorme   petit   beau
pequeño   grande   hermoso   entonces

DERIVATIVES

Give three derivatives of each of the following:

1. long: (a) longueur   (b) longtemps   (c) allonger
2. land: (a) ländich   (b) Landschaft   (c) Ausländer
3. fort:
4. Frau:
5. aimer:
6. deber:

MATCHING

Put the proper number after the expression in the second column that corresponds to the expression in the first column.

1. soñar con	He is afraid.
2. dar un paseo	to dream of
3. Salí	to take a walk
4. Tiene miedo.	I went out.

FILL-INS

1. Replace the blank by the correct form of the word in parentheses.
(beau)   Cette demoiselle est . . . .
(bello)   La muchacha es . . . .

2. Replace the blank by the proper form of the verb.
   (venir) Il .... chez moi demain.

3. Replace the blank with the correct form of the word for the English word:
   Nous n'avons pas .... (any) livres.
   Esta mujer lee .... (many) libros.

SUBSTITUTION EXERCISES

1. Replace the italicized noun with the proper pronoun and re-write the sentence.
   1. Il me prête *le livre*.
   2. Me presta *el libro*.
   3. Giovanni dà *il libro* a Giorgio.

2. Substitute the future for the present in the following sentences:
   1. Ils *savent* parler français.
   2. El padre *habla* a sus hijos.
   3. Tante Marie *kommt* mit ihrer Tochter.

3. Change the tense of the italicized words to the future:
   1. Il *viendrait* lui parler.
   2. Ils ne *savaient* rien.
   3. Nous *avons* pu partir.
   4. Le *da* el libro.
   5. *Sale* a las ocho.
   6. *Ha* visto a su padre.

CORRECTION

Underline the error and write the correct form above it.
1. Tiengo bastante.
2. Tiene la sombrero en la cabeza.
3. Las puertas fue abiertas por Juan.

TRUE-FALSE QUESTIONS

Circle *T* if the following statements are true; *F* if they are false.
1. Pascal invented the adding machine.   T F
2. Gauguin painted only scenes of Paris.   T F
3. Proust is an interesting contemporary musician.   T F
4. Sarmiento was a native of Chile.   T F
5. Rubén Darío was born in Nicaragua.   T F

TESTS OF GENERAL COMPREHENSION

FRENCH

Following are characteristic questions from examinations that test general comprehension.

1. "Assez travaillé pour aujourd'hui!" Elle roulait son fil et la voilà qui s'avançait de son pas vif, alerte, qui faisait cliqueter le dé et les ciseaux dans la poche de son tablier.
   Quel était le métier de cette femme?

2. Sur la fin de la maladie du Roi, quand M. de Chavigny vit que les médecins jugèrent que le Roi était hors d'espérance de pouvoir échapper, il se chargea de l'avertir de l'état où il se trouvait; ce qu'il fit en adoucissant la rudesse de cette nouvelle autant qu'il fut possible.
   Quelle est la nouvelle que M. de Chavigny donna au Roi?

3. Ecrivez à côté de l'expression entre parenthèses l'expression contraire ou opposée:
   1. Il se promène (souvent ....) quand il a (beaucoup de temps ....).
   2. Elle est arrivée (à la fin ....) du concert que nous avons trouvé si (ennuyeux ....).
   3. Je suis (ravi ....) de vous voir (en bonne santé ....).
   4. Elle est (assise ....) maintenant.

5. Il partit (la veille ....).
6. Peut-il (prêter ....) la somme exigée?
7. Pourquoi (pose-t-il ....) cette question?

4. Ecrivez la forme correcte du verbe:
   1. Si vous (éteindre ....) la lumière, peut-être partiraient-ils.
   2. A notre arrivée hier soir, nous (se mettre ....) à table et nous avons (prendre ....) un bon repas avant de (se séparer ....).
   3. Cette femme (naître ....) vers la fin du XIX⁰ siècle dans une ville bien (connaître ....,) de l'Europe centrale.
   4. Qu'est-ce que vous auriez fait, si vous (avoir ....) l'occasion de le voir?
   5. Que ferons-nous pour qu'ils (faire ....) ce qu'ils devraient? Nous (plaindre ....)-nous d'eux, s'ils ne le faisaient pas?
   6. (Aller ....)-, si tu; veux.

5. Ecrivez le mot, pronom ou adjectif, que le sens exige:
   1. Ce sont les livres .... je vous ai parlé. Ils sont plus intéressants que .... que vous avez demandés.
   2. De .... parle-t-il? En tout cas, il .... parle avec emportement.
   3. .... leçon est la moins difficile parmi .... que le professeur a données pour demain?
   4. .... est regrettable, c'est votre manque de tact.
   5. Ecrivez à Jeanne et remerciez- .... de son charmant cadeau.
   6. J'ai acheté deux jouets pour les enfants. Je vais .... donner pour Noël.

6. Mettez les mots entre parenthèses à la place convenable, en recopiant toute la phrase:
   1. (le) Envoyez chercher ....

2. (trop) Il arriva de bonne heure ....
3. (très) Ton conseil est à propos ....

7. Ecrivez dans l'espace indiqué la traduction en français des mots donnés:
    1. (by) Je suis plus grand que lui .... toute la tête.
    2. (with) Près d'elle marchait un petit garçon ....
    3. (asked) Plus tard le général a .... plusieurs questions.

8. Ecrivez des phrases en vous servant des expressions suivantes et traduisez vos phrases:
    1. à partir de ce moment: Phrase: ....
    ....
    Traduction: ....
    ....
    2. entendre parler: Phrase: ....
    ....
    Traduction: ....
    ....
    3. à quoi bon? Phrase: ....
    ....
    Traduction: ....
    ....

9. Traduisez en anglais:
    Ce fut une dure journée, celle du retour de Gildas Maguern, dans la ferme de ses parents. Pour la première fois, depuis le commencement de "sa" guerre, il revenait à Penmur. Les autres soldats de la commune, on les avait vus une fois ou deux, racontant la vie des tranchés bien plus que les combats, buvant avec les amis dans les auberges, fiers de l'intérêt qu'on attachait à leurs moindres propos, toujours en mouvement par les chemins et les champs, flanqués d'un groupe de parents ou d'amis: pas lui. Son capitaine lúi avait dit, un jour: "Eh bien! Maguern, vous ne demandez pas de

permission?—Pas encore, mon capitaine." L'officier avait regardé, un moment, le jeune Breton qui répondait ainsi en saluant, et peut-être s'était-il dit, cherchant à deviner l'énigme: "Sans famille, probablement, un de ceux qui ne laissent rien derrière eux, quand ils partent. C'est dommage! J'aurais eu plaisir à donner un congé à un brave comme lui!"

Cette fois, la permission avait été demandée et accordée; l'homme était monté dans un train bondé d'officiers et de soldats.

10. Traduisez en français:

I know three boys who are good friends, John, Peter, and Jack. Although they do not always have the same ideas, they like to do many things together—especially they like to play baseball. One day they saw a ball in the street and they all ran to get it, but Peter got there first.

"It is mine," cried Jack.

"No, it is mine," said John; "I saw it before you."

Peter, who had the ball, said, "Let's not fight. We'll decide who is to have the ball after we have played." And that is what they did.

Later, when John threw the ball very fast to Jack, it went up[3] very high and broke a glass[4] in one of the neighbors' windows.

Two boys ran away, fearing the neighbors, but Peter stayed.

"Ah," he said, "they will not say it is their ball now!"

GERMAN

The following test in second-year German is based upon a more comprehensive College Entrance Examination for 1941.

1. Underline the best English translation of the German word.
   1. aus: out of   on   toward   also
   2. wieder: against   again   toward   further

[3] monter.
[4] carreau, *m.*

3. stark: bare strong cold dark
4. Bein: bin bee pain leg
5. Satz: substitute satiety sentence settler
6. fliessen: flow be diligent flee fly
7. reisen: ripen call travel rise
8. eigen: only hasty simple own
9. gefallen: fall please succeed accustom
10. lustig: lost lazy airy merry
11. lächeln: varnish laugh cry smile
12. Narr: scar nose fool nerve
13. Kampf: field battle soldier cramp
14. aufpassen: pass up fit clean pay attention
15. greifen: struggle grasp grieve torture
16. Sinn: sin being sense son
17. Mut: moat mode courage anger
18. gehorchen: obey belong to hear watch
19. Zeile: time line goal page
20. Kissen: carry chest kiss pillow
21. Brücke: bridge back brick brook
22. loben: praise love live run
23. Flügel: wing bird angel flier
24. Seife: silk soap page zeal
25. stören: destroy steer disturb stare

2. Underline the best German translation of the English word.
1. open: auf öfter darauf zu
2. lesson: Lehrer Last Aufgabe Leere
3. show: zeugen zeigen ziehen schauen
4. when: wen denn wann ob
5. also: darum also auch zu
6. angry: zornig eng furchtsam angstvoll
7. tower: Tür Tor Tau Turm
8. earth: Mund Erde Erbse Erbe
9. joy: Freude Freier Freundschaft Friede
10. face: Gedicht Geschichte Fass Gesicht
11. beginning: Gönner Schluss Vorsprung Anfang
12. thought: Andenken Dank Gedanke Gedächtnis

13. knight: Knecht Ritter Messer Nacht
14. moment: Anblick Aussicht Augenblick Bewegung
15. upwards: vorwärts hinab abwärts hinauf
16. fork: Furche Gabe Gabel Löffel
17. horse: Ross Herz Pfad Galle
18. slow: langsam lange sittsam schlau
19. brave: ehrlich edel tapfer gut
20. rob: reiben rauben greifen stählern
21. cease: siegen stehen bleiben aufhören behalten
22. ugly: ulkig hässlich übel heimlich
23. last: lästern verletzen dauern bedauern
24. straight: kürzlich strittig geraten gerade
25. shot: Schutz Schluss Schuss Schatz

3. Write the German equivalent for the English words in parentheses.

1. Du (eat) zu wenig.
2. (Have you . . . remained) auf dem Lande
3. Der Knabe (knows) nicht, wie alt er ist.
4. Wir (intended to) nach Europa fahren.
5. Sage mir, (when) er kam.
6. Darf ich (for) den Zucker bitten?
7. Viele (beautiful) Bilder sind in diesem Museum.
8. Auf dem (highest) Hügel stand ein Haus.
9. (With that) bin ich längst fertig.
10. Wir kamen in (her room) zusammen.
11. Es (happens) oft.
12. Es war nur wegen (the honor)
13. Wenn du ausgehst, (take) nichts mit.
14. (Speak), mein Liebling, ich gehorche dir.
15. Alle (except) den Alten lachten.
16. Er (named) die andern.
17. Was machen Sie (evenings)?
18. Trinken Sie (another) Tasse Tee!
19. Sein Haus ist viel grösser als (ours).
20. Nur die Freunde (will come).

4. Translate into idiomatic English.

Es war auf einer Reise in den Hundstagen gewesen nach meiner Heimat, die ich schon seit zehn Jahren nicht gesehen hatte. Während das Wägelchen, das mich immer zu den Ferien abholte, sich von dem Wirtshaus aus schon in Bewegung setzen wollte une die beiden Braunen davor gerade anzogen, reichte mir der Schenkenwirt, der auch der Postmeister des Dörfchens war, noch schnell ein Paketchen nach, das schon mehrere Tage auf mich gewartet hatte und doch um ein Haar fast vergessen worden wäre. Mein Herz schlug, als ich es zwischen den Fingern fühlte, denn ich wusste genau, was es enthielt. Schweizer Briefmarken, mit denen es beklebt war, hatten mir bereits alles verraten. Und während es nun langsam die Dorfstrasse hinunterging und die Hunde aus den Höfen der bellten und die Kinder auf den Zehenspitzen hinter den Zäunen standen, verbrannt und flachshaarig die Finger in den schmutzigen Mäulern, und über Allem die Sonne schien, sass ich da, das kleine Paketchen vor mir auf den Knieen, sehr vergnügt. Denn hinter dem grauen Umschlag verbarg sich absolut nichts anders als das erste Exemplar meines ersten Werkes. Ich brannte vor Ungeduld hineinzusehen. Hier aber ging es nicht zwischen den Strohdächern und unter den kakelnden Hühnern, nein, erst draussen zwischen den gelben Kornfeldern, wo der Himmel voll Lerchen hing und die Blumen vom Wegrand grüssten. Ich war damals eben noch sehr, sehr jung.

5. Do not translate. Read the passage carefully and answer the questions in English.

Nicht weit oberhalb des herrlichen Tales bei Algund, in welche die Legende König Laurins Rosengarten versetzt, befindet sich auf einem reizenden Hügel das kleine Kirchlein von St. Peter. Von dieser Kirche, die die älteste der Gegend ist, erzählt man sich nun folgendes: die Zwerge dieser Gegend behüteten sich nämlich schon lange, eine Kirche zu bauen, wurden aber in ihrem Bestreben von den Riesen auf dem

Schloss Tirol fortwährend daran gehindert. So ofte nämlich der Bau bis zur Aufsetzung des Daches fortgeschritten war, streckte ein Riese, der auf dem ungefähr eine Viertelstunde weiter östlich liegenden Schlosse wohnte, seinen Arm herüber und warf mit dem Finger den ganzen Bau wie ein Kartenhaus über den Haufen. Endlich kamen die kleinen Zwerge auf einen glücklichen Gedanken. Sie beschlossen, die Kirche in einem einzigen Tag und einer einzigen Nacht mitsamt dem Dach zu vollenden, was ihnen auch gelang. Als die Riesen tags darauf nach spätem Erwachen die Kirche vollendet erblickten, behamen si für diese Schnelligkeit und Klugheit der kleinen Zwerge, sowie für den schönen Bau eine so grosse Achtung, dass sie denselben fortan in Ruhe liessen.

1. Wo leigt die Kirche von St. Peter?
2. Was können Sie über das Alter dieser Kirche sagen?
3. Wie wurden die Zwerge am Bau ihrer gehindert?
4. Wo lag das Schloss der Riesen?
5. Welchen glücklichen Gedanken hatten die Zwerge eines Tages?
6. Warum haben die Riesen die Kirche nicht wieder zerstört?

6. Translate the following passage into German:

The sun was just going down as the old woman opened the door of her little house. Her large black cat jumped down from the table and ran under the bed. When everything had become quiet again she closed the door, threw her coat over a chair and went into the kitchen. The fire was still burning and in front of it sat her grandson. He had fallen asleep. "Karl!" she called loudly, laying her hand on his shoulder, "you must hurry. At a quarter of six the pastor will be here. Go up and change your clothes. And don't forget what I told you." He got up without looking at her. "Every time when we have visitors I have to comb my hair." She laughed. "Well, nobody will come next month, for we shall be in the country. But until then I expect you to do everything you can to help me."

SPANISH

The following are typical questions from a recent comprehensive test in Spanish.

1. Five English words are given at the right of each of the following Spanish words. Select the best translation of the Spanish word and draw a line through its number in the column at the extreme right.

1. Fondo: 1. bottom 2. found 3. lining
   4. bottle 5. fudge   1 2 3 4 5
2. Coger: 1. lion 2. cough 3. catch
   4. peck 5. cage   1 2 3 4 5
3. Fechia: 1. fake 2. date 3. tag 4. deed
   5. faith   1 2 3 4 5
4. Temprano: 1. temple 2. tempest
   3. time 4. easy 5. early   1 2 3 4 5
5. Salud: 1. salad 2. sold 3. hearth
   4. save 5. health   1 2 3 4 5
6. Probar: 1. test 2. proud 3. tease
   4. weight 5. probable   1 2 3 4 5
7. Poder: 1. power 2. powder 3. pods
   4. foot 5. pass   1 2 3 4 5
8. Seco: 1. such 2. wet 3. sick 4. dry
   5. second   1 2 3 4 5
9. Sal: 1. sea 2. salt 3. sun 4. enter
   5. send   1 2 3 4 5
10. Reina: 1. rain 2. rein 3. queen
    4. rent 5. quarrel   1 2 3 4 5
11. Rato: 1. rate 2. rat 3. while 4. wheel
    5. turn   1 2 3 4 5
12. Sencillo: 1. sense 2. simple 3. penny
    4. without 5. wheel   1 2 3 4 5
13. Serio: 1. serious 2. series 3. sorry
    4. be 5. match   1 2 3 4 5

14. Tardar: 1. delay 2. afternoon 3. tart
    4. late 5. chew   1   2   3   4   5
15. Suave: 1. suede 2. smooth 3. sleep
    4. sweet 5. sweat   1   2   3   4   5

2. Read the first of the following passages carefully and answer the questions on it in English. Treat the other passages in order in the same way. Work as far as you can in 15 minutes. It is not expected that most candidates will be able to complete this section.

1. Cuando volvieron de la iglesia celebraron con una merienda espléndida el bautizo. La casa estaba llena de invitados; entraron todos en el comedor. Sobre el blanco mantel resaltaba la límpida cristalería. Y acá y allá, la nota pintoresca de un pomposo, oloroso, ramo de flores. Todos estaban alegres, animosos. Venía al mundo un nuevo ser. Se celebraba su entrada en la vida. ¿Que había en el mundo para este niño?
  a. ¿Qué hicieron al volver de la iglesia?
  b. ¿Qué se veía en el comedor?
  c. ¿Por Qué estaban todos alegres?
  d. ¿Qué pregunta se hacían?

2. Callados, muy quedos, besando apenas al suelo con su breve pie y extendidas las manos en la obscuridad, iban los Reyes Magos en busca den un virtuoso niño a premiarle con dulces y juguetes, cuando el delantero tropezó con el lecho en que reprosaba Elena, dormida.
  a. ¿Por qué andaban con tanto cuidado los Reyes Magos?
  b. ¿Para qué venían?

3. Mi íntimo amigo, Leiva, suele invitarme a comer los jueves, y a la hora del café cuenta historias de cuando era pobre. Se complace en repetir que, no un día sino varios, tuvo que ir pidiendo limosna por las calles. Tales relatos adquieren picante sabor al ser escuchados en el palacio suntuoso donde vive actualmente Leiva, pues es, por el gusto artís-

tico, una maravilla, y, por la magnificencia, un alarde de
millonario.
  a. ¿Qué historias cuenta Leiva?
  b. ¿Qué repite con gusto?
  c. ¿Por qué adquieren sus relatos picante sabor?

4. Oyóse de pronto el sonido de una campilla, y la gente se
   dirigió hacia un lugar alto para ver lo que era. Vieron al
   cura del pueblo, que ascendía por el monte, acompañado
   del sacristán, a la luz de un farol que llevaba este último.
   Con la cabeza inclinada hacia el pecho, el cura empezó a
   rezar el oficio de difuntos.
   a. ¿Cómo se sabe que algo extraordinario pasaba en el
      pueblo?
   b. ¿Le parece que ha sido un suceso triste o alegre? ¿Por
      qué?

5. En Armenia la joven que desea casarse prepara un platito
   de pan que coloca en la terraza de su jardín. En seguida se
   esconde y observa lo que va a pasar. Bien pronto llega un
   cuervo, se come el pan y se echa a volar. El instante es
   solemne: si el pájaro va muy lejos, es mal presagio; la joven
   no se casará en el año próximo. Si, por el contrario, el
   cuervo se posa en una casa vecina, todo irá bien. El casa-
   miento se efectuará muy pronto.
   a. ¿Qué hace la joven que desea casarse?
   b. ¿Qué significa para una muchacha cuando el pájaro se
      posa en una casa vecina?
   c. ¿Cómo sabe una joven de Armenia que no va a casarse
      en el año próximo?

3. Write in the blank space the correct translation of the English
   word or words in parentheses.
   1. Un tío (of ours) se fué a Cuba   . . . .
   2. Las chicas no han llegado todavía; no
      queremos entrar (without them).   . . . .
   3. Termine Vd. su carta (before going out).   . . . .

    4. (It was five o'clock) cuando cerraron las
       puertas.   ....

    5. Me quedo con (these) pañuelos. ¿Por qué
       valen más que (that one)?   ....

    6. ¿(Didn't you like) los conciertos? A mí, sí.   ....

    7. La carta (is not) terminada todavía.   ....

    8. Los niños tienen una pelota. ¿Quién
       (gave it to them)?   ....

    9. ¿Conoce Vd. al (Captain) Pérez?   ....

   10. ¿(Whose) son estos guantes?   ....

4. In the blank space write the translation of the English word or words in parentheses. In each case use the Spanish verb whose infinitive is given at the left.

    1. (saber) (We shall know) el resultado
       mañana.   ....

    2. (hacer) Dijeron que (they would do it)
       con mucho gusto.   ....

    3. (venir) Yo (came) lo más pronto posible.   ....

    4. (salir) El hombre gritó—¡(go out) en
       seguida!   ....

    5. (colocar) (Let us put it) cerca de la
       ventana.   ....

    6. (escoger) (Choose) lo que quiera.   ....

    7. (componer) Un vecino me (repaired) el
       reloj.   ....

    8. (ofrecer) Yo (offer) cuanto tengo por el
       automóvil.   ....

    9. (irse) El pidío que nosotros (go away).   ....

   10. (seguir) (Go on) leyendo, haga el favor.   ....

5. Illustrate with a sentence the correct us of each of the following idioms. Translate each sentence into English.

    1. hay que ....

    2. dejar de ....

    3. respeto a ....

    4. estar para ....

5. en fin ....
6. tener en cuenta ....
7. oír decir ....
8. puesto que ....

6. Write the opposite of the following:
   1. lejos de   3. temprano   5. tanto mejor
   2. a la derecha   4. hace frío   6. mañana
                                         7. alguno

7. Put into the plural all the words in the following sentences whose meaning permits it.
   1. Póngalo Vd. aquí.   ....
   2. Tengo un buen lápiz.   ....
   3. Se lo escribo.   ....
   4. Fué conmigo.   ....
   5. Me la pidío.   ....

8. Translate the following into Spanish:
   1. Good morning! How are you? Very well, thank you.
   2. This house and that one are mine. Where is yours?
   3. I arrived a week ago.
   4. I want to buy as much as you.
   5. What time is it? It is about 3 P.M.

9. Put the following sentences into the negative:
   1. He visto algunos aeroplanos.
   2. Alguien vendrá.
   3. Alguna vez viajaré por aquellos países.
   4. Díganoslo.
   5. Creo que vendrá.

Following is a partial list of published tests in foreign languages:

American Council Alpha and Beta Tests in French and Spanish, World Book Co., Yonkers.

American Council Alpha Aural Comprehension Tests in French, Teachers College, Columbia University.

Columbia Research Bureau Tests in French, German, Spanish, World Book Co., Yonkers.

Cooperative Tests in French, Spanish and German, Cooperative Test Service of the American Council on Education, New York.

Educational Testing Service, 20 Nassau Street, Princeton, New Jersey.

Every-Pupil Tests in French, German, and Spanish, Bureau of Educational Measurements, Kansas State Teachers College, Emporia.

Indiana State High School Tests in French and German, Division of Education Reference, Purdue University, Lafayette.

Lundeberg and Tharp, *Audition Test in French*, Ohio State University, Columbus.

Miller and Nielson, *Outlines and Tests on French Civilization*, Appleton-Century-Crofts, New York.

French Comprehensive Test, Secondary Education Board, Milton, Massachusetts.

* 20 *

DEPARTMENTAL SUPERVISION
AND CURRICULUM
CONSTRUCTION

What are the duties of the supervisor or chairman of a language department, and what should his relationship be to his fellow teachers? It is on *his* interpretation of his duties that the success or failure of his department often rests. In most instances he will have qualities of leadership, but they must be marshaled carefully if he wishes to work in harmony with his colleagues and make his department function efficiently.

The duties of a supervisor or chairman of a modern-language department are, generally speaking, threefold: (1) administrative duties as chairman of the department and director of the course of study; (2) duties toward his teaching force, particularly the supervision of their work; and (3) duties toward the student body whom he should seek to interest and to whom he should try to provide the maximum return for their effort and study.

In the first capacity, the supervisor should present a program of study which does more than merely fit the requirements of his city or state syllabus. For example, it may have as one objective definite preparation for any tests—city-wide, state-wide, or nation-wide—which the students will be likely to take. But, although this particular aim must not be overlooked, the general course of study must go far beyond this lesser objective, for its purpose is primarily to teach the language in all its phases and to the greatest possible extent. Depending on the size of his department, the supervisor should prepare a detailed program containing the material to be covered in every course offered by his department for at least one semester. This program, while general in nature, should indicate in detail the amount of reading, grammar, or cultural material to be covered each day so that at the end of the semester all students will be equally prepared as far as possible. Besides this general program, which is primarily planned as a guide for the teacher, there should also be a number of carefully outlined study plans for each type of lesson which new teachers or student teachers can use, so that they will lose no time in starting their work effectively. These study plans should be so organized that the work covered in the first semester leads naturally into the work for the following semester, and so on, until the entire course of study is completed. In addition to the daily assignments, the study plans should state the general objectives for each term so that each instructor will have equal opportunity to give his students the same proficiency in the language as his colleagues.

In his relationship with his teaching staff, the head of the department should endeavor, as far as possible, to encourage the instructors in their particular fields of interest and to assign them to teach the courses in which they seem to be most effective. He should never fail to remember that the success of his department will depend on the wise and efficient use of the many talents that he will have at his disposal. By basing teaching assignments on the natural abilities of his staff, instead of on seniority alone, he can often achieve a far greater degree of success for his department, and far more harmony.

If every instructor has before him a schedule of the work that is to be covered each day, and material that will enable him to handle this work effectively and with some variation, the supervisor's task in observing the work accomplished will be greatly facilitated. Some supervisors prefer to enter a classroom ostensibly to ask the instructor a question but, instead of interrupting him, allow him to continue his teaching, meanwhile observing the quality of the work and the reactions of the students. Other supervisors are more direct in this respect; they enter the classroom and observe everything openly—the motivation and presentation of the lesson, the oral and written drill, the general attitude of the class, the good teaching techniques shown by the instructor, etc. The training students have had in self-reliance, their ability to take over the class themselves if the instructor has to leave the classroom, and the organization of the class for such an emergency are all points a well-trained supervisor can note in a full hour's observation of the teaching procedure. Some supervisors combine both methods in order to increase their opportunities to help and advise the members of their staff. If the supervisor shows a constructive and friendly attitude toward all the teachers and a sympathetic understanding of the problems that may be confronting them, and if he can avoid the appearance of dissatisfaction because one of his staff members surpasses him in some branch of the work, his whole department will be likely to work as a unit and to work far more effectively. Under such supervision, each teacher will feel that he has a very definite part in the success of the department as a whole.

This general spirit of cooperation can be carried over also to correcting departmental, city, state, or national examinations so that there will be no possibility of variation in standards of marking. When cooperative departmental or committee correction is frequent, the standards of each instructor will be likely to conform to those of the department or the school as a whole.

The relationship between the department head and the students in his department is that of arbiter of any differences which arise between them and their instructor; but he must maintain a reputation for understanding and supporting the teaching staff in any difficulty that results from misunderstanding on the part of the students. He should also unify the work of the department, and make the students aware of this by organizing departmental bazaars, plays, assembly programs, club meetings, departmental dances, outings, visits to museums, occasional trips to see foreign motion pictures, and dinners. It is the chairman's duty to keep the students aware that his is an active department, on the alert for such extramural opportunities as local, state, or national contests in which the students may compete. He should make the students realize at all times the value of the subject his department is teaching; and if they are interested in jobs, he should try to keep in touch with business offices which may have positions available. The chairman of a department on the college level should maintain close contact with schools that may need teachers and with commercial houses and government bureaus that may employ graduates.

A detailed record of each student's grades in every course he has taken in the department, and a character study based on each instructor's opinion of him should be kept for at least 5 years after he graduates. Such records will prove valuable in recommending students for jobs.

Besides the threefold duties already discussed, the supervisor also has a duty to his superiors in the school or school system; he should at all times serve as the representative of his teaching staff, his department as a whole, and the students taking courses in it. He should cooperate with the administration as far as possible so that neither his department members nor he himself will be overlooked when important decisions are made. He should try to make sure that his department has an active part in school affairs, that the opinions of his teaching staff are respected by other departments, that the prestige of his department is never endangered by any indifference, on his part, to the affairs of the school as a whole. His task is difficult and he must maintain his leadership not only within his school but within the community. He must represent his department in meetings of the learned societies composed of other members of his profession; it is his duty to take an important position in these programs. He should keep his department and himself before the community not only by his personal contribution but also by his willingness to keep abreast of the times. It is particularly important, as he gets older, that he try to understand the viewpoint of the younger members of his staff, but at the same time uphold the basic values that tradition and experience have shown to be essential to creating and administering a good department.

* 21 *

THE MODERN-LANGUAGE
TEACHER AND HIS SUPERIORS

A number of years ago the *French Review* published a very interesting questionnaire for self-examination prepared by Simeon Klafter, then first assistant in modern languages in a New York City high school. At approximately the same time there was published a statement of what supervisors or inspectors of teachers in the New York City schools used as a basis for judging a good teacher. The purpose of these two publications was to acquaint teachers, particularly student teachers, with what their superiors expected of them. Although this material seemed trivial to some, it was often invaluable as advice to beginning teachers or to those seeking advancement. Because self-analysis or self-criticism is always difficult without some form of direction, it is hoped that the suggestions made in this chapter will serve as a guide. There are, of course, variations in requirements and emphasis from time to time, but on the whole the ideas expressed here should be helpful to every teacher.

The modern-language teacher should first fully understand the importance of the language he is teaching and be convinced of its value to his students. Before beginning to teach, he should familiarize himself thoroughly with the course of study prepared for his particular school by both city and state so that he will never dwell on unessentials or, conversely, fail to teach what is needed for students to pass the required examinations. At the beginning of the school year the wise teacher will study the curriculum carefully and divide the material to be covered during the term into daily lessons. If possible, he should prepare, well in advance, special material—exercises, sentences for translation, etc.—in addition to what the textbook provides, so that his teaching will be enhanced and given a personal quality. Assignments should be planned so that the prescribed material will be completed by the end of the term. When the textbook used does not follow the curriculum requirements, it is best to base the teaching procedure on subject matter rather than on the sequence of the material in the book. The teacher should always try to make the pupils understand the importance of each day's work, help them find the essential points in each lesson, and show them how to master these points.

Good teaching is based on the principle that drill—that is, the repeated use of a grammatical rule, patterns of speech, or a word or expression—fixes the rule, pattern, or word more firmly in mind than merely memorizing it. Drill must be organized so that it is thoroughly effective. Some forms of rapid-fire drill may so terrorize or bore the students that they are useless. If it does not stimulate, it should be abandoned. The blackboard should be used constantly so that every student will *see* as well as hear, and *write* as well as recite orally. Presenting students' work on the board will eliminate future errors—at least to some extent. The teacher should never leave uncorrected work on the board; in other words, he should never have more work put on the board than he is sure he will have time to correct. He should also plan time for review drill on grammatical points that have caused the most trouble.

Regular progress in reading is essential so that comprehension of the text may be achieved quickly. If the students fail to show progressive comprehension, it is proof that they have not mastered the essential vocabulary in previous lessons. Daily drill on new as well as old vocabulary must then be made a part of every lesson.

The foreign language should be used almost entirely in class so that the student's progress in aural comprehension will parallel the rest of his language learning, i.e., so that his total progress, not written proficiency alone, can be recorded.

Professor Brooks suggests banishing English from the classroom entirely for a period of 4 weeks, at least as an experiment. He is convinced that thereafter no teacher will return to English. He urges spending 5 minutes every day talking in the foreign language on an unannounced subject, and never repeating in English, even in summary form, what has been said in the foreign tongue. This procedure is extraordinarily effective. It is important to make the subject always so interesting to the student and to inspire him so that he will want to do more than the daily assignment.

The textbook can be either a tool for the teacher or a prop for him to lean upon. It is unwise for any teacher to let himself be controlled by the textbook; he should use it only for the greatest benefit of the class as a whole.

Questions and tests form a definite part of the course. Their purpose should be to help the students understand the work and to build up their confidence. Tests should be given frequently, but they should not repeat the same subject matter unless a majority of the class has failed to understand something tested previously. Care should therefore be taken to avoid useless sentences and questions.

Verbs should be taught effectively, not merely mechanically. Teaching them should be not a chore but a vital part of language instruction. If poor results are obtained, a different method of teaching verbs should be devised so that they will become as familiar to the student as any in his own language. Every student should be able to use verbs correctly, regardless of whether it is in conversation, translation, or oral composition.

In presenting a new lesson the teacher should always take great care to use practical sentences that will help the student understand the new material. This will facilitate his learning to study well. The teacher must of course give him careful directions on how to use his textbook and how to prepare a lesson. At the beginning of each term the teacher may need to devote as much as an hour of classroom time to this. Every lesson should be presented in as interesting and logical a manner as possible, and there should always be a motive behind the presentation of very lesson. Its place in the whole curriculum should be brought out so clearly that the student will see its relationship to what has preceded and will understand that it is part of a complete structure whose object is practical language learning.

To test aural proficiency as well as grammar, the teacher should give many dictations regularly so that they will become an increasingly effective teaching device.

Listening-comprehension tests given on tape or directly by

the teacher should be used regularly to evaluate the progress in aural comprehension of the class.

When necessary, phonetics should be used to aid in pronunciation. Passages can be assigned for memorizing, both to make pronunciation easier and to impart easy fluency in using the language.

Frequent pronunciation tests on tape, followed by self-analysis and criticism as well as teacher analysis should be given; or if no recording machine is available, regular classroom tests should form part of each weekly, or certainly monthly, program.

Every lesson must be carefully prepared so that the teacher will lose no time in class fumbling around for a starting point. Before the class begins, he should know how long to allow for explaining the next lesson and how long to allow for correcting work on the blackboard.

In large classes the teacher should take care to determine beforehand the order to be followed in calling on students, so that everyone in the class will have a chance to recite. A rotating class list may be prepared each day, or name cards may be used. When students are called upon in an orderly fashion, they will be more likely to prepare assignments regularly instead of taking a chance of not being called on. The teacher should examine them each day on different subjects or different phases of the same subject—pronunciation, vocabulary, or proficiency in speaking or writing—noting each student's record and his previous recitation record. He should insist on daily homework even if to obtain it he has to reduce assignments to a minimum at first. When students realize that they are gaining in ability, they usually undertake more work willingly.

As was said earlier, every classroom should be provided with pictures, posters, and similar materials that portray the civilization of the country. Such material usually interests students and, if carefully selected, subconsciously increases their knowledge.

A good teacher insists that all work that is handed in be well written and well presented; he insists on complete answers to questions, on complete coordination during unison recitations, on correct English at all times, and on good posture and behavior. The teacher who is not intelligently exacting about these details of classroom procedure usually loses control of his class or at least fails to obtain the maximum results from his students.

No teacher should repeat incorrect answers given by the pupils. He should discourage students from raising their hands to answer questions except when he has specifically asked them to, because in a large class this often leads to confusion and disorder.

Any good teacher is serious about his work. He is conscientious about it at all times and cooperates with other instructors both in his own and in other departments. He tries to increase his knowledge of his subject so that he will become a better teacher and scholar and give more to his students. If he can pass his own enthusiasm for his subject on to his students, half of his battle as a teacher is won.

Boards of education and examining inspectors have a tendency to evaluate a new teacher, at least partly, on the neatness and cleanliness of his classroom. At the beginning and end of the hour they will look to see whether the blackboard has been cleaned. They also invariably look around the room to see whether there are papers, bits of chalk, or pencil shavings on the floor. Such points, in their opinion, indicate that the teacher lacks control of the class, and they appraise him accordingly. They also note his personal appearance, his neatness, and his good taste in dress.

When the students are sent to the board to translate sentences, these inspectors notice whether the sentences are written on the board in order and numbered and whether the pupil's name is put above each exercise so that the board work can be corrected and graded quickly, easily, and with maximum advantage to the students. They maintain that a teacher should insist that both board work and notebooks be written carefully and clearly, that all the paper used for homework should be of the same size, and that collecting papers and notebooks in the classroom be orderly. Almost without exception they expect a foreign-language classroom to have a bulletin board on which cultural materials are displayed. They also expect news items relating to the particular country to be clipped and put on the bulletin board. All this material should be carefully labelled so that the pupils can learn something from looking at it, and reference should be made to it in class so that the students will make a habit of looking at these exhibits. They may ask how frequently these displays are changed. They expect to find, in a very conspicuous place in the classroom, a map of the country and to see the instructor point to it whenever the textbook suggests it.

A superintendent inspecting a class will note whether the work has been organized carefully, whether material (tests, assignments, etc.) to be distributed to the class has been mimeographed or typed—for this is greatly preferred to putting it on the board for the students to copy, being less time consuming.

It is expected that a pleasant and reciprocally courteous atmosphere will prevail in the classroom and that the pupils will show respect for their teacher and feel that he is just toward all of them. The inspectors feel that he should be tolerant, understanding and broadminded, that he should never indulge in cheap or vulgar humor nor show undue familiarity. They also give careful attention to how the teacher uses his voice, his power to hold the attention of his students by modulating it properly, his correct use of English, and his ability to use the foreign language easily and with confidence.

Oral and written exercises should always fit the capacity of the average pupil. Whenever possible, superintendents try to learn whether written exercises are collected when assigned, and returned, carefully and fully corrected, the next day. Merely mechanical, routine correction is considered to reflect some lack of interest on the teacher's part, both in his subject and in his pupils, although in some cases it may be the direct result of an excessively heavy teaching schedule or of over-crowded classes.

The presentation of a lesson should stem from an experience that most members of the class have probably had. It should never be awkward and pedantic. If a reading lesson is in progress, the elements dealing with culture and civilization should be touched upon very definitely. Class work should always be done mainly by the students, although led by questions from the teacher. The teacher should not lecture or talk during the entire hour; his voice should be heard as little as possible.

The laboratory has become such an integral part of most language courses that now every teacher is expected to know how to use and direct the use of the tape recorder. He should be able to insert tape, wind it, regulate its speed, rewind it, record on it successfully, and teach others to do the same. The tape recorder is invaluable for several purposes: pronunciation exercises, dictations, and aural-comprehension training exercises and tests; questions as part of the preparation of an assigned reading lesson; oral reading by the student; and patterns of speech as part of teaching structure, grammar, verb forms, vocabulary, and so forth.

Tapes can best be made in a small room without an echo. Tone and volume must be regulated for the best recording; this can be learned first from an expert and then from experience. Coughing, rustling papers, dropping pencils, and other noises must be avoided, for such interruptions distract the student's attention and reduce his power of concentration —essential for this type of teaching and learning. Tapes should be recorded louder than is necessary, and no unit should exceed 15 minutes, since interest lags after that time. Therefore, teaching through several short units is more effective than through one long unit. Dictations should be recorded clearly at normal speed with a native or near-native non-dialectic pronunciation; this can be done by following the procedure described in Chapter 12. In recording exercises with repeat pauses, as well as for drill or responses, more time should be allowed than is actually necessary. A good formula to follow is to count to 3, mouth the probable response inaudibly, and count to 3 again before answering a question. If insufficient time is allowed for the student's response, he becomes discouraged and the effectiveness of this technique is destroyed. Sentences, questions, and responses should be short. All directions to students which apply to his participation in a tape exercise should be clearly stated in

English, not in the foreign language; and all models in the foreign tongue that serve to guide the student in pattern exercises should be repeated, preferably 3 times.

When not in use, tapes should be stored in separate boxes away from heat and sunlight, with each box and tape carefully labeled. A leader tape should carry identification and be attached to the front end to prevent the first few phrases from wearing away. Different languages and tapes for different classes should be stored in separate sections. Ink marks on the tapes help to distinguish sections of materials recorded, and a scratch mark across the tape's label indicates where the material ends. Copies should be kept of all material recorded, so that it can be replaced should a part of the tape deteriorate.

A competent operator should always be on hand when students are using the laboratory, to supervise and repair the apparatus or tapes when necessary, and to instruct students in the proper use of the machines.[1]

A final requirement for the teacher in a public high school is membership in professional associations. He is supposed to keep up on his subject by participating in the work of these societies and, if possible, contributing to professional journals.

In short, the teacher who is recommended highly must be conscientious, efficient, effective, and interested in his profession, his students, his classroom, his personal appearance, his school, and the community.

In 1955, the Steering Committee of the Foreign Language Program of the Modern Language Association of America prepared a statement of what it considered to be the necessary qualifications for secondary-school teachers of modern foreign languages. This statement was endorsed by every language

[1] Edward Stack, *The Language Laboratory and Modern Language Teaching*, Oxford University Press, 1960.

teachers' association in the United States, and it now constitutes a new standard by which modern-language teachers, whether old or new, are judged.[2]

1. Aural Understanding

Minimal—the ability to get the sense of what an educated native says when he is enunciating carefully and speaking simply on a general subject.

Good—the ability to understand conversation at average tempo, lectures, and news broadcasts.

Superior—the ability to follow closely and with ease all types of standard speech, such as rapid or group conversation, plays, and movies.

Test—These abilities can be tested by dictations, by the *Listening Comprehension Tests* of the College Entrance Examination Board—thus far developed for French, German, and Spanish—or by similar tests for these and other languages, with an extension in range and difficulty for the superior level.

2. Speaking

Minimal—The ability to talk on prepared topics (*e.g.*, for classroom situations) without obvious faltering, and to use the common expressions needed for getting around in the foreign country, speaking with a pronunciation readily understandable to a native.

Good—The ability to talk with a native without making glaring mistakes, and with a command of vocabulary and syntax sufficient to express one's thoughts in sustained conversation. This implies speech at normal speed with good pronunciation and intonation.

Superior—The ability to approximate native speech in vocabulary, intonation, and pronunciation (*e.g.*, the ability to exchange ideas and to be at ease in social situations).

Test—For the present, this ability has to be tested by interview or by a recorded set of questions with a blank disc or tape for recording answers.

[2] *The Bulletin of the National Association of Secondary School Principals*, vol. 39, no. 214 (November, 1955).

3. READING

Minimal—The ability to grasp directly (*i.e.*, without translating) the meaning of simple, non-technical prose, except for an occasional word.

Good—The ability to read with immediate comprehension prose and verse of average difficulty and mature content.

Superior—The ability to read, almost as easily as in English, material of considerable difficulty, such as essays and literary criticism.

Test—These abilities can be tested by a graded series of timed reading passages, with comprehension questions and multiple-choice or free-response answers.

4. WRITING

Minimal—The ability to write correctly sentences or paragraphs such as would be developed orally for classroom situations, and the ability to write a short, simple letter.

Good—The ability to write a simple "free composition" with clarity and correctness in vocabulary, idiom, and syntax.

Superior—The ability to write on a variety of subjects with idiomatic naturalness, ease of expression, and some feeling for the style of the language.

Test—These abilities can be tested by multiple-choice syntax items, dictations, translation of English sentences or paragraphs, and a controlled letter or free composition.

5. LANGUAGE ANALYSIS

Minimal—A working command of the sound patterns and grammar patterns of the foreign language, and a knowledge of its main differences from English.

Good—A basic knowledge of the historical development and present characteristics of the language, and an awareness of the difference between the language as spoken and as written.

Superior—Ability to apply knowledge of descriptive, comparative, and historical linguistics to the language-teaching situation.

Test—Such information and insight can be tested for levels 1 and 2 by multiple-choice and free-response items on pronunciation, intonation patterns, and syntax; for levels 2 and 3, items on philology and descriptive linguistics.

6. CULTURE

Minimal—An awareness of language as an essential element among the learned and shared experiences that combine to form a particular culture, and a rudimentary knowlege of the geography, history, literature, art, social customs, and contemporary civilization of the foreign people.

Good—Firsthand knowledge of some literary masterpieces, an understanding of the principal ways in which the foreign culture resembles and differs from our own, and possession of an organized body of information on the foreign people and their civilization.

Superior—An enlightened understanding of the foreign people and their culture, achieved through personal contact, preferably by travel and residence abroad; through study of systematic descriptions of the foreign culture; and through study of literature and the arts.

Test—Such information and insight can be tested by multiple-choice literary and cultural acquaintance tests for levels 1 and 2; for level 3, written comments on passages of prose or poetry that discuss or reveal significant aspects of the foreign culture.

7. PROFESSIONAL PREPARATION

Minimal—Some knowledge of effective methods and techniques of language teaching.

Good—The ability to apply knowledge of methods and techniques to the teaching situation (*e.g.*, audio-visual techniques) and to relate one's teaching of the language to other areas of the curriculum.

Supervisor—A mastery of recognized teaching methods, and the ability to experiment with and evaluate new methods and techniques.

Test—Such knowledge and ability can be tested by multiple-choice answers to questions on pedagogy and language-teaching methods, plus written comment on language-teaching situations.

It is not an easy task, this teaching of languages, but it is a task that is worth while and one that, even in this modern world, has many gratifying compensations.

BIBLIOGRAPHY

Alpern, H., and Katsh, A. I., *Audio-Visual Materials in Foreign Language Teaching*, Report of the Sixteenth Foreign Language Conference, November, 1949. Published by Department of Foreign Languages and Literatures, School of Education, New York University, 1950.

Andersson, Theodore, *The Teaching of Foreign Languages in the Elementary School*, D. C. Heath & Company, 1953).

Angiolillo, P. F., *Armed Forces Foreign Language Teaching*, S. F. Vanni, New York, 1947.

Bagster-Collins, E. W., *The History of Modern Language Teaching in the United States*, The Macmillan Co., 1930.

Baker, Florence M., *The Teaching of French*, Houghton Mifflin Company, 1931.

Bent, Rudyard K., and Kronenberg, H. H., *Principles of Secondary Education*, McGraw-Hill Book Co., 1941.

Bloch, Bernard and Trager, George, *Outline of Linguistic Analysis*, Linguistic Society of America, 1942.

Bloomfield, Leonard, *An Introduction to the Study of Language*, Henry Holt & Co., 1933.

Bloomfield, Leonard, *Outline Guide for the Practical Study of Foreign Languages*, Linguistic Society of America, 1942.

Bodmer, F., *The Loom of Language*, W. W. Norton & Company, 1944.

Britton, K., *Communication, A Philosophical Study of Language*, Harcourt, Brace & Co., 1939.

Brooks, Nelson, *Language and Language Teaching*, Harcourt, Brace & Co., 1960.

Carroll, John B., *The Study of Language*, Harvard University Press, 1953.

Cole, R. D., and Tharp, J. B., *Modern Foreign Languages and Their Teaching*, D. Appleton-Century Company, 1937.

Coleman, Algernon, *An Analytical Bibliography of Modern Language Teaching*, University of Chicago Press, vol. I, 1933, vol. II, 1937.

Coleman, Algernon, *Experiments and Studies in Modern Language Teaching*, University of Chicago Press, 1934.

Coleman, Algernon (ed.), *The Modern Language Study*, The Macmillan Co., vols. I-XVII, 1927–1931.

Coleman, Algernon, *The Teaching of Modern Foreign Languages in the United States*, The Macmillan Co., 1929.

Coon, Horace, *Columbia, Colossus on the Hudson*, E. P. Dutton & Co., 1947.

Cornelius, Edwin T., *Language Teaching*, Thomas Crowell, New York, 1953.

Cosenza, Mario E., *The Study of Italian in the United States*, Italy-America Society, 1924.

De Sauzé, E. B., *The Cleveland Plan for the Teaching of Modern Languages*, J. C. Winston Company, 1929.

Doyle, H. G., *Spanish Studies in the United States*, Government Printing Office, Washington, D. C., 1926.

Duff, Charles, *How to Learn a Language*, Blackwell & Mott, Ltd., Oxford, 1948.

Dunkel, H. B., and Agard, F. B., *Second Language Learning*, Ginn & Co., 1948.

Elliott, A., Thomas, C., *et al.*, *Methods of Teaching Modern Languages*, D. C. Heath & Company, 1904.

Freeman, S. A., *What Constitutes a Well Trained Teacher*, Modern Language Journal, vol. XXV, 1940.

Gleason, H. A., *An Introduction to Descriptive Linguistics*, Henry Holt & Co., 1955.

Gouin, François, *The Art of Teaching and Studying Languages,* tr. by Howard Swan and Victor Bétis, G. Philip & Sons, London, 1905.

Grundy, John B., *New Ways of Teaching French,* Longmans, Green & Company, 1932.

Gullette, C., Keating, C., and Viens, C., *Teaching a Modern Language,* F. S. Crofts & Co., 1942.

Hagboldt, Peter, *Language Learning,* University of Chicago Press, 1935.

Hagboldt, Peter, *The Teaching of German,* D. S. Heath & Company, 1940.

Handschin, Charles, *Modern Language Teaching,* World Book Company, 1940.

Handschin, Charles, *The Teaching of Modern Languages in the United States,* U. S. Bureau of Education, Bulletin no. 3, 1913.

Huebener, Theodore, *The Cultural Phase of Modern Language Teaching,* Foreign Language Monographs, no. 1, New York City Board of Education, 1937.

Huebener, Theodore, *How to Teach Foreign Languages Effectively,* New York University Press, 1959.

Huse, H. R., *The Psychology of Foreign Language Study,* University of North Carolina Press, 1931.

Huse, H. R., *Reading and Speaking Foreign Languages,* University of North Carolina Press, 1945.

Jespersen, O., *How to Teach Foreign Languages,* George Allen & Unwin, Ltd., London, 1947.

Johnston, Marjorie C., *Modern Foreign Languages in the High School,* U. S. Department of Health, Education, and Welfare, Bulletin no. 16, 1958.

Johnston, Marjorie C., and Seerley, C. C., *Foreign Language Laboratories in Schools and Colleges,* U.S. Department of Health, Education, and Welfare, Bulletin no. 3, 1959.

Jones, John, *An Exposure of the Hamiltonian System of Teaching Languages,* Longmans, Green & Company, London, 1826.

Kaulfers, W. V., *Modern Languages for Modern Schools,* McGraw-Hill Book Co., 1942.

Kaulfers, W. V., and Roberts, H. De W., *Cultural Basis for the Language Arts: An Approach to a Unified Program in the English and Foreign Language Curriculum,* Stanford University Press, 1937.

Kaulfers, W. V., and Roberts, H. De W., *Foreign Languages and Cultures in American Education,* McGraw-Hill Book Co., 1942.

Loftfield, Gabriel, "The Direct Principle in the Teaching of Modern Languages," *Scandinavian Scientific Review,* vol. 3, nos. 3 and 4, 1924.

Marty, Fernand, *Language Laboratory Learning,* Audio-Visual Publications, Roanoke, Va., 1960.

Matthew, R. J., *Language and Area Studies in the Armed Services,* American Council on Education, 1947.

Miller, G. A., *Language and Communication,* McGraw-Hill Book Co., 1951.

Newmark, Maxim, *Twentieth Century Modern Language Teaching,* Philosophical Library, New York, 1948.

Ohio Council on Modern Language Teaching, *Proceedings of the Ohio Workshop on Modern Language Teaching,* Ohio State University, 1940.

Olinger, H. C., *Methodology in Language Teaching, French Review,* vol. XII, 1939.

Palmer, E. E., *Development of the Eclectic Method of Teaching French in the United States since 1875,* unpublished Ph.D. thesis, New York University, 1937.

Palmer, H. E., *The Oral Method of Teaching Languages,* W. Heffer & Sons, Cambridge, 1923.

Palmer, H. E., *The Principles of Language Study,* World Book Company, 1921.

Palmer, H. E., *The Scientific Study and Teaching of Languages,* World Book Company, 1917.

Palmer, H. E., and Redman, H. V., *This Language-Learning Business,* World Book Company, 1932.

Pei, Mario A., *Languages for War and Peace,* S. F. Vanni, New York, 1943. New edition entitled *The World's Chief Languages,* 1948.

Pei, Mario A., *The Story of Language*, J. P. Lippincott Co., 1949.

Peyre, Henri, *The Need for Foreign Languages in America Today*, Bulletin of New England Modern Language Association, December, 1950.

Politzer, Robert L., *Teaching French: An Introduction to Applied Linguistics*, Ginn & Company, 1960.

Prendergast, T., *Handbook to the Mastery Series*, D. Appleton & Company, 1869.

Rice, W. H., *Planning the Modern Language Lesson*, Syracuse University Press, 1947.

Sauveur, L., *Introduction to the Teaching of Living Languages without Grammar or Dictionary*, Schoenhof & Moeller, Boston, 1874.

Sauveur, L., *A Summer School for Teachers*, Amherst College, Lafayette College, Wooster University, 1879.

Seybolt, R. F., *Some Studies in American Cultural Education in the Private School*, Bureau of Educational Research, Bulletin no. 287, University of Illinois, September, 1925.

Spell, J. R., *Spanish Teaching in the United States, Hispania*, vol. X:141–159, May, 1927.

Stack, Edward M., *The Language Laboratory and Modern Language Teaching*, Oxford University Press, 1960.

Stern, S., and Méras, B., *Etude Progressive de la Langue Française*, W. R. Jenkins, 1882.

Sturtevant, E. H., *An Introduction to Linguistic Science*, Yale University Press, 1947.

Sweet, H., *A Practical Study of Languages*, Henry Holt & Co., 1900.

The Teaching of Modern Languages, UNESCO, 1955.

Thomas, C., *et al.*, *Report of the Committee of Twelve* of Modern Language Association of America, D. C. Heath & Company, 1910.

Voss, B. J., *Essentials of German*, Henry Holt & Co., 1936.

West, M. P., *Language in Education*, Longmans, Green & Company, 1929.

West, M. P., *On Learning to Speak a Foreign Language*, Longmans, Green & Company, 1934.

Index